The Die Song

The Die Song

A Journey into the Mind of a Mass Murderer

Donald T. Lunde
and
Jefferson Morgan

W·W·Norton & Company
New York·London

Library of Congress Cataloging in Publication Data

Lunde, Donald T
 The die song.

  1. Mullen, Herbert William.   2. Crime and
criminals—California—Biography.   3. Murder—
California—Case Studies.   4. Criminal psychology
—Case studies.   I. Morgan, Jefferson, joint author.
II. Title.
HV6248.M82L86   1980   364.1′523′0924   [B]
ISBN 0-393-01315-4   80-47

1 2 3 4 5 6 7 8 9 0

For Marilynn and Jinx

Contents

Acknowledgments

No book ever gets written without the help and advice of a number of people, but in this case the list is a particularly long one.

We are grateful to Jim Jackson, Harold Cartwright, Steve Wright, and psychologist David Marlowe, who worked tirelessly on the defense; to Peter Chang, Chris Cottle, and Art Danner, who mounted a very able prosecution, and to Judge Charles Franich, who conducted the trial in a patient and evenhanded manner.

All of the members of the Santa Cruz Police Department and the Santa Cruz County Sheriff's Department, especially Sergeant Terry Medina, were cooperative and helpful. They have every right to be proud of their investigation.

For their valuable counsel and encouragement, we both owe debts of gratitude to Carl Brandt, Frank Cooper, and Starling Lawrence, one of the best editors in the business.

A Brief Explanation

Many readers may wonder how, after nearly a decade, the authors were able to re-create what people said and did during the terrible events depicted in this book. From literally thousands of pages of witnesses' statements, investigative reports, autopsies, and the like, details emerged that made invention unnecessary.

Finally, it must be remembered that there was one eyewitness to all of the murders—the killer himself.

The Die Song

"... *I cried by reason of mine affliction unto the Lord, and He heard me; out of the belly of hell cried I, and thou heardest my voice.*"

—THE BOOK OF JONAH

1
The Drifter

WHITEY WAS THIRSTY. He was also cold, damp, and dirty from having slept in the rain beneath a redwood windfall in Henry Cowell State Park. Oddly enough, he wasn't particularly hungry, although he had not eaten since the day before. Mainly he was thirsty, but there was nothing he could do about it because he was broke. He had spent his last cent the previous afternoon on the bottle of muscatel he had finished before lapsing into unconsciousness. He had awakened feeling congested and dehydrated and stiff in his joints. He was more irritated than worried about his plight. Experience had taught him he wouldn't starve, but he really needed a drink and he was, as always, mildly angry with himself for not shepherding his meager resources. Of course, thrift had not been on his mind when he had curled up under the log with the warming companionship of the bottle, savoring the sweet, tepid liquid that would blot out his memory and cast him into a dreamless sleep.

It was just daylight when he woke up. After relieving himself copiously, he walked through the silent, dripping forest to the San Lorenzo River. He knelt, removed his battered felt hat, splashed water on his stubbled face, dried himself with a grimy handkerchief, and, cupping his hand in the slow-moving stream, tried to rinse the filthy taste from his mouth.

Whitey shivered. Although the main part of the storm had passed over the shoreline during the night, the October sky was still dark and threatening, and the gusty wind was raising a light chop on the gunmetal-colored water of northern Monterey Bay.

Idly, for he knew nothing was there, he went through his pockets. He had long ago given up carrying a wallet. He had lost enough of them in boxcars and hobo jungles to realize that the fewer temptations one put in the way of his fellow pilgrims the better. When he had any money he either stashed it someplace or hid it in different places in his clothing. The only thing he found in his mudcaked jeans was a prescription from the county hospital for an athlete's foot remedy. He had picked up the fungus a couple of weeks earlier in the county jail. The prescription was made out to Lawrence White. He used his real name so seldom he had forgotten what the middle one was.

He fished through an empty pack of Camels, crumpled it, and threw it away. It was time to move on, he decided. The winter rains would soon hit California's central coast, and the police would be even more aggressive about rounding up those who sought refuge in doorways and under bridges. He didn't want to go back to the jail in Santa Cruz. It was overcrowded and full of hard cases, including a few who would be waiting for him if he came back. The prospect of a month of clean sheets and regular meals had seemed almost attractive when he had pleaded guilty to common drunkeness six weeks ago, but a few days later he had found himself in the middle of a riot in the day room. Several mattresses were burned, a television set was broken, and Whitey had a deep gash on his head before order was restored by a phalanx of club-swinging deputies. They took him to the county hospital to have the cut stitched up, and then he was transferred to the county rehabilitation center near La Selva Beach to finish out his sentence.

Yes, it was definitely time to move on. Whitey had a sense of the seasons as acute as any wild animal. For more than forty years, since running away from home as a teen-ager in Oklahoma, he had followed the harvest. Now he would go south, maybe to the Coachella Valley. He would need a little money to get there. They were still picking apples in Watsonville, and perhaps he could hook on for a few days in the orchards. But even traveling the twenty miles to Watsonville wouldn't be easy. Times had changed since he had fled the Dust Bowl. In 1972 people were not nearly as willing to pick up hitchhikers, especially around Santa Cruz. Whitey didn't read the papers much, and he was a loner who had learned that making friends was a luxury drifters could ill afford. Besides, it was usually dangerous. But he had heard talk in the jail about young women disappearing from local roads over a period of months. The residents were jumpy and distrustful, particularly of the hippies who had gravitated to the beaches and wooded hills around Santa Cruz.

At fifty-five, Whitey was hardly a hippie, but he wasn't exactly clean-cut either. His life had not been easy, and years of labor and self-abuse had made him look older than he was. He smiled at the thought that anyone would think of him as a danger to young girls, but he knew he would probably have to come up with bus fare to get to Watsonville. He decided to walk down Highway 9 into town to see if he could panhandle it from the shoppers along the Pacific Street Mall.

Puffing slightly from the exertion of clambering up the embankment to the highway, Whitey set off for Santa Cruz four miles down the hill. It had warmed up a little. His clothes had dried, his hangover was abating, and his mood improved. He was looking forward to getting back out on the road.

It is understandable that the disenchanted and the flower children who had elected to live according to the gospel of Timothy Leary migrated to Santa Cruz County. Separated from the southern end of San Francisco Bay by the Santa Cruz Mountains, the region has hundreds of square miles of sparsely settled wilderness where communes could be established with only minimal attention to shelter. There is an abundance of clear running water, and for the most part the soil is rich and friable, ideal for vegetable gardens and the cultivation of marijuana. The long coastline south of San Francisco is indented with uncounted hidden anchorages well suited to smuggling, a trade that flourished almost from the time of the earliest white settlements.

The influx of what the entrenched freeholders call "longhairs" or "undesirables" started in the early 1960s. They were attracted not only by the forgiving climate and bucolic solitude but also by a lack of the more sophisticated enforcement of narcotics laws that made life uncomfortable in the cities.

By 1972 it was reliably estimated that as many as 17,000 nameless men, women, and children were living in shacks and lean-tos hidden in the glens and along the creeks of the Santa Cruz Mountains, unknown to any authority, including the police or the post office.

Whitey hardly noticed the blue and white station wagon as it passed him and rounded the curve. Although he didn't know it, he was walking through a section of the park called *Cañada del Rincon en el Rio*—literally, "little canyon of the corner in the river." Highway 9 roughly follows the course of the San Lorenzo as it winds from the foothills to the bay at Santa Cruz.

Whitey stopped when he saw the car parked alongside the road ahead of him. The hood was up, and someone was bending over the fender, apparently trying to diagnose a mechanical problem. The motorist was a short, slightly built young man. Whitey stood for a moment, sizing him up. He considered crossing the roadway to avoid an unwanted conversation but changed his mind. He was pretty handy around automobiles, and perhaps he could help get this one started. From his clothes it didn't appear as if the kid would be carrying enough money to offer him a reward, but looks could be deceiving, and at worst he was likely to get an invitation for a ride into town.

It's Friday the 13th, he thought. Maybe it'll turn out to be my lucky day.

"Something the matter, son?" he asked as he walked up to the car. The young man lifted his head from under the hood, turned, and grinned sheepishly.

"I don't really know," he said. "She just conked out on me."

"Let me take a look. '58 Chevy, ain't it?"

"Yeah. Thanks a lot." The young man moved aside, and Whitey peered at the engine. He glanced at the ignition wiring to make sure it was all in place and followed the wire from the coil to the distributor to see if it had worked loose. He began to unsnap the clamps on the distributor cap.

"Maybe the points closed up," Whitey said. He heard no reply. "Sometimes they . . ."

A sharp, sickening pain racked Whitey's head, and he heard what sounded like a loud crack. His eyes widened, but his vision blurred, and he began to feel himself falling, almost as if he were plunging into a deep pit. Blood spurted from his mouth where he had bitten through his tongue. He clawed at the fender, trying to hold himself up. The pain came again, this time with a searing light. Then he saw or felt nothing.

His teeth bared, the young man struck again and again. Blood, hair, and then brain tissue clung to the baseball bat as he continued to bludgeon the man who already lay dead at his feet. At last he stopped. He was panting. He looked around. He was alone except for the body. Methodically, he put the bat on the floor of the back seat and closed the door.

Grasping Whitey under the armpits, the young man began to drag his corpse toward the brush along the road. He was surprisingly strong for his size and had little trouble. When he reached the bushes he partially lifted the body and rolled it down a small incline. It disappeared into the dense vegetation, totally concealed from the road.

The young man shut the hood, slipped behind the wheel of the station wagon, and turned the key. The engine started immediately. He made a U-turn and drove north without haste. After a few miles he turned left, then right, and finally into a residential lane. He pulled into an empty carport, found a rag, took the bat out of the station wagon and tried to wipe it clean. After vigorous rubbing, a light red stain remained on the wood. He picked up a piece of sandpaper and abraded the spot until the color disappeared. He threw the rag and the sandpaper into a garbage can and walked into the house. It was almost time for lunch.

Santa Cruz is the third oldest secular community in California, after San Jose and Los Angeles. Although the San Lorenzo River was discovered and named by Spanish explorers in 1769, it was not until 1791 that the Franciscan friars founded *Misión de la Exaltacion de la Santa Cruz* on its north bank. The Spanish set out to convert, baptize, and exploit the Costanoan Indians, a peaceful Stone Age people who fished the coastal streams and tide pools and gathered acorns from the live oaks that grew on the inland slopes. The Indians' pastoral existence was a fragile one, and they were no match for the colonists nor their Mexican and American successors. By the census of 1910 the race was extinct.

In spite of an imperial decree against building towns on Indian lands, the Spanish started a pueblo across the river from the mission and named it Branciforte in honor of the viceroy of New Spain. Eventually it would merge with the town that grew up around the mission, and Santa Cruz would spread north and south of the San Lorenzo estuary.

John Chilton had driven that Friday afternoon from his home in Felton to the turnout on Highway 9 that marks the head of the Rincon Trail, a path that leads through the Cathedral Redwoods, a spectacular grove in Cowell State Park. The rain had stopped the night before, and it was a good day for a hike. He had taken only a few steps when he saw the crumpled form. He called out. The man didn't move. Chilton backed away, turned, and ran toward his car.

The red light on the ambulance blinked silently as it pulled past the parked black and white sheriff's patrol car and started down the road toward Santa Cruz. There was no need for a siren, since the man in the plastic coroner's bag in the back was beyond help. Detective Terry Medina watched the departure, then turned his attention to the brush near where the body had been found. To all appearances he had been just a harmless wino, but somebody had sure as hell been mad at him. His skull was caved in. Medina joined several deputies who were combing the bushes for a murder weapon.

It took two days for a fingerprint check to reveal that Whitey had been in jail in September. At the time he was booked, he had given the name and address of a sister in Chicago as his next of kin. Medina's superior, Lieutenant Ken Pittenger, chief of investigation for the Santa Cruz Sheriff's Office, routinely sent a teletype to the Chicago police asking them to notify the woman. The answer said the street White had listed did not exist.

The detectives found a few Skid Row derelicts who had seen Whitey around, but nobody well enough acquainted with him to know his first name. Although they put the case in the active investigation file, Medina and Pittenger had a hunch after a few days that whoever had killed Whitey was long gone, and that the murder probably would never be solved.

On October 20, 1972, a week after his death, Whitey was buried at Oakwood Memorial Park following a perfunctory, county-paid service at the Wessendorf and Holmes Chapel.

No one came to the funeral.

2

One Case in a Million

THE SPANISH first saw the great stands of redwoods in the mountains behind Santa Cruz and gave them the name *palos colorados*. But it was the Americans who built the first sawmills, after they had conquered California. Lumbering and such other enterprises as lime kilns, tanneries, and cement quarries left behind small hamlets in the uplands—Boulder Creek, Ben Lomond, Felton, Scott's Valley, Soquel—and coastal villages, such as Davenport north of Santa Cruz, where schooners landed to carry away the produce of the pioneers. To the south, in the lush valley formed by the Pajaro River, Watsonville became a center for shipping the fruits and truck crops grown on the farms around it. In the high mountains, grapes were grown to make wine.

Although most of Santa Cruz's early trade with the outside world was by sea, the county that was created with statehood in 1850 was not long isolated from its landside neighbors. The first stagecoach rattled across the mountains to San Jose and San Francisco in 1854, and stage lines prospered until they were replaced by a passenger railway, which in turn succumbed to the automobile. One of the best whip hands was Charley Parkhurst, a hard-drinking, tough-talking expatriate of New Hampshire who was not above using muscle to get his way at the roadhouses along his route. Nicknamed "Cock-eyed Charley" or "One-eyed Charley" because of a peculiar squint, he retired eventually to a little cattle ranch in the mountains. Upon Charley's death in 1879, a startled undertaker discovered she was a woman. Having been a conscientious citizen who cast a ballot in every election after voting for President Grant in 1868, Charley was the first female to enjoy the franchise in the United States.

The murder of Lawrence White caused no stir in Santa Cruz. It rated only a few paragraphs in the county's two daily newspapers, and except for the detectives, it went virtually unnoticed.

In October of 1972, Santa Cruz was winding down from its annual summer occupation by the hordes of tourists who thronged to the amusement park along the boardwalk fronting the long, white public beach. Most of the 32,000 permanent residents of the coastal resort were looking forward to the unhurried commerce of the off-season. Except for fair-weather weekends, the old roller coaster and other concessions would be shuttered and wrapped in foggy stillness relieved only by the tread of an occasional security guard. Spring seemed a long way off.

Indifference greeted White's violent death because of his anonymity, not because the people in Santa Cruz were blasé about murder. On the contrary, many of them were still haunted by the savage killings almost exactly two years earlier of a prominent eye surgeon and his family. National notoriety, unwanted and unwelcome, had followed the discovery October 19, 1970, of the bodies of Dr. Victor Ohta, his wife, their two young sons, and his secretary floating in the swimming pool of the Ohtas' spectacular home overlooking the bay. Each of the five victims had been tied up and shot. Several fires had been set in the house, but when firemen arrived their trucks were impeded by the doctor's Rolls Royce, which the killer had parked to blockade the driveway. Under the windshield wiper they found a chilling, typewritten note that evoked the horror loosed by Charles Manson and his followers a year before:

halloween . . . 1970

today world war 3 will begin as brought to you by the pepole of the free universe.

From this day forward any one and ?/or company of persons who missuses the natural environment or destroys same will suffer the penalty of death by the people of the free universe.

I and my comrads from this day forth will fight until death or freedom, against anything or anyone who dose not support natural life on this planet, materalisum must die, or man-kind will.

KNIGHT OF WANDS
KNIGHT OF CUPS
KNIGHT OF PENTICLES
KNIGHT OF SWORDS.

The last reference to the suits of the tarot suggested a group of maniacs. Fears of another homicidal cult subsided four days later, however, when sheriff's deputies arrested John Linley Frazier, a twenty-four-year-old recluse with a long local record of juvenile offenses and drug use who lived most of the time in a dilapidated cow shed down the hill from the Ohta home.

Psychiatric examination revealed Frazier to be suffering from paranoid schizophrenia in the extreme. Using the Bible and elements of the occult, he had evolved a delusion that it was his holy mission to rid the world of those guilty of "polluting and destroying the earth," deciding in the process that the last Book of the New Testament, the Revelation of St. John the Divine, was directed to him, also John:

"And he sayeth unto me, Seal not the sayings of the prophecy of this book; for the time is at hand.

"He that is unjust, let him be unjust still; and he which is filthy, let him be filthy still. . . .

"For I testify unto every man that heareth the words of the prophecy of the book, If any man shall add unto these things, God shall add unto him the plagues that are written in this book. . . ."

As it became apparent to them that John's behavior went beyond the temporary effects of the drugs he used, his mother and his wife, whom he left several months before the murders, tried desperately to get psychiatric treatment for him. They were unsuccessful, partly because he refused to cooperate but also because California's dwindling mental care facilities put any substantive therapy out of reach.

Ronald Reagan, the certain winner of a second term as governor in the upcoming November elections, had assembled an unlikely coalition of conservatives who wanted to curb public health spending and liberals opposed to the "warehousing" of mental patients in "snake pits." Plans were drawn for the elimination of state psychiatric hospitals, but most of the promised community treatment centers that were to replace them would never materialize.

Frazier, whose increasingly weird behavior alienated him from even the most tolerant who inhabited the dreamy underworld of drug dealers and dropouts, became more and more paranoid, convinced that "they" were plotting to destroy him, to keep him from carrying out God's will.

It was imperative that he act at once, before his imagined enemies could stop him.

Frazier was unacquainted with the Ohtas, who in turn were unaware that their movements were being watched from a covert in a redwood grove in the gulch below their house. Frazier was waiting for the moment when he would sacrifice the intruders on the hilltop, destroy their blasphemous works, and return the land to its natural state. On a dreary Monday he went to the house while it was empty, lay in wait, took each member of the family and the secretary captive as they came home, executed them, and set the house on fire.

In spite of his own bizarre actions in court and professional testimony that he was acutely psychotic, Frazier was found sane by a jury under California's then definition of legal insanity, taken from the so-called M'Naghten Rule set down in England by Lord Chief Justice Tindal a century and a quarter earlier: ". . . a defect of reason, from disease of the mind, (such that a defendant would) not know the nature and quality of the act he was doing, or, if he did know it, that he did not know he was doing what was wrong."

Frazier was represented by Jim Jackson, the public defender for Santa Cruz County, who had engaged me as a psychiatric consultant. At that time I was assistant professor of psychiatry at the Stanford University Medical School in Palo Alto, just across the mountains from Santa Cruz.

About a year before Frazier was arrested, I had reluctantly accepted a court appointment from a friend of mine, a superior court judge in Oakland, as an alienist (the quaint, century-old term for psychiatrist that lawyers refuse to give up for some reason) in a criminal trial. During my testimony in that case, I had noticed a number of rather well-dressed people in the audience. Since the matter was neither controversial nor publicized, I decided they weren't reporters. It was later that the judge told me they were lawyers, on hand to see how Don Lunde, the new shrink, handled himself under cross-examination. I guess I passed, because in the ensuing months I found myself being asked to consult in dozens of criminal cases, hired either by the court or by the attorneys for the prosecution or defense. What had started as a casual favor for a friend would, in the coming years, take up more and more of my time.

Jim Jackson was a large, ruddy man with a wild mane of red hair and a bristling mustache. Blunt and occasionally given to tirades in court, he was a member of the private law firm of Britton and Jackson, which handled the county's indigent defendants on a contract basis. In spite of his sometimes bombastic demeanor, he was highly regarded as a brilliant and tenacious advocate. I had liked him instinctively.

Before moving to Santa Cruz Jackson had spent several years working as a deputy district attorney in Alameda County. When he was assigned to defend Frazier, he called his ex-boss in Oakland and asked him to recommend a forensic psychiatrist. The latter suggested my name.

During questioning by Jackson I argued that Frazier's delusional system mandated the killing of certain people as a moral obligation. Therefore he didn't know right from wrong.

Under cross-examination by District Attorney Peter Chang, who asked whether Frazier "was capable of knowing the acts violated the standards of conduct that had been formulated by society," I was forced to admit he was.

Frazier was condemned to die in the gas chamber. The sentence later was reduced to life in prison.

Jackson and I both were disturbed by the case, the lawyer because the nineteenth-century test for legal insanity had once again proved to be worthless, I because I saw Frazier as another proof that the mental health system had broken down. Had treatment been available for him, five people would still be alive.

During the trial I became friends with Jim, Harold Cartwright, his principal investigator, and Peter Chang, the prosecutor. We all knew the mass murder was an isolated episode in a small town, and we didn't expect ever to be in the same courtroom again. However, we did continue to see one another socially. The first time we all got together was for dinner at Jackson's house a month or so after the Frazier jury came in with its guilty verdict.

Peter had been deeply affected by the case, to the extent that it changed his views on capital punishment. He was rare among DA's, having opposed the death penalty all of his life. But the savagery of the Ohta murders had led him to demand that Frazier be executed.

Although Peter was convinced to a moral certainty that Frazier was the killer (everyone was before the trial was over, since I testified that he had confessed to me during a psychiatric examination), the only hole in the prosecution's case was that no murder weapon had ever been found.

After dinner at Jackson's house, some of us may have had a little too much to drink. As we sat long into the night, debating and reliving the trial, I mentioned that Frazier had told me where he had thrown the gun. Up to that time I had felt professionally constrained not to reveal it.

The next day, the district attorney sent a man to find the revolver. It was in the middle of a thicket of poison oak down the hill from the Ohta house.

Peter and I remained friends anyway.

Even though the facts showed that the slaughter of the Ohta family was the random act of a madman who had lived in the Santa Cruz area since childhood, the tragedy further hardened community prejudice against hippies and other members of the "counterculture."

They were suspicious rather than terrified. It had been, after all, one case in a million.

3

The Hitchhiker

IN THE END it was its splendid geography that gave Santa Cruz its primary industry, tourism. As early as 1869 the town of Capitola just to the south was subdivided as a summer resort, and by the turn of the century guest houses and hotels thrived, and the mountains were dotted with vacation cabins. The boardwalk grew along the beach between the municipal pier and the mouth of the river. In 1924 a group of local entrepreneurs started the annual Miss California contest there. The initial winner, a petite blonde named Faye Lanphier, went on the following year to become the first Miss America in Atlantic City, a place whose blandishments Santa Cruz worked hard to copy.

California's runaway growth after World War II more or less bypassed Santa Cruz. Although the population increased as developers built homes for the affluent drawn to the sheltered beauty of Monterey Bay, by 1972 fewer than 125,000 people lived in a county a quarter of the size of Delaware.

Many of the newcomers were students who attended either Cabrillo College, a two-year institution between Soquel and the beach community of Aptos, or the University of California's new Santa Cruz campus. The latter accepted its first applications in 1964 during the early days of the national turmoil and academic unrest triggered at its sister campus in Berkeley. Conceived as a cluster of small residential colleges in a dramatic setting among the redwoods high above the city and the bay, U.C. Santa Cruz offered the informal structure and freedom that students were demanding at larger universities.

Mary's soft leather bag slapped against her hip as she jogged to catch up with the old station wagon that had stopped about 100 feet past her. She was lucky, she thought, to get a ride so quickly.

Ordinarily Mary Margaret Guilfoyle would not have been hitch-hiking, but she was in a hurry and there was no time to wait for the next bus from Cabrillo College into Santa Cruz. Today was Tuesday, October 24. She had a 3:30 P.M. appointment for a job interview at the State Department of Human Resources on May Avenue, and she didn't want to be late. She needed another job to augment her earnings as a part-time teaching assistant at the junior college where she was a student.

Even though she was rushed, Mary knew better than to get into a car with a strange man without looking him over carefully. Several young women had disappeared hitchhiking, and the dismembered bodies of two of them had been found that summer up in the hills. They had only been teen-agers, and probably didn't know what was happening. At twenty-four, Mary had been on her own for nearly six years. Still, it paid to be cautious. She approached the open window on the passenger's side, bent over, and regarded the driver warily.

He was young, about her own age she guessed, and not much larger than she was. That was a plus. If he tried anything she could probably handle him. His long brown hair was combed straight back. She couldn't tell if it was damp from hair dressing or just dirty. His large brown eyes seemed to be examining her as carefully as she was him.

Mary Guilfoyle was a beautiful woman, and she knew it. She stood 5 feet 7½ inches barefoot, which she often was, and her 115 pounds fit attractively into the size 8 red minidress she was wearing. It was a breezy, Indian summer day with the temperature near eighty, and she didn't need a sweater or jacket. Her wavy, sandy-colored hair fell below her chin, framing her face, and her green eyes crinkled at the corners when she smiled. After a few seconds, he grinned in return. She decided he was all right.

Mary began to ask if he was driving into Santa Cruz, but he interrupted before she could finish. "Where are you going?" he asked.

"Downtown," she replied. "To the state employment office."

"I'm going right by there."

"Hey, great." She opened the door and climbed in next to him. "Thanks."

The car pulled away from where it had stopped on Soquel Drive below the modern buildings of the campus. Neither of them spoke. In a minute they were approaching the intersection with Park Avenue.

"Maybe it would be a little quicker if we took the freeway," she suggested hopefully.

"Oh, yeah," he said absently. "Sure." He turned to the left on Park and then right on to the ramp leading to the northbound traffic on Highway 1.

Mary decided against trying to start a conversation. The old car was pretty dirty and littered with papers. She noticed a battered brown briefcase in the back, and wondered if he might be a student at Cabrillo. She didn't remember seeing him before. He seemed content not to talk, and that was just fine. She sensed the same awkward tension she had detected before on the rare occasions when she had thumbed a ride with a man. She didn't feel threatened by it, but she would be glad when the trip was over.

Mary settled back for the six-mile drive. After about five minutes he flicked on his right turn indicator. He was getting off the freeway at Emeline Avenue rather than going on to the main interchange at Ocean Street.

"Is this the right way?" she demanded.

"It's shorter," he answered. Since she didn't have a car, Mary didn't drive much, but she realized they were close to the employment office. She relaxed, and her thoughts wandered. After her appointment, she would take a bus across town to the little apartment she shared with her boyfriend on East Cliff Drive in Twin Lakes. Suddenly she was aware the car had stopped. She looked around. They weren't at the state office.

"What's going on? . . ."

She never saw the hunting knife he had brought up from under the front seat. He grunted with effort as he struck across her chest with it clenched in his right hand. The blade pierced her heart, killing her instantly. She fell forward without a sound, and he raised the knife and stabbed her twice in the back. With the force of the blows she slipped from the seat to the floor. The young man put the knife beside her and started driving again. He was gratified to see there was no blood on the upholstery.

Half an hour later the blue and white station wagon was slowly following the sharp turns of Smith Grade as it descended from its junction with Empire Grade in the hills northeast of town. After crossing Majors Creek about five miles from the turnoff, it glided to a halt on the right side of the road. The driver got out and looked around. There were no cars coming, and he had seen none for several minutes.

He half-dragged and half-carried the body down a shallow bank about 125 yards into a copse with a small clearing shielded from the road by brush and fallen trees. He laid the dead girl on the ground, which was still damp and steaming slightly from the rain the night before. Gently, he spread her knees and knelt between her legs. The knife was steady in his hand as he gazed at the body and pondered where to begin.

Blood erupted through the light fabrics of her dress and panties as the blade sliced deeply across Mary's lower abdomen and then from her belly up to her sternum. The second incision cut cleanly through the center of her bra, which fell apart, exposing her breasts. He placed the knife on the dirt. His fingers slipped as he tried to pull apart the crimson muscle wall and blood flowed over his hands. He was aware of a faint metallic smell, and was a little surprised at the residual warmth of her body as he groped inside it. He withdrew the stomach and part of the small intestine. He tried to find the liver and kidneys, and then reached up under the rib cage. He felt a spongy mass and heard a gurgling as his fingers encountered the lungs. Finally he stood. Blood soaked his sleeves to above the elbows, and his jeans were damp with it. He looked with detachment at the grotesque shambles at his feet. The girl's eyes were open, staring back lifelessly. It would be dark soon, time to leave. He took off his shirt and, using a corner that had not been stained, wiped the knife as clean as he could. It had not gone well. He started back to the car.

As the noise of the engine died away in the distance, the sounds of the forest that had been stilled when the intruder came gradually returned. It was twilight. Crickets began to chirp, and the sparrows scolded a raucous blue jay that hopped around the body. First one and then several vultures circled overhead, and the leaves rustled softly as the first small animals ventured timidly into the clearing, attracted by the buzzing of the flies and the scent of decay.

4
The Priest

JEFF TOWLE was alarmed when Mary didn't return to the apartment on Tuesday night. She had said she would be home early. The next day, after learning from her supervisor that she had failed to appear at the college Wednesday, he became frantic.

The detectives at the sheriff's office were sympathetic but did not raise his hopes. They told him bluntly that girls dropped out of sight all the time. The younger ones were usually runaways. Often they were never seen again.

But Jeff knew that Mary had not wandered off. What had started a few years earlier as a common interest in poetry and literature had blossomed into love and a permanent commitment. He began calling their friends, hoping in vain she might be staying with one of them for some reason, at the same time knowing it was not so because she would have telephoned him.

He dreaded calling her parents, who lived in upstate New York.

Along with most of coastal California, Santa Cruz has been visited periodically by catastrophic earthquakes since the beginning of the

Cenozoic Era. The San Andreas Fault, that great fissure that runs from the Sea of Cortez north to Alaska, transects the eastern side of the Santa Cruz Mountains about fifteen miles north of the city.

In the fall of 1800, three years after the first adobe houses were built at the pueblo, the mission fathers recorded that the ground shook intermittently for twenty days, and huge cracks appeared in the earth near the Pajaro River. Damage also occurred during the big tremors of 1838 and 1865, and during the 1906 earthquake that left San Francisco in smoldering ruins.

In the 1920s a few scientists began to speculate that the primeval convulsions that had created the continents might have been the result of shifting land masses, terrestrial plates floating on the molten core of the planet. They were dismissed by most of their peers as harmless eccentrics. In 1953, two California geologists put forth the idea that land on the west side of the San Andreas Fault had been moving horizontally northward for as long as 150 million years, and that Monterey Bay had been 225 miles south of its present location between 38 and 58 million years ago. Not all their colleagues concurred. In the 1960s, however, the theory of continental drift began to be generally accepted.

By 1972 it was known that the San Andreas Fault forms the boundary between the North American plate, which appears to be stationary, and the vast Pacific plate that is moving north, creating the grinding stress that builds up to earthquakes. Santa Cruz, and the rest of the coast between San Francisco and Mexico, is actually on the eastern edge of the chunk of the earth's crust upon which ride the islands of the Pacific. It is a place in but not of North America.

In the early 1970s seismologists from all over the world began concentrating their studies on the area just east of the Santa Cruz Mountains, generally agreeing it would be the epicenter of the next major California earthquake. They were unwilling, however, to be as precise as a man named Reuben Greenspan, a self-styled mathematician who dwelt as a hermit with his string of mules in a remote corner of Death Valley and who had been "predicting" earthquakes for forty years. In 1972 he confidently foretold that a cataclysm of enormous magnitude would occur between Santa Cruz and San Francisco at 9:00 A.M. January 4, 1973. The newspapers and television reporters found the old desert rat colorful and cooperative, and his prediction received widespread attention.

But the people of Santa Cruz are Californians, after all, and Californians regard earthquakes as a fact of life, just as Midwesterners live with the threat of tornadoes.

Almost no one took Greenspan seriously.

The place appeared to be empty when the young man entered. He had not seen any passersby when he parked on the quiet residential street in Los Gatos, nor had anyone come out of Saint Mary's Catholic Church as he walked up the steps. He hesitated inside the large open doors, wondering where everyone was. Even though it was a Thursday afternoon, it was November 2, All Souls Day, and he had not expected the church to be deserted. Dipping the fingers of his right hand in the water in the stoup, he quickly made the sign of the cross, genuflected automatically in the direction of the tabernacle on the altar, and started walking slowly down the center aisle.

After a few steps he paused again. There was a light burning over the confessional to his left. A priest was inside, waiting to hear penitents. He was not alone after all.

The young man reached under the left side of his dark jacket and felt the reassuring smoothness of the knife handle above the leather sheath on his belt. His eyes rested on the light. Bending momentarily to lift a kneeler that was in his way, he edged clumsily through two pews to the side aisle. Holding his breath, he jerked on the door to the priest's compartment. It was locked. Frustrated, he rattled the knob, trying to force the latch. The expression on his face turned to one of uncertainty. He started to turn away.

Inside the confessional Father Henri Tomei, the church's assistant pastor, was startled by the commotion. He slipped the bolt, opened the door, and stepped outside. There was a young man standing there. His nostrils caught the faint odor of whiskey.

When he heard the rasp of the bolt, the young man froze. The door swung open, revealing a man in a cassock. He was short, squarely built, with gray hair. Before the priest could speak the knife ripped upward into his chest. The force of the thrust carried both men back into the confessional. The wounded man grappled silently with his attacker, who was suddenly alarmed at his strength. He knew the blade must have reached the heart. Why had the priest's powerful hands not gone slack? The knife clattered to the floor, and the young man tumbled out of the booth to recover it. He felt a sharp pain. The priest had managed to kick him above the ear. He got to his feet, shaking his head to clear it. Father Tomei had turned and was grasping the bench, trying to pull himself up. The young man hacked downward with the knife, but it glanced off the base of the priest's skull.

Father Tomei's eyes rolled. *"Mon Dieu,"* he whispered.

The knife struck twice more, and the struggle was over.

The young man rose from his knees. The body was crumpled in the doorway, the legs protruding into the aisle. He tried to kick them inside so he could close the door. Someone screamed. He turned slowly. No one was there, but he heard retreating footsteps. He sheathed the knife, wiped his sweating palms on his dark pants, and walked to a side exit at the rear of the church. There was nobody around when he stepped into the cool sunshine. Moving more quickly now, he got into the blue and white station wagon and drove away. Within a few blocks he was on the main commercial artery of Los Gatos, and a few minutes later pulled on to Highway 17 toward Santa Cruz twenty miles to the west. He was unconcerned when a black and white patrol car passed him going the other way with its red light and siren on.

The young man drove over the pass, through tall trees and past autumn-colored vineyards. With indifference born of familiarity he ignored the magnificent view from the summit of mist-covered mountains. Driving carefully, he took the Mount Hermon turnoff at Scott's Valley. When he reached the driveway, he left the car outside and found a hose. Opening the two front doors, he directed the full force of the spray on the floor mats for several minutes. Then he scrubbed the soaked carpeting vigorously with a stiff brush. The ten-day-old bloodstains left by Mary Guilfoyle had turned brown. He could not eradicate them completely. He turned off the water, coiled the hose, and left the car open so the floor would dry.

Father Richard Howley, the pastor of Saint Mary's, was in his office when he heard Mrs. Margaret Reed, a parishioner from the nearby town of Saratoga, shrieking and pounding on the door of the rectory. He ran to the church and found Father Tomei.

"Call an ambulance," he barked at Clara Pederson, the parish secretary and housekeeper who had followed him. "Call the police." He pulled a purple stole from his pocket, kissed the cross embroidered on it, and draped it around his neck. There were tears in his eyes.

By the time the ambulance arrived, Father Howley had almost finished administering Extreme Unction. He rode with his friend to Los Gatos Community Hospital, where Father Tomei was pronounced dead shortly after 4:00 P.M.

Sergeant Jim Shea was among the first policemen to get to Saint Mary's after the call came from Mrs. Pederson. He and the other detectives learned a short time later that Father Tomei was dead. They sealed off the church and began searching for evidence.

Los Gatos is a small city in Santa Clara County over the ridge from Santa Cruz that grew from a single sawmill built in 1850 into a quiet, predominantly residential community of about 24,000 by 1972. Although essentially a suburb of San Jose, it retained a rural character more in keeping with its name, derived from the mountain lions that roamed the foothills well into the twentieth century. The small Los Gatos police department is modern and efficient, but it had never had to deal with a crime that created the outcry caused by the priest's murder.

The detectives began by taking a statement from the shaken Mrs. Reed. As she entered the church she caught only a glimpse of the killer, who was stomping Father Tomei. She said he was white, young, slender, about six feet tall, wearing a black shirt or jacket, black trousers, and black laced boots. Shea gave the description to the reporters who had begun to besiege the church.

"So far there doesn't appear to be any motive at all," he told them. "He was stabbed, but we haven't found a weapon." He refused to speculate whether the murderer had been waiting in ambush inside the confessional.

From Mrs. Pederson and Father Howley the detectives pieced together Father Tomei's last hours. He had said two masses in the morning and was scheduled to celebrate a third in the evening. All Souls and Christmas are the only two days of the year Catholic priests may offer more than two. Later in the morning he visited patients at two convalescent hospitals and conducted a funeral. After a late lunch with Father Howley, he had told Mrs. Pederson he was walking over to the church, less than twenty yards from the rectory.

"I'm going to see if there's anybody there for confession," he had said. "I'll be right back."

At 6:00 P.M. the church bells tolled for the mass, but police guards kept worshippers away from the building. As news of the murder spread, some of the parishioners gathered outside to pray. The officers watched them closely for any sign that one of them might be the killer.

The preliminary report from the coroner said a broad, sharp object had run through Father Tomei's heart, and that he had been stabbed twice in the back and once in the back of the head. Police technicians rolled a set of fingerprints from the body for comparison with any found at the scene of the murder. Fingerprints also were taken from Father Howley and other members of the church staff. All of them were checked against those lifted from the confessional. One incomplete set was different. It was sent to Sacramento and to the FBI in Washington at the same time analysts began comparing it with prints on file in Los Gatos and the rest of Santa Clara County.

The next day Police Chief Harold Johnson appealed to the residents of Los Gatos to report anything they might have seen in the neighborhood of the church near the time of the murder. Although the department received hundreds of calls, none of the information was useful. No one had seen a car or a stranger answering Mrs. Reed's description. Johnson didn't give up hope that another witness might turn up.

"Most of what people are telling us are just little vignettes that each person thought might be helpful," he told the reporters. "They may prove the lifeblood of our investigation."

5
The Mistake

THE BRUTAL SLAYING of a priest in his confessional on one of the holiest days of the Christian calendar drew a huge amount of publicity. The outrage and revulsion were especially intense because Father Tomei was internationally known and exceptionally well liked. Although the police were under great pressure to solve the crime, they could find no apparent motive and hardly any clues.

Henri Tomei had been born in France sixty-five years earlier. His mother had died when he was a small child, and when his father was drafted to serve in the French army at the beginning of World War I, he placed the boy in an orphanage. The father died a short time later. According to his friends, Henri had decided by the time he was seven that he wanted to be a priest.

Ordained when he was twenty-four, Father Tomei never forgot his days in the orphanage. For nearly thirty years he worked among the dispossessed street urchins of his native Marseilles. A natural musical talent and puckish personality not unlike that of one of his heroes, Maurice Chevalier, combined to help him mold a ragged group of undisciplined boys into Les Petits Chanteurs de Lazare, a choir that gained international recognition. He composed hundreds of hymns sung in Roman Catholic churches throughout the world. One of the most famous, "The Virgin of Peace," was written in the waning days of World War II, after he and several companions survived an Allied air raid by huddling together under a truck. After the war he was appointed music director of the Archdiocese of Marseilles and toured several countries, including the United States, with his little singers.

In 1959 a heart ailment had forced Father Tomei to take a leave of absence from Marseilles. The only surviving members of his family, some uncles and cousins, lived in Northern California. After visiting them there, he asked for an assignment near San Francisco. In 1961 he was posted as associate pastor of Mount Carmel Parish in Redwood City, and in 1964 he moved to Saint Mary's.

Although he didn't talk about it much, Father Tomei risked his life several times during the war as a member of the French Underground. He remained fiercely patriotic, and after moving permanently to the United States, he kept his French passport and citizenship. When Georges Pompidou visited San Francisco in the late 1960s, he greeted Tomei warmly at a reception.

Hundreds of mourners, including San Francisco Mayor Joseph Alioto and the city's entire French consular corps, overflowed Saint Mary's for the Mass of the Resurrection offered November 7, 1972, by the archbishop of San Francisco. At its conclusion they filed past Father Tomei's coffin, draped with the Tricolor of France.

None of them noticed the plainclothesman across the street filming them as they entered and left the church.

The night of Father Tomei's funeral, Marilynn and I were propped up in bed, reading. She was scanning the evening paper. I was going over my notes for a lecture the next day. It was late, and our five sons were all ensconced in their various bedrooms, presumably sleeping. We were enjoying the luxury of the nocturnal quiet.

In the years we had been married, Marilynn had come to understand that psychiatrists occasionally have to deal with violent people. She put down the newspaper.

"Do you think there's any chance you might end up working on this case?" she asked. "For either side?"

Some of my students had been asking me a similar question, but framed differently: "Hey, do you think the guy who knifed the priest is crazy?" I gave the same answer.

"I don't have the faintest idea," I replied, turning off the light and reaching for her.

"Anyone who would do a thing like that has to be insane," she insisted.

"Not necessarily," I said, kissing her. "Besides, from what the papers say, they don't have much chance of catching the killer."

The investigations into the deaths of Father Tomei and the disappearance of Mary Guilfoyle proceeded independently as 1972 came to an end. Lawrence White's case had been dropped.

A week after Mary vanished, her boyfriend and her supervisor at work placed an advertisement in the Santa Cruz *Sentinel.* Under a badly reproduced picture of her smiling winsomely from behind a tree was the plea: URGENT, HAVE YOU SEEN THIS GIRL? It was followed by a description and the two men's telephone numbers. No one called.

By late November students and teachers at Cabrillo College, dissatisfied with what they thought the sheriff's office was doing, raised a fund to hire a private detective. He talked to everyone he could find who knew her and tried to trace her movements the day she failed to come home. The investigator finally agreed with the authorities that Mary had probably been kidnapped while she was hitchhiking. He also concluded that she undoubtedly had been murdered.

As Christmas vacation approached, the sheriff's office, Santa Cruz police, and administrators at both Cabrillo and the University of California issued repeated warnings against hitchhiking. Some car pools were set up, and students, especially young women, were advised against traveling alone. Still, on any given day, scores of solitary coeds could be seen standing along the highways near the two campuses, waiting patiently for free rides.

In Los Gatos, the sensation engendered by the murder of Father Tomei began to die away. After sitting through several showings of the videotape the police had made at the church during the requiem mass, a tired Mrs. Reed told them she was sure the killer had not attended the service.

The frustrated police went over the case again and again. The fingerprints found on the confessional could not be identified. Whoever the murderer was, he had no criminal record, nor had he ever held a job that required him to be fingerprinted. A painstaking investigation of the priest's life revealed no hidden secrets. It seemed that no one on either side of the Atlantic had any reason to want him dead.

There was a flurry of renewed interest in the Guilfoyle case just after the New Year, when another Cabrillo coed, Cynthia Schall, disappeared while she was hitchhiking to school. Neither the Santa Cruz police nor the sheriff's detectives could find any link between the two apparent kidnappings. A few days later parts of a woman's body that had been hacked apart began washing up along the coast.

It took several weeks for the medical examiner to determine that the remains were those of Cynthia Schall.

On December 29, 1972, Reuben Greenspan, the crusty, sixty-seven-year-old seer who had predicted an earthquake the following week along the San Andreas Fault, held a press conference to announce that he had made a mistake.

Described by one journalist as a man "who looks like an Old Testament prophet temporarily wearing twentieth-century garb," the bearded Greenspan, wearing a neat dark suit, appeared before 100 sometimes hostile reporters. None of them told him the zipper in his trousers was halfway open. Although he obviously was ill at ease, he was not rattled by their questions.

Greenspan said he had started predicting earthquakes in the 1930s using a complicated mathematical formula with which he calculated the maximum tidal strain at different points on the earth's crust caused by the sun and the moon. He supposedly had presaged tremors accurately in the Pacific before World War II, but most of his forecasts after 1935 failed to come true. His reputation had been revived when he successfully predicted the Los Angeles earthquake of February 9, 1971. But this time, he said, he was wrong.

"I goofed," he told the reporters. "I just plain goofed. I made an error in my calculations. I made a mistake and I apologize. I do my work in Death Valley, where the temperature gets up to 135° in my room and the perspiration drips all over my notes." He blamed his error on his having to work out extremely complex computations with paper and pencil.

The old recluse denied that he had ever claimed any of the academic credentials that newspapers over the decades had attached to him. His background, he said, was in marine navigation.

Finally he said he was going back to his cabin in the desert, forty miles from the nearest post office.

"Sometimes I talk to my mules," he added wistfully. "I want to go back where God, man, and the devil can't find me."

The young man reread the account of Greenspan's recantation in the next morning's edition of the San Francisco *Chronicle.* Sipping his coffee, he went over the article a third time.

It was confusing. Greenspan obviously knew the real answer, knew why the earthquake wouldn't happen.

He wondered why he had lied to the reporters at the news conference.

6
The Dealers

KATHY FRANCIS was not fully awake when the knock came. It had been raining incessantly for two days, and even though it was almost 9:00 A.M., the sky was gloomy and it was pitch dark inside the cluttered little cabin. Rain always made her sleepy, and the boys were still snoring fitfully in their bunk.

She heard the tapping on the door again. One of the kids stirred, disturbed by the noise. Annoyed, she swung her legs off the folding couch that served as a double bed, sat on the edge, and ran her fingers through her disheveled brown hair. It couldn't be Bob, she thought. He wasn't due home until that night, and besides he would walk in without knocking. It probably wasn't the police either. They would bang harder.

Anxious to answer the door before whoever it was knocked again and woke her two sons, Kathy rose and padded in her bare feet across the cold floor of the unheated shack without taking the time to light a candle. Clutching the top of her mismatched pajamas closed against her chest, she opened the door a couple of inches and peeked outside. The light was bad, and her brain was still a little numb, but she thought she recognized the young man standing on the porch. She couldn't quite remember where she had seen him.

"Hi," she whispered sleepily, her voice thick.

"Hello," he answered. "Is Jim Gianera here?"

"No."

"When do you expect him?" the man asked. Consciousness was returning slowly, but Kathy still couldn't recall who he was. He seemed to be very polite.

"They haven't lived out here for months," she said.

"Where can I find them?"

Kathy regarded the young man with some suspicion. He was wearing a blue-checked overcoat, his long hair was combed, and he was clean-shaven. She doubted he was a narc. His appearance was too neat. They were always dirtier and more outlandishly dressed than the drug dealers they tried to infiltrate. Anyway, if he had wanted to make a buy, he probably would have asked for Bob rather than Jim.

"What do you want with Jim?" she demanded.

"I just wanted to talk to him. I'm an old friend."

"Yeah. I guess I've seen you around."

"Yeah." He waited. Kathy shivered in the damp cold. She wanted to go back to bed.

"He and Joan moved into their house over on Western last October," she said.

"Oh. I didn't know it was finished."

"It wasn't, really, but enough for them to move in."

"Do you know the address?"

"It's 520."

"Five-twenty Western Drive," he repeated.

"Yeah."

"Thanks. Sorry I bothered you."

"That's OK, cousin. 'Bye."

Softly, she shut the door and tiptoed back to the still-warm couch. She could hear snuffling from the bunk in the other room. She pulled the blankets over her head and closed her eyes. Shit, she thought, I hope they go back to sleep. It's too early to hassle with kids.

Outside, the young man stood for a moment in the protection of the dripping overhang, waiting for the rain to let up long enough for him to slosh down the muddy road to his car without getting soaked.

The January downpour had turned the steep dirt driveway into a slippery quagmire, and he had not been able to make it up the hill with the station wagon.

He took in his surroundings. The atmosphere around the tiny log building smelled faintly of mildew. Near the porch a couple of dingy sheets hung soddenly on a drooping clothesline, next to a surfboard leaned against the wall. Tacked to a corner was a tattered color picture of Christ over the words, "He is risen." Near the door he could see a crude, hand-lettered sign asking visitors not to smoke inside because one of the children was ill.

The cabin, nearly obscured on three sides by brush and berry brambles, was one of a handful of rustic dwellings that shared a common address on Branciforte Drive, a highway that winds from Santa Cruz into the mountains past the municipal golf course in DeLaveaga Park. Up the hill from the porch stood a house trailer. A small brick house and another trailer were above that. Although the mailbox was on Branciforte Drive, the primitive residences actually were off a side road leading to the Mystery Spot, an old house that had become a tourist attraction because it was set at a cant that made it appear things rolled uphill.

The young man waited patiently, his shoulders hunched and his hands deep in his pockets, until the rain slackened. He started down the hill.

Upstairs in the house on Western Drive, seven miles from the little cabin, Joan Gianera was looking forward to a steaming, cleansing shower. It was one of the few luxuries she could afford these days. The utility company had turned off the electricity nine days earlier because she and Jim hadn't been able to pay the bill, but the gas was still on and the house had hot water.

They were having enough trouble without having to live in the dark. It was partly his fault. If he hadn't been so moody about not finding carpentry work, they wouldn't have fought so much. She didn't like the idea that Jim and Bob Francis could only seem to make money dealing dope. Not that she had any objections to marijuana, but hauling and selling it was dangerous. If they didn't get arrested, they were going to get into trouble with some of the heavy types they did business with. Their mutual worries had often led to violent arguments between Joan and Jim, and brief separations.

Joan closed the door to the small upstairs bathroom, took off her clothes, and dropped them on the floor. She gazed at herself in the mirror over the counter opposite the toilet. She thought the woman who looked back at her was unremarkable: twenty-one years old, 5 feet 3, 115 pounds, long brown hair, a lean body with small breasts and hip bones that protruded slightly above her groin. She shaved her legs because of her dancing classes, but curling tufts of fine body hair were visible under her armpits.

She had kept a doctor's appointment on Wednesday, January 24, and later had a dancing lesson, so she had asked her parents, who lived not far away, to babysit with their eighteen-month-old daughter, Monica. That was yesterday. The baby had stayed all night with her grandparents. As soon as she had showered, Joan would pick her up.

Downstairs, James Gianera sat glumly in the kitchen, his jacket draped over the back of a chair. He could hear the water running in the shower upstairs. Although gray light came through the window by the refrigerator, the corners of the room were in semidarkness. Maybe when Bob Francis got back from his trip there would be enough money to pay the light bill, he thought. They hadn't made a score in a long time, and the debts were piling up. He had even had to borrow one of Bob's trucks, the twenty-five-year-old pickup, to get around. His own panel truck had broken down. It was parked out front, useless, and he couldn't afford to get it fixed. Well, things would improve when the estate was settled, he thought. His inheritance wouldn't amount to much, a few thousand dollars, but it would solve their problems for a while.

He rose and walked into the living room, where it was brighter. His practiced eye roamed around the walls and up the open stairway, catching tiny flaws in construction that no one else would see. It was a good house. He was a skilled carpenter, and it was a good house. He vaguely resented the fact that it belonged to Joan's father, but if he hadn't put up the money, they never would have been able to build it. It had been a family project, and during the summer Bob had helped Jim and his father-in-law close it up in time for them to move in before winter.

He started slightly when he heard a knock at the door. He opened it to find a young man standing outside on the cement walkway.

"Oh, hello," Gianera said. "It's been a while." He did not invite the visitor inside. The man looked at him steadily.

"I'm really pissed about the time I've been wasting," he told Gianera.

"I don't know what you're talking about," Jim said curtly. A bell rang. "Just a minute," he said. "I've gotta get the phone." As Gianera retreated into the kitchen, the young man stepped inside and closed the door. Jim answered the telephone. It was Joan's mother, Elanor Foster.

"I was just wondering when Joan planned to pick up the baby," she said. "I thought maybe she'd like to go to lunch."

"I'm not sure," Jim said. "She's upstairs in the shower."

"Have her call me when she's finished."

"Right."

When he turned after hanging up, Jim was surprised to see the young man standing in the living room. He suddenly felt uneasy.

"Do you know where Jeannie is?" the visitor asked conversationally.

"No. Don drove by a few weeks ago. Maybe she's down in Big Sur." There was an awkward silence. "What do you want?" Jim asked. He took a step forward.

The young man was considerably shorter and lighter than Gianera's 5 foot 10, 180-pound frame. He stepped back defensively and pulled a small black revolver from his belt. "You're claptrapping me," he screamed.

Jim saw the gun, turned, and ran into the kitchen. He heard a pop and felt a sting on his right arm. He jerked the refrigerator door open to shield himself. The second shot struck him in the left elbow, shattering the bone. He lurched against the refrigerator, spilling some of its contents, and groped wildly for a weapon. As the young man advanced, Jim's hand found a plastic milk bottle. He tried to hurl it, but it slipped from his bloody fingers and tumbled to the floor.

Blindly, Gianera charged his attacker, who sidestepped backward and fired again. The bullet smashed through a rib and punctured Jim's lung as he scrabbled at the other man's coat. He reeled back against the stairway. Grasping the railing, he pulled himself up and stumbled frantically up the stairs. He had to get to Joan. A fourth shot slammed into the door jamb above the landing.

Joan had turned the water off and was drying herself when she heard what sounded like firecrackers downstairs, followed by crashing noises and a thumping on the stairs. Clutching a gaily colored bath towel, she opened the door. Jim was staggering around the corner of the landing. Blood oozed from the left side of the ski sweater he was wearing. His eyes were bulging. There was another explosion and crimson blossomed over his mustache and sideburns. She dropped the towel as the weight of his body struck her, pushing her back. He tried to slam the bathroom door, but someone was outside blocking it. Horrified, she watched her husband drop to his knees and fall forward, blood pumping from the corner of his mouth. She looked up. There was a man with a gun. Before what was happening fully registered, he shot her through the left chest, and she fell backward. She tried to roll over, to cradle her husband's head, to protect him.

"Jim, I love you," she gasped. "I love you."

The young man heard the naked woman moaning softly. He jerked the hunting knife from the sheath on his belt and stabbed her once in the back. Her body arched spasmodically. He knew Gianera was dead, but he was not sure about her. Carefully, he swung open the cylinder of the little revolver, shook out the empty shells and reloaded it from a box of cartridges he took out of his pocket. Rapidly he fired three times though the woman's neck. Then, aiming precisely, he shot her over the left eye.

The killer stepped back out of the bathroom and made a quick search of the only other upstairs room, a bedroom with a sliding glass door leading to a deck. In addition to a bed, there was a sleeping bag on the floor.

Returning to the bathroom, he picked up the cartridge casings and then walked down the stairs. He looked through the rooms on the first floor. The crib in the one next to the kitchen was empty. He reloaded the gun again in the living room but didn't count the empty shells when he retrieved them from the deep pile carpet and put them in his pocket. As he stuck the revolver back in his belt, he noticed a button was missing from his coat. He looked around but couldn't find it.

The telephone rang. Instinctively he took a step to answer it, then checked himself. It was time to leave.

As the young man stepped out the front door and closed it behind him, two large, friendly dogs romped up to him, wagging their tails. The yard, enclosed by a high wire fence, was cluttered with scraps of lumber left over from construction. He fumbled momentarily with the latch on the tall wooden gate. It was on the outside, and he had to reach up and over to manipulate it. He shooed the dogs away so they wouldn't escape as he left and locked the gate.

It had stopped raining, but he was sure it would start again soon.

Kathy had not been able to go back to sleep after all. The brief intrusion had been enough to rouse one of the boys and, inevitably, they were fighting in a matter of minutes. Grumpily, she had put on her pink slippers, lighted a new candle and an oil lamp, and poured out their breakfast cereal. It was too wet to send them outside, so she didn't bother to make them get dressed. Little Daemon was wearing a sweater and pajama bottoms. When she told David to put on something more than his jockey shorts, he said he wasn't cold. She shrugged and didn't insist.

Kathy dreaded the day before her, imprisoned by the rain with two boys, nine and four years old. David's cold would keep him home from school again. She found some kindling and built a fire in the stove. Sometimes she thought she couldn't cope any longer. If she didn't stay stoned most of the time, she thought she would go crazy. Life was getting to be a real bummer.

After breaking up another wrestling match between the boys, she put them both back up on their bunk, gave them a Chinese Checkers board and some marbles, and ordered them to be quiet. Amazingly, they obeyed. She sat down and began eating a dried fig from a carton on the counter in the kitchen. She looked at the brown and withered Christmas tree still standing amid the debris in the living room where she and the kids had decorated it six weeks ago. When the rain stops I guess I'll have to take it down, she thought.

The young man parked the station wagon at the bottom of the hill again and walked toward the cabin. It would be troublesome if he got stuck in the mud.

He strode to the door and, without hesitation, turned the knob and shoved it open. It jammed on a warped spot in the floor, and he had to push his way in sideways. Kathy, taken off guard, rose from her chair. The boys looked up from their game.

"Could I have a couple of words with you?" he asked.

"Yes . . ." My God, she thought, he has a gun.

With incredible speed he fired four shots. The first hit Kathy in the left chest, the second passed through her brain. The third bullet struck four-year-old Daemon in the left eye. The fourth opened a neat hole in David's forehead.

The boys lay crumpled on the bed. Marbles spilled from David's lifeless hand. Kathy had slumped to the floor, still clutching the dried fig. The young man slipped the revolver back into his belt and withdrew the knife. He bent over and stabbed Kathy in the chest, and then stabbed each child in the back.

He left less than a minute after he had arrived, scraping the door shut.

7

Three Bodies

ABOUT 11:30 A.M. Larry Hill heard dogs barking outside the house. He and Chris had been up late the night before, and they had slept late. He looked outside and saw a red truck. Three men got out, and one of them started toward his front door. He went to meet him.

"We're from the Branciforte Fire District," the man explained. "I'm Captain Larsen. We're checking house numbers. Do all these places have the same address?"

"Yes."

"Who lives there?" he asked, pointing to the cabin down the hill.

"Bob and Kathy Francis and their two kids." Two young volunteer firemen went to the door of the cabin and knocked. There was no answer. "Bob's away, I think," Hill told the captain. "I guess she and the boys went out."

Inside the cabin the oil in the lamp had been consumed, and it had flickered out. The candle guttered in the kitchen, casting a shadowy light on the three still forms. The only sound was the ticking of Kathy's big wristwatch. If anyone had been able to see through a window, it would have looked as if they were sleeping.

Susan Harmon brought Christopher home from the doctor at 1:30 P.M. His foot had been swollen painfully when he woke up that morning, and it was obvious the cut he got the day before had infected. The doctor had cleaned the wound and injected him with an antibiotic, and by the time they got back to their house trailer above the Francis place, he was feeling much better. The rain had stopped, and he wanted to go outside.

Susan knew that David had stayed home that day too, since she usually drove both boys to school. She told her son he could go and ask Mrs. Francis if David was well enough to play.

Christopher walked the hundred yards to the cabin. He and David were best friends, even though David was two years older. He knocked on the door, but no one came.

"David, are you home?" he called.

Disappointed and lonely, the little boy trudged back up the hill, talking to himself.

Bob Francis was getting impatient. The deal wasn't turning out the way he had expected. He had dropped off seven pounds of grass the day before, but the client still had not come up with the money. He said he would have it by midnight. Bob knew he was good for it, but it meant it would be the middle of the night before he got home. He might even have to spend another night in Berkeley, and he'd been gone two days already.

Wednesday morning Bob and Jim Gianera had driven up to Ben Lomond to pick up the shipment. He had dropped Jim off at his parents' home before leaving to make the sale in Berkeley. When the client told him he wouldn't have the money until the next day, Bob decided to drive on up to Marysville. He had heard that several of his connections there had been busted in a big raid, and he wanted to find out what had happened. He stayed the night with friends and returned to Berkeley on Thursday. After finding out late in the day that it would be another several hours before he could collect, Bob called his supplier and told him he wouldn't get back to Santa Cruz until Friday. He thought he had better let Kathy know. She always worried when he was late, afraid that he was in jail.

Nancy Crowly received the call about 9:30 P.M. The house she and her daughter shared with Steve Houts had the only telephone in the odd little compound off Mystery Spot Road. Steve needed it for his job as a sign painter. Sometimes it was more of a nuisance than a convenience, since their ever-changing neighbors often used them as a message center. This time it was Bob Francis.

"Could somebody go up and tell Kathy I might not be home tonight?" he asked. "If I do make it, it'll be late."

"Sure," Nancy said.

"Tell her not to worry," Francis added.

"I'll go," Houts said.

It was a fairly long hike up the hill to the cabin, and it was muddy. Steve decided to drive up in his Volkswagen bus. He saw no lights when he parked in front of the cabin. She must have gone to bed early, he thought. There was no answer to his knock.

"Kathy," he called, "it's me, Steve." Still no answer. He banged on the door again, then opened it a crack. "Kathy? Anybody home?"

The headlights of his van illuminated the bed, which was near the door. There was no one in it. He pushed the door open a little further and stepped inside. There was a dim light from a candle burning in the kitchen. Kathy was curled up on the floor. She must be stoned, he thought. He walked over and shook her shoulder. He could feel her skin through her pajamas. It was cold. "Kathy . . ." He saw dried blood on her lips. The hair prickled on the back of his neck.

"David," he shouted. "Deamon!" He ran into the little room next to the kitchen where he knew the boys' bed was. They were in it, but there was no blanket over them. He touched them. They were both stiff.

Houts ran outside. There was a light on in Thatcher Clarke's trailer. He started running, slipping and falling in the mud. Clarke heard him screaming and came out to meet him. He was groggy, as if he had been asleep.

"What's the matter, man?"

"I think everyone in that house is dead," Houts yelled.

Clarke rubbed his eyes. "Oh, no. I thought something weird was going on there today."

Houts turned toward his car. "I gotta call the cops," he said.

"No, wait . . ."

"Waddaya mean, wait?"

"Man, I mean what's going on?" Houts thought Clarke was having a hard time grasping what he was telling him.

"Listen," he repeated, "I'm going down to call the cops."

"What for, man?" Clarke called after him.

Houts was already in the bus. As he turned it around, he saw Clarke running up the road.

"My God, what happened?" Nancy asked after Steve hung up the phone.

"They're all dead."

"She's been awful depressed lately," she said. "She must have killed the kids and then committed suicide."

Sheriff's detective Mike Aluffi pulled into the muddy driveway off Mystery Spot Road at 10:20 P.M. His headlights shone through the falling mist, picking up the familiar forms of Al Stevens, a patrol division lieutenant, and three other officers. Stevens was standing next to a patrol car talking into a radio microphone.

"What we got?" the detective asked.

"Three DOA's. A woman and a couple of kids."

"The dispatcher said 187."

"The guy who found the bodies said he thought it might be murder-suicide. I didn't stay inside long enough to see if she had a weapon."

"Who found them?" Aluffi asked.

"A man named Houts. He lives down the hill there. He was waiting for us outside his place when we got here about five minutes ago. After I made sure everybody in there was dead, I chased the neighbors away and told them to go home and wait for us to talk to them."

Aluffi gazed around. It was difficult to see the other dwellings in the darkness. "Very many people live around here?" he asked.

"Hard to say. Looks like a bunch of crash pads full of hippies."

"Who'd you call so far?"

"Everybody."

"The technician rolling?"

"Yep. And Lieutenant Pittenger. And the captain. And the assistant sheriff. We'll have all the help we need."

Terry Medina was at home watching television when the telephone rang about 10:30 P.M. It was another sheriff's detective, Sergeant Brad Arbsland.

"I'll be by to pick you up in about twenty minutes," Arbsland said.

"What's going down?"

"A triple homicide."

"Wonderful," Medina observed dryly. He knew he would be up all night.

Pittenger, the chief of investigation, was at the cabin when Arbsland and Medina got there, along with over a dozen other officers and detectives. Since the place had no electricity, they were waiting for the fire department to bring up some portable generators before going inside. The lieutenant told the investigators to start interviewing the neighbors.

When Medina and another detective walked up to the house where Houts and Nancy Crowley lived, they saw a frightened-looking young couple standing in front, looking up the hill. "You Mr. Houts?" Medina asked the man.

"No. Steve and Nancy were babysitting for us. We just got back from dinner at Zachary's."

"That's right," Houts interjected from the doorway. "They just got here."

"OK," Medina told the nervous couple. "You can leave. I'm Detective Medina," he added to Houts. "Mind if we come in?"

"No." Houts stepped back and opened the door wider. Nancy was standing behind him. Medina nodded to her and opened his notebook.

Terry Medina was accomplished when it came to questioning young members of the counterculture. His dark good looks and open, pleasant manner inspired confidence, and his youthful appearance discouraged any generational distrust. An experienced detective at twenty-six, he had nonetheless grown a mustache to make him look older.

"The lieutenant told me about how you found the body," he said. "I want to ask you some preliminary questions before we get back to that."

Nancy told him that she had moved into the house with her daughter, Sara, the previous May, some months after the Francises set up housekeeping in the cabin up the hill. At that time another couple lived with Bob and Kathy—Jim and Joan Gianera. The Gianeras had moved out last fall. Medina made a note of the names.

"When did you move in?" Medina asked Houts.

"Last month."

"You two married?"

"No."

"How about the Francises?"

Houts shrugged. "I doubt it," Nancy said. "We never asked." Medina wondered if anybody bothered to get married anymore.

"Did you know them very well?"

"Yes," Nancy said. "We were pretty good friends. Kathy took care of Sara sometimes."

"Do you think she might have been depressed about anything?"

Nancy hesitated. "I think she was a very weak individual," she said finally, "mentally, I mean. She was worried all the time, and constantly depressed over what a drag it was raising the kids. Bob was gone a lot, and that bothered her too."

"Is he the boys' father?"

"No. Well, yes, Daemon is his, but the oldest belongs to Kathy and her ex."

"You said Bob is gone a lot."

"Yeah," Houts said. "He just, like comes and goes. If he's going to be gone longer than he thought, he usually phones here and asks one of us to give Kathy the message. He's done that a lot in the last couple months."

"What kind of guy is he?"

"Real mellow," Houts answered. "Kind of calm."

"Does he do anything for a living?"

"He's a kayak builder," Houts said. Medina smiled.

"Where does he go on these trips?"

"I don't know for sure. Marysville, I think, and Berkeley." There was a pause. "You know, I said Bob was mellow. For what it's worth, though, I don't think he likes cops much." Who does these days, Medina thought.

"Any particular reason?"

"No. He just had a couple of traffic beefs. It made him uptight."

Medina asked the couple for a list of the other people living in the area. Then he routinely broached the subject of narcotics.

"They may blow a little grass now and then."

"Ever seen anything else? Smack? Reds? Whites?"

"No," Nancy said. "I'm almost positive they weren't into anything hard, at least not since they moved here. I made sure, you know, because of Kathy babysitting Sara."

"When did you last see Kathy?"

"About 6:30 Wednesday night. She dropped Sara off and picked up some kindling."

"How'd she seem?"

"Really depressed," Nancy said. "She was really bummed out."

Patiently, Medina took the two back over the events of the evening —Francis's call, finding the bodies, Houts's conversation with Thatcher Clarke. They repeated their suspicion that Kathy might have killed the boys and herself.

"Did either of you see any strange cars up that way today?" Medina asked. He glanced at his watch. "I mean yesterday."

"Well, sometime between 8:00 and 10:00 in the morning I saw an old station wagon go by on the way up to Kathy's," Houts said. "It was like a '58 Chevy, maybe gray and white. I'm not sure."

"How many people?"

"One guy driving."

"Did you get a good look at him?"

"No."

"Ever see the car before?"

"No. I'm sure of that."

Thatcher Clarke had also seen the car, but he wasn't certain of the make. He told Detectives Aluffi and Arbsland, who found him in his trailer, that he thought it might have been an old Rambler. He was positive about the time, though. It had been 9:00 A.M.

"What did the guy do?" Aluffi asked.

"He tried to drive up the hill, but couldn't make it because of the mud. He backed down, and then walked up to Kathy's house."

"What did he look like?"

"He was short, medium build, straight haircut. I think he was a Mexican," Clarke added. "He was pretty well dressed, too."

"How old?"

"In his twenties or thirties."

"What did he do?"

"He knocked on the front door, and Kathy opened it. He stayed on the porch talking to her for about five minutes and then he left."

"Did you see him drive away?"

"Yeah."

"And he didn't go inside?"

"No." The detectives were disappointed. Whoever it was, he probably wasn't a suspect.

At about 12:30 A.M. the fire trucks ground up the hill with generators, and lights were set up. Detective Jim Pummill and evidence technician Ben Seibel went inside. Pummill's eyes fell on a nude photograph of a woman pinned on the wall. He could see that it was the same person who lay on the kitchen floor.

"All right," he said, "take pictures of everything. We won't move the bodies until the medical examiner gets a look at them." He began taking measurements and sketching a floor plan of the cabin.

Aluffi and Arbsland finished questioning Thatcher Clarke and started toward the next place, where Larry Hill lived with Christine Archer. Clarke, whose trailer was the closest other residence to the Francis cabin, had told them that Kathy and Bob had been arguing quite a bit lately over the fact he was away so often. Perhaps to mollify her, he said, Bob had told her they might move to Hawaii.

He also gave Aluffi the name and address of David's father, Robert Hughes, who lived in Albany, a small town near Berkeley. Clarke, who said he was a friend of the family, told the detectives that Hughes was a musician, a bassoonist who was assistant conductor of the Oakland Symphony.

Hill and Christine Archer didn't have much to add to what the investigators already knew, other than telling them about the survey by the fire department. Aluffi made a note to interview the firemen who had been there.

While Aluffi walked back down to the cabin to report to Lieutenant Pittenger, Arbsland went on to the second trailer to get a statement from Sandra Harmon. Clarke had told them he had driven her and her son, Christopher, to the doctor during the day Thursday.

"Do you have any idea who might want to kill them?" Arbsland began.

"No. They didn't have any money for anybody to steal. I think Kathy was collecting welfare, and Bob just sort of did odd jobs."

"Did either Bob or Kathy seem to be afraid of anyone?"

"No," she said, "they were real friendly with everyone. They weren't hiding or anything like that."

"Do you think he might have been dealing dope?"

"No. They smoked grass, but that's as far as it went."

"Did you know her previous . . . David's father?"

"His name is Bob Hughes. He's a composer or something. They got along great as far as I could tell."

"How about Bob and Kathy."

"They had their problems, I guess, but I think they got along OK. She told me Tuesday they were going to sell her car and his two trucks and move to Hawaii. She was real happy about it."

Aluffi had walked back down to Houts's place to use the telephone. He called the Albany police and asked them to notify Robert Hughes of his son's murder and to tell him to call the sheriff's office in Santa Cruz.

About 2:30 A.M. a crew arrived from Smith's Mortuary and removed the bodies. The pathologist who would perform the autopsies had done a preliminary examination in the cabin. He told Lieutenant Pittenger it looked as if all three victims had been both shot and stabbed. They had been dead for more than twelve hours, he added.

"That means Francis could have killed them, gone somewhere, and then called Houts to work up an alibi," Pittenger said. "Get an APB out on him."

"Do we tell the reporters he's a suspect?" someone asked.

"Let's just say we want to talk to him. We don't want to scare him away."

For the next hour, the investigators searched through the disorder in the cabin. They found no murder weapon, nor any other usable clues, other than a photograph of Bob Francis.

"Bring that along," Pittenger said. "We'll probably need it."

8
They Had No Enemies

BY DAYLIGHT, word of the murders had started to spread. Although the discovery of the bodies had come too late to make the morning newspapers, Bay Area radio stations carried sketchy stories about the triple slaying.

In the predawn hours, Lieutenant Pittenger assembled his investigators at the sheriff's office to compare notes and make assignments. The all-points bulletin was issued for Robert Francis, who had no local criminal record. It said he was "wanted for questioning." The teletype didn't identify him as a suspect, but it suggested approaching him with caution nonetheless.

Detectives Medina, Arbsland, and Aluffi returned to the cabin just after sunrise and relieved two uniformed deputies who had been guarding it through the night.

As soon as it was light enough to see, the three began a careful search outside the building, sweeping the area in circles. They found nothing that could have been used as a murder weapon. At 7:30 A.M., they went back to talk to Larry Hill and Christine Archer. With their permission, they searched the little brick house. They didn't discover anything to indicate the two had lied about anything. As they were leaving, two other detectives, Pummill and Don Smythe, drove up the dirt road. The five men gathered around the car.

Medina sighed. "It looks like this one isn't gonna be neat," he said. "I guess it's time we start doing it the hard way." They decided to split up and start canvassing every house from Branciforte Road to the Mystery Spot and all the side roads in between. As Pummill and Smythe trudged down the hill, Medina, Aluffi, and Arbsland turned toward Thatcher Clarke's trailer. They were intrigued by the account Houts had given of Clarke's reaction to the murders, his reluctance to call the authorities.

Medina was not surprised to find Sandra Harmon with Clarke. Other neighbors had already told him the two sometimes spent the night together. While Medina and Aluffi questioned Clarke, Arbsland took the young woman outside and talked with her alone.

"How'd you happen to move in here?" Medina asked.

Clarke shrugged. "It's sort of a long story."

"We got all the time in the world."

Medina thought Clarke looked uncomfortable. "My ex-wife had some friends down here, and we came down and visited them once. I just liked the area, and decided I'd try it out for a while."

"Where's your ex-wife?" Medina asked.

"She lives in Sacramento."

"Who are these friends you mentioned?"

"A guy named Charlie Oliver and his old lady, the woman he lives with."

"How'd you happen to find this place?"

"Charlie knew about the trailer and told me it was for rent."

"Did you know the Francises before you moved here?"

Clarke seemed embarrassed. "You know, that's a strange thing," he said. "I hadn't met Bob before, but I thought I recognized Kathy. Just before I moved in, I found out she used to live with a friend of mine in Berkeley named Bob Hughes. We had met years ago."

"So you did know her."

"Well, I hadn't seen her in years."

"Hell of a coincidence."

"Yeah, really."

Medina changed the subject. "You mind if we look around your trailer?"

"What for?"

"We won't know unless we find something, will we."

Clarke hesitated. "Sure," he said finally. "Go ahead." He stood by as the two detectives began opening drawers and cabinets. From under the bed Medina retrieved a hammer with a steel handle. He tied a small tag to it, numbered it and initialed it. "You mind putting your initials on that card?" he asked Clarke.

"Why?"

"It's your hammer, isn't it?"

"Yeah."

"We just want to make sure you get it back, that's all."

Aluffi called Medina back into the bedroom. Under a counter near the bed he found a faded pair of blue jeans. There were spots near the left hip pocket and the front left thigh. "Looks like bloodstains," Aluffi said. Medina folded the pants and tied a tag to a belt loop. He watched Clarke carefully as the latter initialed the card. His hands were steady.

"Last night, when Houts came up here after finding the bodies, did you ever tell him not to call the police?" Medina inquired.

"I don't . . . I didn't mean . . . did he say that?"

"I'm asking you."

"Look, man, I was half-asleep. I didn't know what was going on. I didn't want him not to call the cops. When I finally flashed on what was happening, I ran around to the other places to make sure everyone else was all right."

"Would you object to taking a polygraph examination if we decided it was needed?" Medina asked evenly.

"What's a polygraph?"

"A lie detector."

"No." Clarke blurted defiantly. "I wouldn't mind at all."

"We'll be in touch," Medina said.

The detectives had drawn a blank with the neighbors. Everyone who knew Bob and Kathy said that they liked them and knew of no one who would want to murder her. Nobody had seen or heard anything unusual on the day of the crime.

When they returned to the cabin they found Medina, Arbsland, and Aluffi inside searching it again. They collected a blue suitcase full of old letters and snapshots, a large pocket knife, some sharp leather-working tools, and a rusty hunting knife. None of it looked promising.

Clarke and Sandra Harmon came to the door and asked if it was all right for them to leave. Medina gave them permission.

A group of reporters and photographers arrived. One of them started to walk through the door. The detectives pushed him back.

"Don't touch anything," Medina said. "You can take all the pictures you want outside."

"What about the dead woman's husband?" someone asked. "Is he a suspect?"

"Any statements will have to come from downtown."

Another officer had been in his car, talking on the radio. He approached Medina and drew him aside, out of hearing of the reporters.

"The lieutenant wants me and Smythe to go back to the office," he said quietly. "You guys are supposed to stay here and finish up."

"What's happening?"

"He's not sure. The Santa Cruz PD just started working a double homicide."

"Do they think? . . ."

"Yeah. That maybe it's tied to this little party."

"Sweet Jesus."

9

The Link

ELANOR FOSTER had choked back nausea as she stood, swaying, in the doorway to the bathroom, her hands over her eyes. She turned and ran, stumbling blindly, down the stairs and into the kitchen. She dialed the telephone number of her husband's office in Santa Cruz.

"Herb," she sobbed, "I'm at Joan's house. You've got to come, quick."

"What's the matter?"

"Joan is dead."

"My God!"

"Joan and Jim are both dead, up in the bathroom."

"What happened?"

"I don't know," the terrified woman replied. "It's horrible."

"I'll be right there."

Mrs. Foster sat huddled at the base of the stairs, her coat pulled around her, and gazed without seeing at a milk bottle smeared with dried blood. I must be strong, she thought, but her mind kept returning to the grisly scene upstairs, and she was overcome with fear and revulsion.

Elanor Foster was unprepared for brutality. She and her husband had raised their children with the gentle teachings of the Society of Friends, and in a world of increasing violence, she had felt safe. The Fosters practiced their faith both in and out of Quaker Meeting. For years he had worked for Goodwill Industries, a vocational rehabilitation organization. He was the personnel manager in Santa Cruz. In 1970, tormented by the carnage in Vietnam, he had run unsuccessfully for Congress as a Peace and Freedom party candidate.

She wondered what they would tell Monica. The baby was only a year and a half old, but she was bright and active and would be afraid when she finally realized her mother would never come back. Joan had been so young when Monica was born, barely twenty. Elanor had been twenty-five when she had Joan. It was difficult now to grasp that the cold, stiff form on the bathroom floor had been the warm, sweet-smelling infant she had cuddled against her breast that summer so long ago.

When Herbert Foster arrived at the house, he embraced his wife. She could not go back upstairs. He looked in the bathroom and returned to the first floor. There were tears in his eyes.

"We have to call the Gianeras," he said.

Mrs. Foster had not been alarmed when Joan failed to call her back right away on Thursday. There had been no answer when she telephoned later in the morning, again that afternoon, and a third time in the evening. When she was unable to reach her Friday morning, however, she had started to worry. She called Jim's mother, Georgia Gianera, at the family's home in Ben Lomand, but Mrs. Gianera told her that Jim had said nothing about going out of town for any reason. About 9:00 A.M. Friday Mrs. Foster left Monica at home with her older son and drove to the house on Western Drive. She wondered whether their telephone might be out of order.

She was surprised to see the garage door open when she got there. The gate was latched, and the dogs were inside the fence. She knocked several times on the front door and then tentatively tried the knob. It was unlocked.

A frightful foreboding gripped her when she saw a wicker chair overturned in the living room, and the bloody handprints on the gaping refrigerator. She looked in the baby's room, but it was empty. When she saw blood spattered along the stairway wall, she ran up the stairs. Then someone was screaming. It took her a moment to realize it was she.

Mrs. Gianera got to the house just before 10:00 A.M., accompanied by a neighbor. She needed a few minutes to compose herself after seeing the scene in the bathroom. Gently, she covered Joan's nude body with the big bath towel and went downstairs.

"Where are the police?" she asked.

Herb Foster looked up, almost as if he were startled. "Oh . . . we haven't . . . we better call them."

There were three police cars parked outside the house by the time Lieutenant Chuck Scherer got there. A beefy man with receding, close-cropped hair and a habitual cigar protruding from the side of his mouth, Scherer was almost a caricature of a big-city detective. In fact he was tough, smart, and street-wise, a dependable cop admired by both his men and his superiors. He slammed the door of his car and walked briskly to the front door. The dogs, seeming to sense his authority, did not approach him. Inside, he found Herb Foster sitting on the living room floor, his head cradled in his hands.

One of the first patrolmen to answer Foster's call showed Scherer an expended .22-caliber shell casing and a single leather button, both found on the living room carpet. A bullethole had been located in the wall outside the bathroom, and an officer had dug out the slug with his pocket knife. It appeared to be .22 caliber also.

"Has anything else been touched?" Scherer asked, looking around at the disarray in the living room and kitchen.

"No, this is just the way we found it. Looks like somebody might have been searching for something."

"Maybe. Have all the witnesses been questioned?"

"All but two. There were a couple of hippie types here when we got here, but they split before we could talk to them."

Another patrolman joined the conversation. "They were Gianera's brothers, George and Mickey," he said. "I overheard one of them tell their mother they couldn't stick around because they had some place to go. She asked them about the car, and they said they'd hitchhike so she could keep it to go pick up their father."

"Whatever they had to do must have been important, with their brother dead upstairs," Scherer said.

"We're not a hundred percent sure that is Gianera. The lower part of his face is shot up pretty bad."

The lieutenant ordered lights set up in the bathroom so pictures could be taken before the bodies were removed. The electricity was off.

"Check the box outside," Scherer said. "See if somebody flipped the main switch. Be careful not to disturb any prints."

An officer came back upstairs in less than a minute. "It's off," he said, "but the box and the switch both have lead wire seals on them. The company must have cut the power."

"Call them and find out anyway."

There were two trucks parked in front of the house. One, a 1953 dark van, was registered to James Ralph Gianera. The name of the registered owner of the other, an antique Chevrolet pickup, had not come back from Sacramento.

The investigators found several marijuana roaches in the upstairs bedroom, along with pipes and a number of small bags of seeds and stem. Scherer went downstairs to talk with Herb Foster.

"You're the father of the victim?" he asked.

Foster was more in control of himself than when Scherer arrived.

"Yes. Joan is . . . was my daughter."

"Were they into drugs much, do you know?" Scherer tried not to be brusque.

The father hesitated. "Yes, I think so. But I think it was tapering off. I . . . I think they were only using pot."

"Had they used anything harder in the past?"

"They had used LSD, and I think speed, but not anymore."

"Heroin?"

"I don't think so."

"Was Jim a dealer?"

"I don't honestly know."

Scherer remembered that nobody had been able positively to identify the body of the man upstairs as Gianera. The parents had assumed it was, but no one had made them go back up for a second look.

"Had the two of them been getting along OK?" he asked Foster.

"They were having some problems," he answered. "Jim was having a hard time finding work, and they argued about it sometimes."

"Do they own this house?"

"No, I do. Jim and I did most of the work ourselves."

When the coroner's crew arrived, they were accompanied by two sheriff's detectives. In Santa Cruz, as in many California counties, the elected sheriff also acts as coroner. Detective Sam Robustelli sought out Scherer after the two corpses had been removed.

"Well, it's definitely a double murder," he said. "There was no weapon under the bodies."

"I understand you guys have one working too."

"Yeah. A woman and her two kids scragged in a hippie pad out by the Mystery Spot."

"Any sign it's connected with this?"

"It's hard to say. We haven't been able to find the woman's common-law husband."

"Yeah? Well. We're not so sure that's Gianera in the meat wagon."

"You think Gianera might have surprised the little woman with a boyfriend?"

"It happens. We'll know more if we can find a set of Gianera's fingerprints."

Robustelli looked surprised. "That shouldn't be too hard," he said. "He and his two brothers are all drug dealers. We've got rap sheets on all three of them."

"That's interesting. Is Jim the oldest?"

"Yeah. I looked them up when we heard the names of the victims here. Mickey is nineteen, and George should be about twenty-two. They live with their folks in Ben Lomond."

"Could you see if your people could pick them up?" Scherer asked the sheriff's officer. "They were here this morning but left before we could talk to them. It'd be nice to know how business has been the last few days."

Robustelli left to radio the request to the sheriff's dispatcher, and Scherer went out in the yard. He poked through the garage, which was full of miscellany, including a kayak. It also contained a collection of power tools. With the door standing open for more than twenty-four hours, he was surprised they hadn't been stolen. As he stepped back through the gate, a car pulled up in front of the house. A man and a woman got out and walked over to the fence.

"Are Jim and Joan home?" the man asked. They appeared to Scherer to be apprehensive. Both of them glanced nervously at the patrol cars.

"Who are you?" Scherer asked.

"We're just some friends."

"I'm a police officer. You live around here?"

"No. At the Mystery Spot."

Scherer was suddenly excited. "What's your full name?" he demanded.

"Thatcher Hall Clarke."

"Age?"

"Thirty-five."

"Well, Mr. Clarke, I'm afraid I have to tell you that both Mr. and Mrs. Gianera have been murdered."

Clarke's hands flew to his face, and he paled visibly. "Oh, my God!" He paused for a second. "I . . . I know who done it."

"OK, Thatcher," Scherer said. "Let's the three of us go downtown."

10
Rumors of a Burn

ROBERT HUGHES, the father of the older murdered boy, arrived at the sheriff's office from his home in Albany Friday morning. Mike Aluffi asked him what he had been doing the previous day. The musician was manifestly distraught but cooperative and free with his answers. He said he had worked at home on a composition in the morning, spent the afternoon at Mills College in Oakland, and performed in the evening with the Oakland Symphony Orchestra.

"It's your statement, then, that you weren't in Santa Cruz either January 24 or 25?"

"Absolutely."

Aluffi studied the man across the desk from him. He had a high forehead, with dark hair. His wide-set eyes were red from lack of sleep. The detective was sure he was telling the truth.

"Do you have any idea who might have had a reason for killing Kathy and the boys?" he asked.

"No."

"Were Bob and Kathy having any problems, do you know?"

"Not any more than any other couple, I guess."

"Were they into the drug scene very heavily?"

"I think only marijuana. About five years ago they were doing acid and that sort of thing, but their attitude changed, and they got interested in health foods. After that I think they only used grass."

"Was Bob a dealer?" Aluffi asked.

"Mainly he did things like cut wood and picked fruit. He sold a little pot, but I don't know how much."

"What kind of a guy is he?"

"He's very friendly, at least to me. I think he's a very nice person. He loved the children and spent a lot of time with both of them."

"Do you think he's violent?"

"Definitely not."

"When was the last time you saw him?"

"Over the holidays." His voice faltered. "I . . . I brought some presents for David and Daemon, for both boys. Then I took the family and a neighbor of theirs to dinner."

"Who was that?"

"Thatcher Clarke."

"What do you know about him?" Aluffi asked. Hughes seemed a little surprised at the question.

"I've known Thatcher a long time," he said.

"When did you first meet him?"

"Several years ago we worked together in San Francisco. He was a choreographer for the San Francisco Ballet Company."

"Were you living with Kathy then?"

"Yes, I was."

"Did you ever see any signs that he might have become interested in her?"

"You mean? . . . No."

"What happened in the intervening years?"

"Thatcher left San Francisco and went to New York. I heard that he got into drugs, left his wife, and went to Amsterdam. I lost contact with him then."

"When did you meet him again?"

"When I found out he was living near Kathy's place."

"That seemed a little remarkable to us."

"I can imagine. I asked Thatcher about it, and he told me that when he came back from Amsterdam, he decided to go back to his wife in California. It didn't work out, I guess, but he had come to

Santa Cruz with her once, and he liked it. When they split up again, he decided to move here. He said he didn't know Kathy lived here until after he rented the trailer. Some guy he was talking to in a bar told him who she was."

"What sort of disposition do you think Clarke has?"

"He was kind of temperamental when he was working with the ballet, but he seemed to mellow out some after going to New York and Amsterdam and getting into drugs."

"Did your son ever say anything to you about any other man visiting Kathy while Francis was gone?"

"No. I think David would have told me. I believe Bob may have been involved with another woman for a little while. And Kathy saw another guy for a short time while they lived up at Dobbins, but that was all past history."

"Where is Dobbins?"

"Up in the Sierra. Near Marysville."

"Why did they leave there and come here?"

"She was from here. His family lives in Idaho. I remember them telling me there was a guy up in Dobbins who was real ornery, and that was one reason they moved."

"You said they didn't have any particular problems. Did Kathy ever mention any trouble?"

"She told me that things had been a little rocky lately, but she was optimistic that they would improve. Bob was happy about leasing some land in Hawaii, and Kathy wrote me that they would be moving there soon."

"Did either of them show any suicidal tendencies?"

"God, no."

Aluffi gave Hughes the description of the man Clarke and Houts had seen visiting the cabin Thursday morning and asked if it sounded familiar. The grieving father thought it over for a minute.

"No," he said finally. "I don't know anybody like that."

Sheriff's Detectives Pummill and Smythe went to Captain Dick Overton's office as soon as they got to the police department. They filled him in on the sheriff's investigation.

"Scherer has a couple of live ones on the grill right now," Overton said. "You guys had better sit in. It looks like we'll be working these two cases together."

Pummill and Smythe recognized Clarke and Sandra Harmon when they walked into the room. "They say that Jim and Joan Gianera used to live up there with Bob and Kathy Francis," Scherer said. "We're going over to the mortuary to have Mr. Clarke here see if he can ID our male victim. We still don't know if it's Gianera or Francis."

The two sheriff's detectives and Scherer accompanied the distressed couple to White's Mortuary, where autopsies on all five bodies had been completed. The attendant pulled back the sheet covering Gianera's face. Clarke turned away.

"That's Jim," he whispered. Pummill made a note of the time and date. It was 12:55 P.M., Friday, January 26, 1973.

Back at the police station Scherer asked Clarke and Sandra Harmon to wait while he briefed Pummill and Smythe on the Gianera murders.

"Francis is looking better all the time," he said. "We just got the word back from Sacramento that the old Chevy pickup parked outside the Gianera house belongs to him."

"We have an APB out for him," Pummill said, "but we're not calling him a suspect, at least not out loud."

Clarke and Miss Harmon had a couple of things to add to their stories. The previous Monday, a woman had visited the Francis cabin and had stayed two days. They thought her name was Charlotte, that she was from Marysville, and that she was out on bail.

"What for?" Scherer asked.

"A dope bust," Clarke said.

"When did she leave?"

"Tuesday morning or evening," Sandy said. "She borrowed a guitar from Bob before she left."

"You seen her since?"

"No. But I think they said she was going to stay with some other friends in Santa Cruz. Maybe it was Joan and Jim."

"You think her arrest might have had something to do with Gianera or Francis? That they might have burned somebody in a deal and she came here for revenge?"

"I don't know," Clarke said.

"Why the hell didn't you mention any of this to us last night?" Pummill demanded.

"Nobody asked us," Clarke said. "I didn't think about it at the time."

The detectives told Clarke and Sandy they could go home but should not leave town. After Pummill and Smythe departed for the sheriff's office, Scherer telephoned the Marysville police. He talked with a Detective Atkins.

"Yeah, we had a pretty big drug deal go down last week," Atkins said. "Two of the people we busted were in their fifties, but another one was a young woman."

"Girl in her early twenties, about 140 pounds, with dirty blond shoulder-length hair?"

"That fits her description."

"Was her first name Charlotte?"

"No, it was Louise."

"Do you know where she is?"

"No, she made bail. She isn't due to go back to court until next week."

"If you find her, hang on to her for us," Scherer said. "We may want to question her."

About 1:00 P.M. Medina and Arbsland heard a car pull up as they continued to dismantle the cabin looking for clues. They stepped outside and saw a man get out of a Volkswagen bus and walk toward Clarke's trailer.

"Can we help you?" Medina called. "We're sheriff's officers."

"I was looking for Thatcher."

"He's downtown right now. What's your name?"

"Charles Oliver. I'm a friend of Thatcher's." He paused. "I heard about it on the radio. I came up to see him. We were all good friends."

"When were you by here the last time?" Medina asked.

"Yesterday afternoon about 3:30," Oliver said. "Thatcher wasn't home, so I went over to see if Bob and Kathy were around. I knocked, but nobody seemed to be here." He looked toward the cabin. "I guess . . . they were in there, huh?"

"Yeah."

"Did you know Bob Francis very well?" Arbsland asked.

"Pretty well. A couple of months ago I went to Marysville with him on a fishing trip."

"You have any idea where he might be?"

"He goes away sometimes for two, three days at a time. You might try a hostel up in Berkeley. I don't know the name of it."

"Is he a dealer?"

Oliver shrugged. "Maybe a little grass."

"Did you know Clarke before he moved here?"

"Yeah. His ex-wife and my girl were old friends. They came to visit us once, and Thatcher decided he liked it here. He showed up about six months ago, and I helped him find this place."

The two detectives watched the van pull away. "I guess old Thatcher's telling the truth," Arbsland said.

"I still want to put him on a lie box," Medina muttered.

After leaving the police department, Pummill and Smythe joined Robustelli and Aluffi back at the sheriff's office. Gianera's two brothers, George and Michael, and a friend, Earl Fisher, had been brought in for interrogation. When they were finished, all five investigators were convinced the murders had been committed by someone in the drug trade.

George Gianera said his brother had met Bob Francis about four years earlier in Hawaii. Later the two couples and Kathy's two sons lived together on a ranch near Dobbins, a small town in Yuba County not far from Marysville. Bob and Kathy had come with them when they moved back to Santa Cruz, where Bob and Jim had started trading in marijuana.

"How much?" Pummill asked.

"Up to one or two hundred pounds at a time. They'd get it in San Diego and run it up to the Bay Area or Marysville to sell it."

"They ever burn anybody you know of?"

"There were two busts that made them look like snitches," Gianera said. "They weren't, but it kind of looked that way."

"Where?"

"The first one was in San Diego about two months ago. Bob and Jim called down there about a shipment, but the guys on the other end told them they weren't gonna be in on the deal, that some other dudes would handle it instead of Bob and Jim. Right after that the guys in San Diego got busted in San Clemente."

"When was the other one?"

"One, maybe two weeks ago up in Marysville. Bob was up there at the ranch, and they told him they weren't gonna let him haul the stuff, so he left. About fifteen minutes later the ranch was raided. I heard they thought he might have snitched them off."

The only information Michael Gianera could add was that Bob and Jim usually made their runs in Francis's 1967 El Camino pickup, and that they were both in it the last time he had seen them, the previous Monday. He said that wherever Francis was, he would be driving it.

Fisher, a twenty-year-old neighbor of the Gianera family in Ben Lomond, knew a great deal about the drug transportation partnership. He said he was sure neither Jim nor Bob had ever been an informant.

"When was the last time you saw either one of them?" Pummill asked.

"Wednesday morning about nine or ten at the Ben Lomand Coffee Shop. Bob seemed fine, but he said he wanted to off the El Camino because he thought it might be hot. He said he had seen the cops driving up and down Branciforte Drive, and he figured maybe they were looking for his car because somebody in Marysville tipped them off."

"What time did they leave?"

"Right after I saw them at the coffee shop. Jim was gonna drop by and see his mother. He had left Bob's old pickup there. We were gonna play basketball that afternoon. Bob left in the El Camino to go north."

"Do you have any idea who might have killed Jim?"

"There's a guy named Bucky up in Marysville who's supposed to be real tough. He had it in for Jim. I guess he thought he had burned the people in San Diego."

"You ever meet this citizen?"

"No, but Jim told me about him. A couple of months ago this dude shows up at Jim's place with a gun. Maybe it was longer ago than that, because they were still living over at the Mystery Spot."

"What happened?"

"Jim wasn't home but Joan was. This guy gave her the gun and said something like, 'You better hold this. I don't want to kill anybody.' It scared the shit out of her, but she took it. Then Jim came home, and he and Bucky got into a beef. Jim pounded him pretty good."

"Do you know Bucky's last name?"

"No."

"Did Bob and Jim deal anything besides grass?"

"I don't think so. They had some pretty weird mushrooms. We all tried them and got real high."

"Which one had them?"

"I don't know, but you might check their freezers."

"How much did Jim and Bob make on a deal?"

"About 250 bucks each."

Pummill regarded Fisher for a moment. "Did they have any other partners?" he asked casually.

"No," Fisher answered quickly. "They worked alone."

11
A Suspect

AT 3:00 P.M. FRIDAY the sheriff's office received a telephone call from a man named Tom Ferris of Soquel, who identified himself as Kathy's stepfather. He filled in a few gaps. Her real name was Kathleen Prentiss. She had grown up in Soquel and stayed with her mother, Lelia, when her parents were divorced. Her father, Warren Prentiss, moved to Los Angeles, and her mother later married Ferris.

He said Bob was likely to be driving a 1967 El Camino. He went to Marysville and Berkeley often, Ferris added, but he had no idea what he did there. He said he thought Bob loved David and Daemon very much.

Early Friday evening a group of police officers went back to the Gianera house, led by Art Danner, the deputy district attorney assigned to both crimes. Danner had gone over the physical evidence that had been collected, and they decided to comb the place again. They brought high-intensity lights and carefully searched both floors of the building, looking in particular for any other slugs that might be compared with the ones taken from the bodies of Kathy Francis and her two sons. The bullets removed from Jim and Joan Gianera and the one dug out of the wall were so deformed that it would take the crime laboratory in Redwood City a long time to analyze them. They found nothing. Discouraged, they decided another crew would try again in the morning.

A few minutes after 10:00 P.M. Friday, a 1967 Chevrolet El Camino nosed into the dirt road near the Mystery Spot. Sheriff's deputies Bob Tanner and Jim Morris, who had been standing watch at the cabin, were sitting inside their patrol car. As the low pickup truck passed in front of them, they got a clear look at the driver. It was a man, and he resembled the description of the dead woman's husband.

Cautiously, the two officers slipped out of their car, ducked behind it, and drew their service revolvers as the El Camino came to a halt at the end of the road.

"All right," Morris barked, "get out and put your hands on the roof." The man swiftly did as he was commanded. Tanner circled behind him, kicked his legs apart, and patted him down for weapons.

"He's clean. What's your name?" Tanner demanded.

"Robert Francis."

Tanner handcuffed him. "We're sheriff's deputies," Morris said, hustling their prisoner toward the prowl car.

"Yeah, man, I know."

The two officers were struck by the fact that Francis showed no surprise or agitation at being arrested, nor did he ask why. On the way to the car he looked at the darkened cabin and asked where his family was.

"They're not home," Tanner told him. They offered no further explanation.

Detectives Robustelli and Howard Sanderson got to the Mystery Spot in less than ten minutes. Robustelli talked with Francis briefly. "You'll have to come with us downtown," he said. "We want to ask you some questions about an incident that happened here."

"Is my family OK?" Francis asked.

"We'll talk about that at the office. We want some answers about a problem. We'll let you know what it is when we get there."

Francis didn't say anything during the short ride to the County Government Center on Ocean Street. Robustelli and Sanderson took him to the detective bureau and gave him a chair. His eyes were bloodshot and dilated. Robustelli could not smell alcohol on his breath. He's on something, he thought.

"Bob, I've got to tell you your wife and two boys were murdered yesterday. Jim and Joan Gianera were killed the same day."

Francis appeared to lapse into shock. His shoulders sagged, and he began sobbing.

"We need to know your whereabouts for the past few days," Robustelli said after a few minutes. Francis stared at his boots and said nothing. Mike Aluffi came into the detective bureau. "He seems to be taking it hard," Robustelli said. "He hasn't said anything. Why don't you give it a shot?"

"Sure." But after trying for some time, Aluffi went to see the captain on duty. "I think we should wait and talk to him in the morning," the detective said. "He's pretty spaced out."

"OK. I'll call Overton at the PD and set it up so they can be in on the interview."

Aluffi went back to tell Robustelli. "Where's his car, by the way?" he asked.

"We left Tanner and Morris out there guarding it. We'll have security on it all night."

"We'll try to get a search consent from him in the morning to go through it."

"Right." The telephone rang, and Robustelli answered it. The call was from a young woman who said she was a friend of Bob and Kathy's. She understood the authorities were looking for him. Robustelli eyed Francis, slouched dumbly in a chair a few feet away.

"You have some information?" he asked.

"Well, I saw Bob about a week and a half ago," the girl said. "He was really grooved about going to the Islands. He said he and Kathy and the boys were going to move out there in a few weeks. Maybe that's where he went."

"Right. Anything else?"

"No. I was just trying to help."

By Saturday morning, the five murders were front-page news throughout the West, joining but not eclipsing stories about the U.S.-North Vietnamese treaty that was to be signed in Paris the following day. Newspapers in San Francisco and Los Angeles head-lined the apparent arrest of Robert Francis and criticized the sheriff's investigators for refusing to talk about it. The reporters had learned the Gianeras and Francises were close friends and theorized that the slayings were connected in some way. They didn't know that Bob and Jim had been part of a drug ring, however, and the murders, coming a few days after the dismembered body of Cynthia Schall had finally been identified, led to speculation that another mad killer was stalking Santa Cruz. Sales of locks, guns, and burglar-alarm equipment, already brisk, went up sharply as soon as the stores opened. But among the inhabitants of the murky precincts of the drug world, there was a different fear. Those who were acquainted with Jim and Bob were sure the killings had been a professional job, and that anyone who had ever talked even accidentally to an undercover narcotics agent had reason to be extremely nervous.

A little after 9:00 A.M. Sheriff's Detectives Medina, Sanderson, and Robustelli persuaded Francis to sign a form assenting to a search of his car. They picked up Seibel, the technician, drove to the cabin, and told the bleary-eyed guards they could go home.

After Seibel photographed the vehicle from every angle, they began systematically to take it apart. Almost immediately they found two expended .22-caliber shell casings, one behind the seat and the other on top of the dashboard.

"That," observed Medina, "is just too goddamn good to be true."

The interior of the passenger compartment was scattered with tools, clothes, papers, and a sleeping bag.

"If he used this for running dope, it has to have at least one place for hiding the stash," Sanderson said. They searched under the hood but found no concealed spaces. While Medina and Robustelli wrestled the seat out, Sanderson and Seibel climbed in the truck bed.

"Here it is," Sanderson called. He had discovered a hidden vault behind the cab, a metal box covered with a lid cut from the bed of the truck. The four screws that held the top in place had been removed. It was empty.

"He must have figured he was going to get picked up," Medina said.

"Or he just made a delivery," another detective ventured.

"Hold on, here's another one." On each side of the bed, the inside panels of the sidewalls had been finely sliced through with an acetylene torch to form camouflaged storage over the wheel wells. Both spaces were bare.

"You might be right. It sure looks like he wanted it to be clean."

"What do you suppose that is?" Sanderson asked, pointing to some reddish brown stains on a large rock in the bed.

"Could be dried blood."

After removing everything from the truck, including the registration proving it was owned by one Robert Clayton Francis, Seibel lifted latent fingerprints from the doors, windows, and the back of the rear-view mirror. Sanderson locked it and flipped the keys to Robustelli.

"You can give those back to the owner the next time you see him," he said.

"Hard to say whether he's gonna need them for a while."

Lieutenant Scherer had managed to get a couple of hours sleep before returning to the police department Saturday morning. On his desk he found a teletype from the Boise, Idaho, police. It said a man named Dennis Francis, age unknown, had come to the station there asking for police protection, claiming that two people had been murdered in Marysville, California, during the night, and that he feared for his life. The message also said that Dennis Francis had told the police that Robert Francis might be on his way to Boise.

"Didn't someone say that Francis's family was from Idaho?" Scherer asked of no one in particular. "Somebody call Lieutenant Pittenger over at the sheriff's office and make sure they canceled that APB." He picked up the telephone and dialed the number for the Marysville police. The shift commander was out, so Scherer talked with the desk officer.

"Yeah, we had a double shooting early this morning, but the two victims weren't killed. It happened in a restaurant parking lot across the river in Yuba City. It was outside our jurisdiction."

"Did they arrest anybody?"

"I think they have one suspect in custody."

"Could it have anything to do with drugs."

"Maybe. From what I understand, nobody's talking."

"What was the weapon?"

"A .22."

Scherer slammed down the telephone, shrugged into his coat, and clamped a fresh cigar between his teeth. "I'm going over the sheriff's office to sit in on the Francis interview," he said. "We may be getting somewhere."

12
A Pattern

BOB FRANCIS sat in the detective bureau surrounded by investigators from the sheriff's office, the police department, and the district attorney's office. He was in better condition than he had been the night before, although his eyes were still red-rimmed and puffy, and he was unmistakably weary. He said he had not been able to sleep. Pittenger cleared his throat and started to read from a card.

"You have the right . . ."

Francis gestured. "Forget it, man, I know my rights. I didn't do anything."

"Do you have any idea who . . ."

"No," he said. "At least nobody who would have a reason, I mean to get me or Jim. We never shorted anybody or ripped anybody off."

"Would anyone have any reason to think one or the other of you might have been a snitch?"

"Christ, no. We never informed or anything else."

"You admit that the two of you dealt drugs?"

"Yeah. Jim and me did deals with grass for a long time, and we milled drugs. I'm not trying to hide anything from you guys. I want to help all I can. I just can't believe it."

"Where did you and the Gianeras live around Marysville?"

"We rented a place on a hundred-acre ranch near Dobbins."

"When did you move?"

"About a year ago Christmas."

Scherer looked at his notes from his conversation with the Marysville policeman. "Was there anybody you knew up there capable of doing something like this?"

"There were two guys who were heavy enough to do it, but they wouldn't have any reason. One is a guy named Bucky, the son of the owners of the ranch, Mr. and Mrs. Burnett. He was always in a beef with somebody. And another guy named Lucky. A real mouthy type."

"Bucky and Lucky?"

Francis didn't smile. "Yeah, I guess it sounds funny. I think Lucky lives in Rio Linda or Sacramento somewhere. From what I understood when I was up there Wednesday, there was a girl who got away when the bust went down, and she's holed up with Lucky in his pad."

"What's her name?"

"Sherry. She's an Oriental. I don't know her last name. But she deals, and she was living with another guy who deals and buys in pound lots."

"There were two shootings last night in Marysville," Scherer said. "You have any idea what it might be about?"

"I was in the slam, remember."

Francis recounted the details of his trip from Santa Cruz to Berkeley to Marysville and back to Berkeley, and told of his telephone call Thursday night to Steve Houts.

"Steve said you told them you might be home late that same night."

"Yeah, well it took longer to get it together, the deal I mean."

"Do you know someone up there named Louise?" Scherer asked.

Francis looked surprised. "Yeah. I stayed with her Wednesday night before going back to Berkeley."

"Was she down here earlier this week?"

"Yes, she was. She was busted along with the rest and was out on bail."

"Do you think she might have suspected you or Jim blew the whistle?"

"No." He was emphatic. "She's a good friend. She knew we were always straight. Besides, she's a student teacher, and she loves kids." Tears welled in his eyes. "She'd never do anything to hurt the kids."

"Tell us more about this guy Bucky."

"He's a heavy user. He drops acid and a lot of other shit. He's real bad news. There was another guy in the valley who was a dealer, and Bucky told him never to come to the ranch. This other guy put him down, you know, and the next thing we know Bucky shows up with a gun and says he's gonna blow this guy away. It was touchy for a minute."

"Did Bucky ever come down here?"

"Two or three times. After we all moved to Santa Cruz, and we were working on Jim and Joan's house over on Western, he showed up one day when Jim and I were working and showed Joan a handgun of some kind. He told her to hang on to it because he was afraid he'd kill Jim, he was so pissed off about something. She did, and they got into it when Jim got home. He had to hit him to get him to go away."

"Where does this Bucky live, to the best of your knowledge?"

"He still lives on the ranch, I think."

Francis looked exhausted. The detectives asked him if he would like to take a break.

"No way. I really want to help you guys. I don't give a shit anymore. I mean, like somebody killed Kathy and my boys and my best friends, and I keep thinking maybe they were after me. Maybe if I'd been there it wouldn't have happened."

"Would you be willing to take a lie detector test?"

"Sure. Anything."

Francis described his business activities, naming every person he thought might have had a reason, real or imagined, for wanting to harm him or Gianera. Much of his story jibed with what the detectives already knew from other witnesses. The rest of it would be easy enough to confirm. Everyone in the room had a growing conviction that he was not the killer.

"Bob, what about robbery?" Scherer asked.

"We didn't have anything worth taking."

"How about the Gianeras? It almost looked as if someone had been looking for something in the house."

"No. They hadn't even been able to pay the light bill. Jim was gonna come into some money, but I'm sure he hadn't got it yet."

"You mean like an inheritance?"

"Yeah. I don't really know, though."

"How much?"

"About three grand."

"Were there a lot of people who knew about it?" Medina asked.

"Not that I know of. A lot of Jim's friends knew about it. Well, yeah, there were a few people who knew about it."

"OK, on Wednesday, the day before it happened, do you recall going with Jim Gianera to his parents' house in Ben Lomand?"

"Right. I dropped him off at his parents' house on Wednesday, about noon sometime, and that's the last time that I saw him."

"Did he mention that he had to sign some papers, or there was something happening about this money he was supposed to get?"

"Yes, I was aware of that for a couple of days, and I even loaned him my truck so that he could take care of his paper work and I wouldn't have to be driving him around and stuff like that."

"Did he say he had to sign some papers that day?" Medina asked.

"I can't remember whether he said he had to sign some papers, or look at some papers or talk to a certain uncle that was handling the situation."

"Did Jim Gianera seem especially anxious to get a hold of the money? Did he give you the impression that he had people to whom he owed money, or that he wished it would hurry up and get there?"

"Well, he seemed anxious about getting, or rather, excited about getting it," Francis answered Medina. "But he didn't seem like he owed any large sums of money to anybody. He owed me around $135, and he also had a truck that had some work to be done on the engine, so that he could take a trip that he'd been talking about, into Oregon, Washington, and Canada."

"Perchance, did you know who would get the money if Jim wasn't available to get it?"

"I haven't any idea," Francis said.

"Did he indicate to you that he had any other bills that he was gonna pay off when he got the money?"

"Well, he said he had a few debts, and like I try to stay out of other people's private business, so I didn't bring that up any further. I figured it was his own business."

Pittenger looked around the room. "All right, Bob, I think that'll be all for now. We'll arrange for a polygraph test. In the meantime, we'd like to keep you on ice, more for your own protection than anything else."

"That's fine by me. I don't want to see anybody."

The investigators kept their seats as Francis was ushered from the detective bureau. Lieutenant Pittenger crushed out a cigarette and lighted a fresh one immediately. A burly man who bore a passing resemblance to the late Alan Ladd, he was given to plain talk.

"Any volunteers to go to Marysville?" he asked. There was a chorus of assent.

The men from the three agencies pooled their information. High on their list of priorities was sending a joint team to Yuba City to find out if the Saturday morning shootings there had any connection with the Santa Cruz murders. The weapon in both cases was a .22, and there was a suspect in custody. They also wanted to find the people Francis had mentioned who might bear a grudge against him or Gianera. Pittenger was elected to lead the detail.

Any doubts about whether the five victims had been murdered by the same person disappeared with the report of the crime laboratory in Redwood City, where the shell casings and bullets recovered from the bodies had been sent for analysis. All had been shot with the same gun. The ballistics experts narrowed it down to one of two German makes of revolver, and said the ammunition had not been new.

To allay fears in the community that the killings were the work of a cult or insane mass murderer, the authorities released most of the facts they had to the press.

The Yuba City lead had not been fruitful. Two teen-agers had been shot by a third during a parking lot brawl.

"Initially we thought the cases appeared similar," Pittenger told the reporters. "But when we dug into it, we found the Yuba City shootings involved only a local beef.

"We just have to keep digging. There are no suspects at this time." Asked about Robert Francis, Pittenger added, "He's pretty shook up about it. His primary concern is to clear this up and try to figure out what to do with the rest of his life."

He said Francis was in protective custody, but refused to say where.

The County Sheriff, Douglas James, issued a press release stating,

"There appear to be drug overtones in the case." Asked to elaborate on the sheriff's statement, Pittenger would only say that the three adult victims were "part of the local drug scene."

At the police department, Captain Overton issued a plea to the citizenry to "keep cool," pointing out there was an obvious "design to the murders. We're not certain what the motive was, but we suspect several things," he said.

Overton recalled that during the panic following the Ohta slayings, there were "many people buying guns who shouldn't have. I'd hate to see that again. Our department is asking for everybody's cooperation. It's our job to protect people, and if anybody thinks that something might happen, he shouldn't hesitate to call us.

"This thing has a pattern to it," Overton assured the reporters. "It's not a case of some crazy man running around shooting people."

13
The Campers

ON THURSDAY AFTERNOON, February 1, Sergeant Dennis Finnegan from the police department and Sheriff's Detective Aluffi met at the district attorney's office in Santa Cruz. Prosecutor Art Danner was waiting for them with Robert Lidburdy, a polygraph examiner from the state attorney general's office. Thatcher Clarke and Bob Francis were being held in separate rooms.

The two detectives briefed Lidburdy and his assistant on the case. After they composed their list of questions, Clarke was brought into the small interview room. The examiner read him his Fifth Amendment rights against self-incrimination, and Clarke signed a card waiving them. Finnegan nodded toward Aluffi, and the two officers left the room as the inquisitors began connecting the sensors.

It was a long wait. Finnegan and Aluffi sat in the inspectors' office, drinking coffee and exchanging notions about the mystery. After Clarke's ordeal was over, Francis was brought into the room with the machine. The detectives witnessed his signature on the waiver card and went back to their coffee cups. Finally, about 5:00 P.M., Lidburdy came to find them. He was carrying several papers, including a long chart bearing lines and numbers.

"Well, you still have an open investigation as far as I'm concerned."

"They're both clean?"

"No deception indicated, as we say in the trade. Clarke has some vague suspicions about different people, but none that he hasn't already talked to you about, I gather. There's no doubt that he had no romantic ties with Kathy Francis. He was a little afraid of Gianera, for some reason. He thought he was a heavy, sort of hostile and potentially dangerous. He also agrees with you that the murders have to be connected with the drug traffic."

"What about Bob?"

"He didn't kill anybody, but I think he's holding out on some details of his business. He also has some suspicions, but he definitely doesn't have any facts regarding a responsible."

"He's been cooperative," Finnegan said.

"Oh, there's no doubt he wants to cooperate. At the same time he's bound by the code. He's telling the truth when he says he never burned anybody, and he doesn't want to start now. In that respect, he's an honorable man. He's a little confused, but I think what he's trying to do is give you any information he believes might possibly be related to the murders, but holding back anything he thinks isn't related that the narcs might find useful."

"I can see his problem."

"If he could talk to somebody he could trust to ignore the drug side of the thing, he might be a little freer. He also might be more relaxed, and remember more. I'll write up a formal report and get it back to Art Danner early next week."

"Thanks. Have a nice trip home."

A few minutes later, Francis walked into the office. "How'd I do?" he asked.

"You passed. We figured you would. But the man said you might not be giving us everything."

Francis thought about that for a moment.

"Look, Bob, this is a murder investigation," Finnegan said with exasperation. "We're not interested in knocking over every nickel-and-dime pot dealer in the neighborhood. We need all the help we can get."

"I'll try."

I was glancing through the afternoon newspaper when the telephone rang in my office at Stanford University on Tuesday, February 6. I had just finished reading a front-page story about the discovery early that day of the body of Ida Anderson Stine floating face up in her bathtub in Capitola just south of Santa Cruz. She was a seventy-nine-year-old widow and former president of the California Women's Christian Temperance Union who taught Bible classes. According to her neighbors, she didn't have an enemy in the world. An autopsy had not been performed by the time the newspaper went to press, but the article said she probably had been raped and strangled.

The telephone bell persisted. I muttered under my breath. My secretary must have stepped out of her office. Reluctantly, I picked up the receiver.

"Hello."

"Dr. Lunde?"

"Yes."

"This is Art Danner at the Santa Cruz DA's office. I don't know if you remember me, but . . ."

"Yes. I remember you very well from the Ohta case." Although I had been cross-examined by the district attorney, Peter Chang, when I had testified about Frazier's insanity, Danner also had worked on the prosecution. I recalled him as a handsome young lawyer, dark-haired and rather intense. "I was just reading the paper. You people are having a hell of a time down there."

"That's not the half of it. Two more coeds from the university disappeared last night while they were hitchhiking home from an evening class."

"No kidding. I didn't see anything about that."

"It was just reported. That's not why I called you, however."

"What can I do for you?"

"Do you remember reading about five murders down here a couple of weeks ago?"

"I think so. You've been having so many lately."

"Yeah, well we think this case is solvable. The three adults who were killed were all into the drug scene pretty heavily. We're sure that's where the motive lies."

"You have a suspect?"

"No. But the common-law husband of one of the dead women

worked as a dope runner with the man who was murdered. He's been very cooperative, even took a polygraph. But we think he might be keeping something back out of fear of burning his friends. The sheriff's office and police have checked out everybody he could think of so far as a potential killer, here and everywhere else, but they all have alibis."

"What do you want me to do?"

"Well, we thought maybe if you talked to him, with the understanding that you're not a cop and would only give us the names of possible suspects, he might be more forthcoming. We've explained your privilege as a psychiatrist to him."

"It seems like an awful long shot, Art."

"Every little bit helps. We're almost positive the murderer is someone he knows."

"Well, I'm terribly busy right now. I don't know when I could get down there."

"No problem. We'll bring him to you."

I flipped through the calendar on my desk. "OK. I don't think it'll do any good, but I can see him after lunch on Thursday."

"We'll have him there. Thanks."

Terry Medina handed me his card. Although we had never been introduced, he remembered me from the Frazier trial. He never said it to me then, but I found out later that he was surprised by my youthful appearance. When I was a student and later an intern, it bothered me a little that I didn't look as old as I was. When I reach that ambiguous plateau called middle age, on the other hand, I suppose I'll find it a blessing. At the time Medina brought Francis to see me, I was thirty-six, the father of five enormous appetites disguised as sons, had served a hitch in the Navy, held bachelor's and master's degrees in psychology as well as my M.D., was a member of the American Academy of Psychiatry and Law, was director of Medical Student Education in Psychiatry and taught forensic psychiatry in the law school at Stanford. Medina didn't know all that; he just thought I didn't look like a psychiatrist. That photograph of Sigmund Freud in his later years, with his elegantly barbered beard, is one of the crosses many of us in my profession have to bear.

There was something else Medina saw no reason to tell me. The DA's office had more than one motive for asking me to talk with

Francis. Although the chance that he had defeated the lie detector was miniscule, it was possible. In the unlikely event that Francis became a defendant in the murders and pleaded insanity, Chang and Danner decided it would be useful to neutralize me as a potential defense witness in advance by hiring me to examine him. If I had been aware of that at the time, I guess I would have been flattered.

The detective gave me a synopsis of the case, then brought Bob in and introduced him. He was a tall man, wearing rather worn clothing, with long hair and a beard. There were several gaps in his teeth, and when we shook hands, I noticed that one of his fingers was missing.

"You can get some coffee down the hall," I said as I showed Medina out of the office. "I'll call you when we're through." I turned to Francis after I shut the door. "OK," I said, "let's start at the beginning."

For the next couple of hours, we talked freely about Bob's role in the drug traffic, concentrating on people who might have had animosity against him or Gianera. I did not turn on my tape recorder, and I took few notes. When the interview was concluded, I wrote a list of names and handed it to Francis.

"Does this look like everyone you know in the world who might have killed your family?"

"Yeah, I think so."

I gave the sheet of paper to Medina when the detective returned to the office. "Anybody on there you hadn't heard of?"

"Doesn't look like it."

"I'm pretty sure he didn't hold anything back."

"Thanks for trying, doc. We'll see you."

"No offense," I said, "but God, I hope not."

The day after my conversation with Francis, a young man parked his old station wagon at a roadside pullout on Highway 9 near the head of the Ox Road Trail in Henry Cowell State Park. A cold wind blew off the bay, and dark clouds scudded from north to south, promising rain. He started up the hill into the trees, wandering aimlessly. After about a quarter-mile, he came upon a muddy road and began to follow it. Something in the forest caught his eye, a glint as if light were reflecting from a window pane. Moving stealthily, he left the road and took cover behind a tree. He listened, but heard no sound save the hiss of tires on the wet pavement as an automobile passed on the highway hidden below.

Creeping silently, the young man approached what at first appeared to be a plastic teepee. As he got closer, he could see it was far more elaborate than that. It was a shelter, pentagonal in shape, roughly twelve feet across, fashioned on a framework of thin limbs gathered from the surrounding woods and tied together with wire and cord. Above sidewalls three feet high the roof angled upward on five sides to a central peak about ten feet off the ground. The frame was covered with large sheets of opaque plastic, giving it the aspect of a great silver tent.

Cautiously, he circled the campsite. There was no one around. On one side of the makeshift cabin a black metal chimney protruded. It gave forth no smoke.

As quietly as he had come, the young man went back to the dirt road and started toward his car. It should not be here, he thought. He would have to come back tomorrow.

The storm had come in from the sea during the night, and by morning rain driven by forty-mile-per-hour winds lashed at the plastic covering the hut. Water crept in at every corner and dripped through the flaps, making the tattered carpet pad that served as a floor soggy. The chill air inside was redolent of dampness, and Scott Card was having trouble getting a handful of twigs to ignite in the tiny stove. The other three youths were awake but remained in their sleeping bags, trying unsuccessfully to stay warm. Young Card was glad he had thought to bring water up from the river the day before. He began to mix a batch of powdered milk from a box between his knees.

At nineteen, Brian Scott Card was the oldest of the four. After he had graduated from high school in Van Nuys the previous June, he and his older brother, Jeff, had set off to backpack through Northern California. In August they found the secluded glade in a seldom-patrolled corner of the state park and built the temporary cabin. In the nearly six months since, the rangers had not found it.

Scott and Jeff had been helped in the construction by a fifteen-year-old nomad they met that summer who told them he was Mark Johnson. They didn't know his real name was Mark John Dreibelbis, or that he had run away from home in Pennsylvania to avoid facing a juvenile court appearance for marijuana possession. Mark was huddled in his sleeping bag reading a comic book, "The Fabulous Furry Freak Brothers," a best seller among members of the acid generation. Jeff had moved out of the cabin a few weeks earlier and was staying with some newfound friends over in Boulder Creek.

The other two campers had arrived the night before. They were Robert Michael Spector and David Allan Oliker, both eighteen, friends of the Card brothers from Southern California. They had left home a couple of days earlier to hitchhike to Humboldt County on the Oregon border, where Rob Spector would register as a student for the spring semester at College of the Redwoods. Dave Oliker, who had dropped out of college for a semester to decide what he wanted to do with his life, had come along for the adventure. The two knew about the cabin from letters Scott had written. The day before, Rob had called his father, a clinical psychologist with offices in Sherman Oaks, and told him they were in Santa Cruz and were going to try to find the Cards. If they did, he had said, they would stay a couple of days before going on to the college in Arcata. In any event, they would be home by the 22nd of February.

"Hey, man, this is really neat," Dave had enthused when Scott showed him around the campsite the evening before. Now he wasn't so sure. He had to go to the bathroom, but he was reluctant to leave the moist warmth of his sleeping bag.

The shelter was well stocked with food, but breakfast would have to wait until Scott got the fire started. He put a batch of damp twigs on top of the stove and rolled up a sheet of newspaper. Suddenly he was aware that someone was standing in the doorway. He had not noticed the flap being pulled back.

A young man stood with his hands in the pockets of his brown raincoat. His dark hair was wet, and rainwater trickled down his cheek. He looked down at the four startled faces blinking up at him.

"This is government property," he said. "You can't camp here. You'll have to leave."

The young man wore no uniform, and the four knew that he wasn't a ranger. "Hey, man," Mark said, "who the fuck are you, Smokey the Bear?"

"If you don't clean up this mess and leave, I'll have to tell the forestry people."

"Shit, man, we're not hurting anybody. Why hassle us?"

"It's not right for you to be here," the young man insisted. "Look at all this garbage." He gestured toward the cartons and other debris scattered on the floor. Mark, Dave, and Rob had pulled themselves out of their sleeping bags and were sitting on them. None of them felt threatened by the short, slight man who challenged them. The odds were four to one, and besides they had the .22 rifle leaning up against the wall in the corner. But they were worried he would turn them in.

"Come on, can't we talk this over?" Scott pleaded.

"No. I'm going to get the rangers."

The young man left the doorway and started walking away. The four youths quickly rose to their feet, and Scott and Mark followed him outside.

"Listen, man, give us some time," Mark said. "Let us have a month."

"No."

"Ten days then. It'll take us that long to get all this shit packed up."

"If I do that, you'll just move to someplace else."

"Come on, man . . ."

"We have nothing to discuss. Get back in the tent."

The two boys shrugged and walked inside. "Do you think he's serious?" Dave asked. "What can they do to us?"

"I don't know, but maybe you and Rob better split. There's no sense in all of us getting screwed."

The four, intent on their troubles, didn't see that the stranger had stepped back inside the entryway, nor did they see the small black revolver he had taken from his pocket. The young man fired six shots so rapidly it sounded like a single explosion. The four crumpled in a tangle of arms and legs. Dave, Rob, and Scott lay unconscious, mortally wounded. Mark was on the ground, groaning. He vomited. Unable to speak, he watched as the intruder pulled a box of cartridges from his pocket and reloaded the gun. He tried to scream but managed only a terrified gurgle. Taking careful aim, the young man fired a single shot into the head of each of the other three. Then he turned the gun toward Mark. Sobbing, the boy screwed his eyes shut. He neither heard the report nor felt the impact as the bullet crashed through his brain.

The young man put the gun back in his pocket and knelt over his victims. He searched the bodies until he found their wallets. He removed ten-dollar bills from two of them and a dollar from a third before pitching them into a pile on the floor. He saw the rifle in the corner, hefted it appreciatively, and placed the sling over his shoulder. He righted a Coleman lantern that had tipped over and gone out when the bodies fell. In the meager light that passed through the plastic tarp, he examined some books stacked near the stove: a hardback dictionary, a pocket thesaurus, and a paperback copy of Isaac Asimov's *Nightfall*.

The killer took a last look around. The acrid smell of cordite irritated his nostrils. He went outside and carefully closed the plastic flap. It had stopped raining, and for a moment, the sun broke through the black clouds overhead.

14
The Arrest

HAD IT NOT BEEN for the shredded clothing and the bra, the young target shooters who had been plinking in the trees off Smith Grade would not have noticed the skeleton of Mary Guilfoyle. It was Monday, February 12, and the schools were closed for Lincoln's Birthday. They drove to a telephone booth and called the sheriff's office. The dispatcher made a note of the location and told them to return and wait for the patrol unit.

The young man looked up, startled by the sound of the squealing tires and siren as the car with the county insignia on the door rounded the corner where Smith Grade met Empire Grade. He put down his ax and wiped the sweat from his forehead with his sleeve. He watched, expressionless, until the automobile passed from sight around a curve. He picked up an armload of firewood and dumped it into the back of his station wagon.

Mary Guilfoyle's decomposed remains were identified with dental charts. News of the grim discovery spread quickly and, in spite of the holiday, a large group of students met at the University of California. The body was the eighth found in Santa Cruz County in less than six weeks, and the two girls who had vanished seven nights earlier, Alice Liu, twenty, and Roselind Thorpe, twenty-two, were still missing. Nine other young women had reported rapes or rape attempts in the university area in the past month. The students voted to mount a massive search of the 2,000-acre wooded campus for the bodies of Alice and Roselind.

The university police chief repeated his warning against hitchhiking. "It's like Russian roulette," he said. "A hitchhiker can get a thousand rides without incident. The next one could result in a bad experience. It's just not worth it."

Fred Perez arose early the next morning, February 13. He had work to do in the driveway of his rental house next door, and he wanted to finish it before it rained. He dressed without shaving, pulled on a pair of work boots, zipped a navy blue windbreaker over his wool shirt, and slammed out the back door of the modest, fifty-year-old frame bungalow on Lighthouse Avenue near Gharkey Street, a block from the ocean. His wife, Margaret, stayed inside.

Perez moved briskly. He regarded himself as being in good shape for a man of seventy-two, and although he had suffered from mild heart trouble, his retirement had been an active one. He was still muscular, packing 190 pounds on his 5 foot 10 inch frame, and he had a full head of steel-gray hair. He wore a pair of dark-framed glasses. Together with his jet-black eyebrows, they gave his rugged features a beetling aspect.

Fred Abbie Perez was heavier now than when he had boxed professionally as a middleweight under the name Freddie Bell after his stint as a Marine in World War I. His strength had come from working on the wharf in the family fish business his grandfather had founded in 1863. The Perezes, one of the county's oldest families, once had owned most of the land on Lighthouse Point. Over the years the orchards had given way to houses, including the one he lived in now.

By 8:00 A.M. Perez had almost finished filling the chuck hole near the curb on the Gharkey Street side of the house he leased to Bob Kardon. His wheelbarrow was in the street behind his parked pickup truck. He didn't look up when the station wagon turned off Lighthouse Avenue and passed him slowly. He didn't see it stop on his side of the roadway a little over 100 feet from where he was grunting rhythmically with the exertion of turning the heavy, wet soil.

It was as if someone had struck him heavily on the right shoulder. He felt a sting, and searing, exploding pain swelled in his chest. He grasped at the air for an instant, then fell sideways and forward. He was unconscious before he hit the ground. A .22-caliber bullet had ripped into his chest and through his right lung, tearing the aorta and shattering the heart.

Across Charkey Street, Joan Stagnaro had just pulled open the drapes in her living room. The front door stood ajar. Hearing a sharp crack, she pushed open the screen door and stepped out on her porch. A blue and white station wagon, maybe an old Pontiac, she thought, was parked on the wrong side of the street opposite her house with the engine running. She saw a single man in the driver's seat. His back was toward her, and he was looking over his left shoulder, through the open rear window. The man sat motionless for several seconds. Mrs. Stagnaro imagined for a moment he might be having motor trouble, but then he turned around, and the car started slowly toward Laguna Street at the other end of the block. As it turned the corner and disappeared, she noticed a red STP sticker near the right front door.

Mrs. Stagnaro turned to go back into the house. Then she saw Perez. Hearing her screams, her two sons ran outside. Frantically, she told them what had happened. The boys ran across the street and knelt beside the man on the ground. He seemed to be breathing, but they didn't touch him. They went back to their house.

Inside, Mrs. Stagnaro was on the telephone. "I think there's been a shooting," she told the police dispatcher. "There's a man lying across the street."

When the car containing patrolmen Rick LeMarquand and Dennis King screeched to a halt next to Perez's wheelbarrow, they saw a man in a brown uniform bending over a still form. It was Chuck Weaver, a sheriff's deputy.

"I was driving by on my way to work," Weaver said as they walked up to him. "I saw this guy on the ground and thought maybe he'd had a coronary."

"We got a report of a shot fired." LeMarquand said. "We'd better take a look." Gently, the officers turned the man over. They heard a faint gurgling from his throat, and saw blood seeping through a small hole in his jacket. LeMarquand felt for a pulse in the neck, but he couldn't be certain the heart was still beating.

He looked up as another police car drew up to the curb and three men got out. Sergeant Dan Fite squatted next to the victim and probed for a pulse. He pulled a flashlight out of his pocket and shined it in Perez's unblinking eyes.

"He's had it," he said to the others. "Call the coroner."

Mrs. Stagnaro was talking excitedly to Officer King. Within two minutes an alarm was broadcast describing the blue and white station wagon.

An ambulance that had been dispatched when the police received the first call turned into the quiet street, red lights flashing and siren warbling officiously.

It began to rain heavily.

Officer Sean Upton was by himself in a patrol car when he heard the bulletin about the station wagon. From the direction it had been going, it sounded to him as if the killer might be headed toward Highway 1. He took up a position near the Mission Street on ramp and waited, his windshield wipers slapping monotonously.

Upton stiffened as he saw a car with an STP sticker on the right front fender pass him and turn on to the highway. "I've got him," he breathed into his microphone as he started after the station wagon. "I'm gonna need cover."

Back at Gharkey Street, Sergeant Fite, who had left his radio turned up, heard Upton's message. He and another detective jumped into their car and started toward the highway. They overheard two other officers closer to Upton radio him that they were on their way to back him up.

Upton followed the station wagon south on Highway 1. He watched the driver, wary of any sudden move. The man seemed oblivious of the prowl car behind him. As the suspect turned left on River Street, Upton heard the voice of Sergeant Burt Witte on the radio. He was right behind him and ready to move in. Upton took a breath and switched on his red light and siren.

The station wagon pulled immediately to the side of the street. Upton heard his own voice booming through a hand-held electric megaphone. "This is a felony arrest," it echoed. "We have you covered. Put your hands on the windshield and don't move."

The driver did as he was told. Covered by the guns of Witte and another patrolman whose car had just arrived, Upton ran to the door of the station wagon, yanked it open, seized the man inside, and forced him to lie face down on the street. The suspect said nothing. Upton patted him down quickly and, finding no weapons, hand-cuffed him and jerked him to his feet. "Get in the back seat," he ordered, pushing him toward his patrol car.

After the prisoner was locked in, Upton walked back to the station wagon and saw a .22-caliber rifle jammed against the front seat with a paper bag over the muzzle. He picked it up gingerly by the barrel. "I think you'd better take this," he said to Fite as he got out of his car.

The young man said nothing during the ride to police headquar-ters, nor while he was being photographed and fingerprinted. Most of the booking information came from his driver's license: name, Herbert William Mullin; age, 25 (DOB 4/18/47); address, 1541 McLellan Road, Felton, CA; WMA: height, 5'7"; weight, 135; hair, brown; eyes, brown; arrest, 187PC (murder).

Upton was ordered to take him to the nearby county hospital for a physical and tests for alcohol or drugs. On the way, the officer tried to draw Mullin into conversation, but the prisoner sat sullenly be-hind the grillework in the back seat and said nothing.

After they got to the hospital, Upton found Police Sergeant Finne-gan and Sam Robustelli from the sheriff's office and asked them to help him guard Mullin during the examination. When Dr. Ronald Turner, the physician on duty, stepped into the room, Mullin had his eyes fixed on the middle distance.

"Do you feel sick at all?" the doctor asked.

Mullin spoke for the first time. His voice was deliberate, the words clipped and precise, the tone without emotion. "I don't have to answer any questions. I choose to remain silent."

"Can I examine him without his consent?" Dr. Turner asked the officers.

"Sure."

"OK, sit him on the table."

Mullin resisted silently, and the three had to hold him. The doctor found him to be in good health, with a normal pulse and blood pressure and no signs of injury, illness, or drug addiction. He could not complete neurologic, vision, or hearing examinations because Mullin refused to speak to him. For the same reason Dr. Turner couldn't make a judgment about his mental state.

When the three officers undressed him, they found four tattoos on Mullin's body. On his abdomen in block letters were the words, "LEGALIZE ACID." Directly below that "Eagle Eyes Marijuana" had been tattooed on the lower part of his belly. On his left forearm were the word, "birth," two crosses and the word, "Maha-shamadhi." When they wrestled him back on to the table, they found the words "Kriya Yoga" tattooed on the inside of his left ankle. Mullin fought soundlessly when Dr. Turner inserted a rubber gloved finger into his anus to examine his prostate. The physician noticed what appeared to be cigarette burns on his penis.

The prisoner balked again when the doctor tried to take a blood sample, jerking his arm away and cowering like a caged animal. Upton telephoned Lieutenant Scherer at the police station. "The doctor wants to know what to do," he said.

"You tell him he has no right to refuse," the lieutenant replied. "The sonofabitch is charged with murder."

While Finnegan and Robustelli grasped Mullin's arms and Upton held down his legs, Dr. Turner drew a blood specimen from the inside of his right elbow. He divided the sample into three test tubes and handed them to the officers.

"That's it," he said. "You can take those to the lab. I'll dictate my report this afternoon."

While Mullin was being examined, Sergeant Fite was dusting the rifle for fingerprints. The station wagon had been impounded at Rossi's Garage until the detectives could get a warrant to search it. While Fite was working on the gun, Sergeant Witte came into the room.

"He had a receipt on him for a .22 pistol he bought from a Western Auto store." he told Fite, handling him a slip of paper.

"December 16th," Fite mused. "That was more than a month before the Gianera and Francis murders. Whaddaya know . . ."

"Too bad we don't have the gun."

"Maybe we'll find it. Give that receipt to Dick Foerster. He's working on the Gianera case."

15
Silence!

As soon as he heard of Mullin's arrest, Terry Medina pawed through his desk at the sheriff's office until he found the list of possible suspects I had compiled after my interview with Bob Francis. He scanned it quickly. He found neither Mullin's name nor one similar to it. Muttering an oath under his breath, he started to crumple the piece of yellow legal foolscap. He hesitated and straightened it out.

"Mullin. Why is that name familiar?" he wondered out loud.

As Medina was putting the wrinkled paper back into the drawer, he saw Sergeant Foerster of the police department coming through the door.

"We think he had another gun," Foerster said. "We found a receipt from a Western Auto store for a .22. It was a Saturday night special. He paid less than twenty-five bucks for it."

"When?"

"December 16th."

"That fits," Medina said.

"I went to the Western Auto store here in town and talked to the owner's wife," Foerster continued. "She said they hadn't sold any guns that day. When I showed her the receipt, she said it was from the associate store in Felton."

"You talk to them yet?"

"I thought maybe you'd like to go along."

"Goddamn right I would."

Medina and Foerster showed the receipt to Anthony Black, the operator of the store in Felton. He said that he had written it personally.

"Those are my initials," he explained, pointing to the box marked "salesman."

"Do you recall the sale?"

"Yes, I think so. Let me get my records." Black came back with his copy of the state registration he had filled out when he sold the gun. The buyer was listed as Herbert William Mullin, 1541 McLellan Road, Felton. He gave his occupation as a sketch artist. The gun was an RG-14, a six-shot revolver with a three-inch barrel manufactured in Germany but distributed by an American company in Florida.

"The crime lab in Redwood City said that was one of a couple of possibilities," Foerster reminded Medina. He turned back to Black. "Do you remember the man who bought this?"

"Yes. He was a short, dark-haired guy. He seemed to be very quiet, kind of a fussy type."

"Did he buy any ammunition?"

"That's another thing I remember. He didn't. He paid for the gun on the 16th, but he didn't pick it up until the 22nd because of the statutory waiting period, you know, for buying concealable weapons. He didn't buy any bullets that day either."

The two detectives ran into Sergeant Arbsland as they walked out of the store.

"We're supposed to go to his folks' house," he told them. "His mother's at home waiting for us. The father is on his way from work."

"Where do they live?" Medina asked.

"On McLellan Road. It's not far from here."

The house was typical of the solidly middle-class rural area. As they got out of the car, Medina was still grappling with the familar ring of Mullin's name.

Mrs. Jean Mullin looked stunned and confused when she opened the door for the three detectives.

"I just can't believe it," she said as she stood aside to admit them. "It just doesn't make any sense."

"Had your son been living here?" Arbsland asked.

"No. He had moved up to San Francisco a couple of years ago, but he came home last September. Then he moved into town about three weeks ago."

"Where was that?"

"The Pacific View Apartments on Front Street. It was apartment number 8, I think."

"When did you see him last?" Medina asked.

"Last Friday."

"That would be the 9th?"

"Yes."

"Did he have a station wagon?"

"Yes, an old Chevrolet. He used it to cut firewood in the hills. He was supposed to . . . to deliver a load for us this morning."

"Where does he cut wood?"

"Oh, around here. Sometimes up on Empire Grade."

Medina caught Arbsland's eye. That was near where they had found what was left of Mary Guilfoyle. Arbsland nodded almost imperceptibly but said nothing.

"How long have you lived here?" Medina asked.

"About ten years."

"Did Herb go to school here?"

"Yes. He graduated from San Lorenzo Valley High."

Medina experienced a flash of recognition. He remembered Mullin now. He had played high school football. Medina had faced him across the line when San Lorenzo Valley played Santa Cruz High. Mullin had been small for a guard, but he was quick and determined. Medina dimly recalled meeting him at a party.

Mullin's father arrived, his face creased with worry. His wife had called him at work to say their son was under arrest. He asked why. The detectives explained briefly, sparing any details. Bill Mullin was an affable, sixty-four-year-old postal clerk who had been looking forward to retirement. Medina thought he took the news stoically.

"Did your son take all of his possessions with him when he moved back out last month?" Foerster was asking.

"No," Mrs. Mullin answered. "He still has some of his things in his bedroom here."

"And he stored some other stuff in the attic and out back," her husband volunteered.

"Had he, uh, been, uh, acting strangely lately?" Medina asked, picking his words carefully.

"Well, I guess you could say that," the father said. "He tried to get his grandfather in Carmel to buy him an acre of land here in Felton, but he refused. That's Jean's father. It upset Herb."

"Anything else?"

"Yeah. Last December he tried to join the Marines. It was a real turnaround, because he had been a CO before."

"A conscientious objector?"

"Yes."

"What happened?"

"He didn't pass the test, for some reason. Anyway, that sort of set him off, too. He found out they wouldn't take him sometime in January. He was very upset, and he was arguing with his mother quite a bit. I finally told him it wasn't working out here, and he would have to find his own place. That's when he moved out."

"OK," Foerster said, shaking hands with Mullin. "I don't think we have to trouble you further right now."

"There's one other thing," the father said. "Herb . . . Herb was a patient at Mendocino State Hospital in 1969." All three detectives knew it as a mental facility.

"What for?"

"It was a self-commitment. He had been using hallucinogenic drugs."

"Thank you both very much," Foerster said. Outside he turned to the other two. "I'll call Art Danner," he said. "We've got enough to get search warrants for this place and his apartment along with the car."

Shortly before noon, Mullin was brought back from the hospital to the police detective bureau, where Lieutenant Scherer read him his rights again.

"Do you know why you're here, Herb?" Scherer asked. Mullin bridled.

"I have the right to remain silent," he mimicked. "I have the right to remain silent on the advice of my attorney."

"Who's your lawyer?"

"Silence!" Mullin barked. "Don't you know what silence means?"

"Would you like to make a phone call?"

"Silence!"

The investigators kept after him for nearly two hours, repeatedly asking him if he knew the reason for his arrest. He steadfastly declined to speak, other than responding occasionally with the single word, "silence." Scherer and the others were unsure who or what they had on their hands, but they strongly suspected Perez was not the only person he had slain.

About 1:30 P.M. Mullin startled them by asking to make a telephone call.

"Who do you want to talk to?" Scherer asked.

Mullin recited seven digits. The lieutenant jotted down the number. "Who's that?" he inquired.

"Silence!"

"We have to have the name of the party," Scherer said. "We have to make a record of the call."

"Silence!"

Scherer shrugged and dialed the number. A woman answered.

"May I ask who this is speaking?"

"Mrs. Mullin," she replied.

"Mrs. Mullin, my name is Lieutenant Scherer. I'm with the Santa Cruz Police Department. As you know, we have your son down here on a very serious matter. He wants to talk to you." He handed the telephone to the prisoner.

"Mom, this is Herb." There was a pause. "I hope you liked your Valentine gift. Can I talk to Dad?" Another pause. "Dad, I think you'd better get hold of Dick Pease."

"When you're finished talking, Herb, don't hang up," Scherer interjected.

Mullin stared at Scherer for a moment, almost smiling. "Just hire Dick Pease," he repeated into the mouthpiece, and then carefully placed the receiver back on the hook.

"OK, Herb, sit down over there." Wearily, Scherer redialed the number. A man answered the telephone on the first ring. Scherer identified himself again. "Mr. Mullin, your son is under arrest for murder," he said bluntly.

"Yes, we know. The police were here this morning."

"If you have an attorney, you should call him."

"Can I come and see Herb?" the father asked.

Scherer looked at the clock on the wall. "If you get here before five, it's OK," he said. "Later than that we don't have enough people working the jail to handle visitors."

After hanging up the telephone, Scherer turned back to Mullin. "Is Dick Pease your attorney?" he asked.

"Silence!"

"Have you talked to a lawyer before, about any of this?"

Mullin began to shout. "I know what my rights are. I have a right to have an attorney, and I have the right to remain silent. Do you know what silence means?"

"We're not getting anywhere," Scherer observed. "Take him back to his cell."

"You people were responsible for the 3 million killed in World War II," Mullin said as he was led away.

Armed with an affidavit from Foerster, Danner had quickly obtained warrants from Charles Franich, a superior court judge in Santa Cruz, to search Mullin's impounded station wagon, his apartment at 81 Front Street, and the family home in Felton. Medina was among those present when the first one was served at Rossi's garage.

Foerster recovered a brown canvas overnight bag from the passenger's seat and handed it to criminalist Paul Dougherty, who was wearing plastic gloves. Inside he found a small cloth sack tied at the top. Inside that was an RG-14 .22-caliber revolver.

"If the ballistics check out, he's killed at least six people in the last three weeks," Foerster said.

After the second gun was found in Mullin's car, Scherer called the county detectives and asked for a conference of everyone who was working on the Gianera, Francis, and Perez murders who wasn't tied up serving the search warrants. Both the rifle and the revolver were sent to the crime laboratory at Redwood City.

After the meeting, Scherer and Sergeant Fite returned to the police station's small cell block. Mullin was screaming and rattling the door of his cell.

"What the hell's the matter now?" Scherer demanded.

"I want to talk to my attorney. Has he shown up yet?"

"No. I'll try to find out where he is." While Fite attempted to calm Mullin, Scherer went back to his office and called Richard Pease, a local attorney who was a former Santa Cruz County district attorney. His secretary reported that he was away, but promised she would have him call the police as soon as he returned. Scherer pondered for a moment after hanging up the telephone, then strode to a filing cabinet and dug out a photograph of the Gianeras' bathroom graphically depicting their blood-spattered bodies. When he returned to Mullin's cell, Scherer let himself in. Mullin was sitting on the top bunk. He looked at the lieutenant quizzically, almost with derision.

"Your lawyer's busy somewhere. He'll call as soon as he gets back to the office." The detective held the picture a few inches from Mullin's face. "Did you know Jim Gianera?" he asked evenly.

Mullin stared at the picture for a few seconds, then turned away. Scherer shifted and shoved the photographs in front of his nose. "I asked you a question," he said sharply. "Did you know this man?"

"Silence!" Mullin said.

"Take him back to my office," Scherer ordered. There, he motioned Mullin to a chair. "Now, then, Herb, having seen that picture, do you have anything that you'd like to discuss with me?"

"Silence!"

"I mean, do you want to waive your right to have an attorney present. Did you kill the Gianeras and the Francis family?"

"Do you know what silence means? I have the right to remain silent."

"You know, Herb, there's a strong possibility we're going to be able to implicate you in the Gianera case and the Francis murders. Why don't you make it easy on yourself?" the detective asked pleasantly.

"Silence!"

Scherer tried to take the measure of his prisoner. He was evidently nervous, although he appeared to be in control of himself. He wondered what would make him crack.

"I'm gonna have to decide what to do with you," Scherer said finally. "I don't know if you'll be safe in the county jail, because there are some inmates who don't like people who kill kids. It's no different from somebody who's a known snitch, you know, someone who has a snitch jacket on him in the jail."

"Silence!" Mullin replied. "I want to go back to my cell."

Scherer sighed. "Lock him up again," he said.

That evening, Bill Mullin arrived at the police station. As gently as he could, Scherer gave the uncomprehending father a sketchy outline of the charges against his son. Mullin had already talked with the family lawyer, who had visited Herb earlier. The lieutenant took Mullin to the cell, let him in, and waited outside.

A normally positive man, secure in his opinions, Bill seemed confused and a little tentative. Herb appeared to be unconcerned, almost relaxed.

"Your mother said to send her true love," the older man offered as he sat down.

"Uh huh."

"We're awfully sorry you're in this deep, deep trouble."

"Yeah."

Bill Mullin looked at his hands in his lap. "Awfully sorry," he whispered.

"Yeah. Did Pease talk to you tonight?" Herb asked.

"Yeah."

"Oh. Uh . . ."

"It's going to be a very costly venture, but we hired him," the father said.

"Did he tell you what I wanted to do?" Herb asked. "Do you agree with that position?"

"No. I think you need psychiatric help more than you need an arraignment before the law."

"Well . . ."

Bill Mullin began to show signs of losing control of his emotions. "Why did you ever buy those guns?" he demanded hoarsely. "Where did you get that rifle?"

"Uh, pertaining to that stuff, you know, uh . . ."

The father clenched his fists. "You're going to talk to me," he cried.

"I'm going to plead the Fifth Amendment."

"You're asking for deep trouble, then. You'd better ask for a psychiatrist before you do that."

"If it's up to me, you know, I mean you guys have an awful lot of power as far as how I act, you know what I mean," Herb rambled. "When I met you, I wasn't even . . ."

Bill's voice contained a tone of resignation. "Never mind," he said.

". . . two weeks old, you know. I mean I can raise my son better than you raised me."

"OK, Herb."

"Other than that, I want to plead no contest and I want to stand on the Fifth Amendment." Herb changed the subject. "My son would have gone to a military academy, you know."

"Is that all you want to say?"

"I'm afraid for Anna, Dad."

The father had never heard the name before. His eyebrows rose. "For whom?"

"I'm going to plead no contest and stand on the Fifth Amendment."

"Is there anything you want me to tell your mother?"

"Just Happy Valentine's Day, and I wish I would have gone to a military academy."

"Anything else?"

"No."

"If I get you a psychiatrist, will you see him?"

"Uh, there's another thing . . ."

"Will you cooperate with him?" Bill persisted. Herb was preoccupied with legal tactics.

". . . it might be mute. You can make a plea of mute and, uh . . ."

"Do you want to talk to a psychiatrist?"

"I'll just plead the Fifth Amendment," Herb said decisively. "I don't have to testify against myself. The Fifth Amendment to the United States Constitution."

In despair, the father rose. "OK, Herb," he said.

Scherer came to the door. "Ready?" he inquired. "All through?"

Bill turned to his son as the door opened. "Good luck," he said. Herb was silent.

"It didn't take long," Scherer observed.

"May God be with you," Bill said. Herb looked away.

"Yeah," he acknowledged.

There were tears in Bill Mullin's eyes. "God be with you."

16
The Lineup

THE NEXT MORNING, Medina sat at his desk going over the lists of evidence retrieved the night before. He had not got to bed until early in the morning, but at that he had been luckier than Foerster, who had stayed up all night examining the items and dictating the inventories after the searches were completed.

Beyond the rifle and revolver, little of apparent value had been found in the car. It was cluttered with tools, papers, rags, and other junk. The rear deck carried a load of freshly cut firewood.

The little apartment on Front Street had been more interesting.

The Pacific View Court and Annex was an old, seedy guest house near the beach. The neighborhood, once a haven for tourists who stayed in respectable little hotels, had become a jumble of cheap apartments and rooming houses populated mainly by the very young or the very old, the former aimless followers of the sun, the latter tied to the place by circumstance, because the forgiving climate made marginal living possible. It was a purgatory of rootless souls.

The Pacific View itself was a two-story frame building with a steep roof of red composition shingles. Mullin's apartment was on the second floor.

From the top of the dresser the officers had taken Mullin's address book, a Bible, and a paperback entitled *Einstein—The Life and Times.* In the closet they found a long coat with a button missing. Above the hangers they noticed a scuttle hole with a trap door and found that it led to the building's attic. Up there they had discovered some women's underclothing, a pair of black shoes, four shirts, a pair of trousers, and a blue jacket.

Medina and Foerster had gone through the drawers of the dresser. In the bottom one they found a can of Winchester gun oil and a stack of newspaper clippings, some of them stories about the recent murders. From the top, Medina had pulled a small brown leather bag full of coins. Something about a leather bag had rung a bell.

Bob Francis had not moved back into the cabin. The detectives had managed to keep him secluded from the press, and after he was cleared as a suspect, he had sought refuge with friends in Boulder Creek. On this morning, Medina telephoned him there.

"Do you remember if there was a brown leather pouch in your house?" he asked. "Maybe one with money in it?"

"I didn't have anything like that," Francis said.

"How about Kathy?"

"No. Wait a minute. Daemon had one. He kept his marbles in it."

"I'll be by later to show you one we found," Medina said. He hung up the phone. He had not mentioned Mullin's name, since it had not been on the list I had compiled with Francis.

Medina returned to Foerster's inventory. As he had dictated it during the night, the police sergeant had closely perused each piece of possible evidence so that he could describe it in detail. One line on the list leapt out at Medina. He stared at the paper.

"One white address book," it said, "containing the name of Jim Gianera, 1965 Branciforte Dr."

"I'll be a sonofabitch," Medina whispered, grabbing the telephone.

Medina, Sergeant Foerster, and Peter Chang, the district attorney, got to Boulder Creek a little before 8:00 P.M. They had spent the late afternoon at the crime laboratory in Redwood City and were on their way back to Santa Cruz.

At the laboratory, criminalist Paul Dougherty told them that he had finished test-firing the revolver found in Mullin's car, and the firing pin impression left on the shell casing was the same as the mark on the empty shell found in the Gianera's living room.

"That cartridge was fired in this gun," he said flatly.

"No possibility it could have been another?" Chang asked.

"No other weapon could have made the mark on that casing."

"What about the bullets taken from the bodies?"

"That work isn't finished yet. I'll call you as soon as we have something definite."

After leaving Dougherty with the evidence taken from the searches of the car and the apartment, along with some of Mullin's personal effects from his parents' home, the three drove to the house where Bob Francis was staying. Medina showed him the leather bag he had found in the dresser drawer.

"That's not Daemon's," Francis said. "I've never seen it before."

"Have you ever heard of someone named Herb Mullin?" Medina asked. "Do you know anybody by that name?"

Francis blinked and thought a minute. "No, but Jim knew a guy named Mullin. I think he told me he was an old high school buddy."

"Did you ever meet him?"

"Yeah, I think I did. I think he showed up for a visit once when we all lived up at Dobbins. That would have been sometime in the summer of '71."

"Do you remember what kind of car he was driving?"

"It seems to me it was sort of a dark-colored Volkswagen."

"Anything else?"

"Right after he got there, Mullin dropped five tabs of acid, and then a little while later, he dropped five more. I want to tell you he got really ripped, higher than a kite. Kathy had to bring him down easy."

"You ever see him again?"

"No. But last December, Jim showed me a letter he said he got from Mullin. No, I guess it was earlier than that, because it was during the time he and Joan were moving into the house. It was weird."

"How so?"

"It was just a weird letter. We laughed about it. For some reason, Mullin wrote to Jim and asked him who he was gonna vote for in the election in November.

"And a little while later," Francis added, "Jim told me he'd seen this guy Mullin around, and that he wanted to buy some LSD."

"Do you remember anything else about him at all?"

"I think Jim told me once that Mullin lived in San Francisco and, if it was the same guy, he showed up one time somewhere in Boulder Creek or Ben Lomond, and he was wearing like real fine clothes. Anyway, he got into a fight with somebody and lost. I don't even remember if Jim was there when it happened."

"OK, thanks," Medina said. "We'll probably be calling you again soon."

"I didn't see today's paper," Francis said. "Is Mullin the one they busted for shooting that old guy yesterday?"

"Yeah."

"You think he killed Kathy and the others?"

"It's beginning to look like it," Chang said.

On February 15, Chang filed a charge against Mullin accusing him of six counts of first-degree murder. Late the night before, the laboratory had reported that Perez had been killed with the rifle found in his car, and that the Gianeras, Kathy Francis, and the two boys had all been shot with his revolver.

The laboratory also had another, equally fascinating piece of information. One of Mullin's fingerprints matched a latent lifted from the confessional in which Father Tomei had been stabbed to death almost four months earlier. The report had been sent to the Santa Clara County district attorney's office. No charge would be filed immediately, since Mullin was already in custody for six other murders in another county.

The courtroom of Santa Cruz Municipal Judge Donald O. May was packed when Mullin was arraigned later that morning. Most of the spectators were reporters. Everyone craned to get a look at the celebrated defendant, who was brought shackled from the county jail. He was clean-shaven, apparently having given up an incipient mustache he had when he was arrested, and his hair was neatly combed as he stood impassively and listened to the charges. When the clerk finished reading, the judge asked Pease, Mullin's attorney, whether his client was ready to enter a plea. Unexpectedly, Mullin spoke. His voice was low but clear and steady.

"According to the Fifth Amendment of the United States Constitution, I cannot be forced to testify against myself," he lectured the judge. "Therefore, I choose to remain silent."

"That's all right, fine," replied May. "All we want to do is assure that you receive your right to a fair preliminary hearing. Mr. Pease, Mr. Chang, when do you suggest we hold it?"

"Whenever it's convenient for the court, your honor."

"All right, March 1st," the judge said, consulting his calendar. "Anything further?"

"There is the matter of bail, your honor," the defense attorney said.

The judge looked at the district attorney. "Mr. Chang?"

"Because of the seriousness of the offenses charged, and the fact he may be charged with a murder in another jurisdiction, the people would oppose bail," Chang said.

"Mr. Pease?"

"We think bail for the defendant would be appropriate, your honor."

"All right, bail is set at $300,000."

Following the five-minute arraignment, Mullin was taken back to the county jail by six heavily armed deputies. Chang and Pease were deluged with questions by reporters as they walked from the courtroom into the hot glare of the television lights.

In the afternoon, Mullin was brought to the sheriff's investigation bureau. His lawyer was already there, along with Medina and Art Danner from the DA's office. The detective turned on a tape recorder.

"Now, then, Mr. Mullin," he said, "later today we'll have a lineup . . ."

"You're doing it all wrong," Mullin interrupted.

"I beg your pardon."

"The presence of Mr. Pease should be acknowledged on the tape."

"OK then, let's have everybody here introduce himself out loud, including you." Once that was accomplished, Medina resumed. "As I said, we'll have a lineup in which you will participate. Witnesses will observe you to determine whether you are responsible for the crime with which you are charged. You are entitled to have an attorney present to observe the proceedings. If you do not have an attorney, one will be afforded to you at no cost to you." He looked up from the card he was reading. "Do you understand these rights?"

"I wish to stand on the Fifth Amendment. I wish to remain

silent." He smiled thinly at Medina. "Would you please recite the Fifth Amendment?" he requested.

"Basically it's the amendment that says you don't have to make any incriminating statements," Medina said. "None will be requested from you, I assure you. The reason we're going through all this is to make sure your civil rights are being carried out in the proper manner."

"I asked you to recite the Fifth Amendment," Mullin said, almost sternly.

Medina was losing patience. "Look, Herb, I don't have a copy on me."

Mullin turned to Pease. "Should I answer his question?" he asked.

"I would advise you to," the attorney said.

"I understand my civil rights," Mullin said. "I'll participate on the advice of my attorney."

Meanwhile, in three separate rooms in the sheriff's office, Sergeant Arbsland prepared Thatcher Clarke, Steve Houts, and Joan Stagnaro for the lineup. Five other prisoners and a sheriff's officer would appear with Mullin.

Mrs. Stagnaro was the first to go into the room after the seven men trooped in, squinting and shading their eyes against the bright lights. Mullin was the fourth in line. Several minutes passed before she handed her card to Arbsland. She had circled "unknown."

Houts also circled "unknown" but added the notation, "Number 5 looked similar, but that's the extent." He told Arbsland the reason he could make no identification was that he paid more attention to the car than the driver.

Clarke circled number three but scrawled a large question mark next to it. The third man in line was the sheriff's deputy. Arbsland swore.

"I circled the number three because I got bad vibes from him," Clarke explained. "The guy I saw at Kathy's house that morning was over fifty yards away. I couldn't see his features."

"You just fingered a cop," Arbsland told him. "We *know* where he was on the day in question."

"I just got bad vibes from him, that's all."

17
A One-Man Crime Wave

IMMEDIATELY AFTER THE LINEUP concluded, Medina took a telephone message for Pease from the attorney's office. He informed the secretary that her employer was in a holding cell conferring with his client.

"What can we tell him?" Medina asked.

"I just wanted him to know the cousin from San Francisco is here, the one who called to say he might have some information about Mr. Mullin."

"Right, I'll see that he gets the word," Medina said, scribbling a note. He handed the piece of paper to a clerk. "Give that to Dick Pease when he's finished talking to Mullin." He turned to Arbsland. "What say we pay a visit to Pease's office," he said.

"We could get in a jam doing this," Arbsland panted as they ran the three flights down to the parking lot.

"What the hell. It's worth a try."

Richard Watson, twenty-nine, was very agreeable when the two investigators asked to speak with him in the attorney's waiting room. He explained that he was a member of the family and that he had grown up with Herb.

"Some people say he's a pretty sharp individual," Medina said. "Would you comment on that?"

"I would say Herb's IQ is probably very good. He's a bright boy, and has been, even in my recent experiences with him. Of course, the fact that he has been using drugs, and apparently had been using drugs for the last several years, has dulled his mind somewhat, but he is basically a bright boy and has always done well in school."

The cousin told the detectives that approximately nine months earlier, while Herb was still living in San Francisco, he had called and asked to see Watson. The two spent about an hour and a half talking at Watson's apartment. He said Mullin was concerned that he wasn't doing anything with his life, that he wanted "meaningful employment." Watson said he suggested that since Herb had studied engineering in college, he might look for a job as a draftsman. He encouraged him to sign up for a couple of refresher courses, but he didn't think Mullin had done so.

"Did he ever talk to you about what his religious beliefs or convictions were?" Arbsland asked, thinking of the murdered priest.

"He had gone the course," Watson replied. "He had, during the last few years I guess, been involved in different phases of religious belief. But he indicated to me that he did a great deal of meditation and spent time by himself doing so. That was not much of a Christian thing, but on ideas and beliefs of nature and so forth."

Medina inquired about Mullin's relationship with his parents. Watson told him it was a close though perhaps not particularly warm family. He suspected they had become somewhat estranged. "By and large, I'd say the family in recent times has just been unable to know what to do with him, and has not been willing to recognize the fact that he may have a psychological problem, even though perhaps most of the drug problem has passed."

Watson added that he had talked about Herb's mental state with their uncle in Carmel. "He and I both came to the conclusion that there should be some way that we could possibly get Herb to commit himself."

"Why . . ." Medina began.

"What the hell are you two doing here?" Pease had just walked through the door and loomed over the three seated men. Medina switched off his tape recorder and grinned innocently.

"Hi, Dick," he said cordially. "You were too busy to come to the phone when your secretary called. We figured that since Mr. Watson had come all the way from San Francisco, we might as well try to save him some time and talk to him while he was waiting."

"You bastards figured you'd come over here and tamper with one of my witnesses, is what you mean," Pease roared.

"Come on, Dick," Arbsland offered soothingly. "He didn't say anything that's gonna hurt your client. We have it all on tape. You can listen to it if you want."

"You're goddanm right I can."

Medina played the recording, and Pease was pacified to a degree. With the attorney present, the detectives asked a few more routine questions and then excused themselves.

"You think it was worth it?" Arbsland asked as they walked back to the car.

"Probably not. But I don't think he'll give us any heat about it."

By Friday, February 16, 1973, the newspapers and wire services had assembled a great deal of information about Herbert William Mullin. The family had moved to Felton from San Francisco in 1963. He was one of two children, with an older married sister now living in Sonoma County. The product of ten years of private Catholic schools, Mullin had entered San Lorenzo Valley High School as a junior and graduated in the top third of his class in 1965. He was a classmate and friend of James Gianera. The two were on the football team together—although he was short, Mullin had played varsity guard.

An active and popular student, Mullin enrolled with a scholarship at Cabrillo College, where he earned an associate of science degree in highway engineering two years later. He transferred to San Jose State College and changed his major to philosophy, minoring in music and astronomy. Apparently turning his back on his strict Christian background, Mullin became intensely interested in eastern religions. He dropped out of San Jose after six weeks and never attended classes again.

The son of a World War II army officer, Mullin reregistered as a conscientious objector. As alternative service, he had worked for Goodwill Industries. He had been arrested for marijuana possession in 1968 but pleaded guilty to a lesser offense and was placed on probation. He was known to use drugs, but the authorities were uncertain to what extent. Recanting his conscientious objector status, Mullin had tried unsuccessfully in the months before his arrest for murder to enlist in the army, the marines, and the Coast Guard.

He had never shown a tendency toward violence.

The reporters besieged the family home in Felton. "We are deeply shocked about this thing," Bill Mullin told them. "I'm going to call my pastor and ask him to convey sympathy to the families of the deceased. It's the only thing I can do."

"The motive for the slayings is not clearly defined," Chang said guardedly in an interview.

Defense attorney Pease told the reporters that when Mullin left high school, "Herb was a bright student and fine athlete and had the world by the tail, according to his teachers. However, he became a loner, a pretty badly confused young man."

The same day as Mullin's arraignment, the naked, headless bodies of two young women had been found in a canyon east of Castro Valley in Alameda County, about seventy miles from Santa Cruz. One was Caucasian, the other Oriental, leading to speculation that they might be the corpses of Roselind Thorpe and Alice Liu, the two coeds who had vanished from Santa Cruz while hitchhiking in the rain the night of February 5.

"We must be the murder capital of the world right now," Chang said.

That night, Jim Jackson and Harold Cartwright came to our house for dinner. During the 1973 winter quarter I had agreed to teach an undergraduate seminar at Stanford called "Criminal Behavior and the Criminal Justice System." It was an informal class that met one evening a week from 7:00 P.M. to 10:00 P.M. at my home. Jim and Harold had agreed to drive over from Santa Cruz to talk to the students about the problems of defending criminals. Marilynn and I had invited them to come early and eat with the family, which delighted our boys. They were especially taken with Harold, a bearded, congenial bear of a man whose easygoing way with children had made him a kind of honorary uncle over the past couple of years.

At the dinner table, Jackson casually mentioned that he didn't think he should discuss Herb Mullin after the students arrived, just in case he ended up defending him. I remarked that I hadn't noticed he had been appointed.

"We probably will be," Jim said, glancing at Harold. "He's virtually without resources, and the family obviously can't afford a long and complicated legal defense that might involve an insanity plea."

I put down my fork. Jackson was elaborately studying his roast beef. "What insanity plea?" I demanded. "Have you seen him already?"

"No, but the word we hear around the courthouse is that he's probably loony."

I rose to answer the doorbell. It was almost seven. "You could be wrong," I said over my shoulder, without conviction. The last thing in the world I wanted at that time was a drawn-out murder case.

On Saturday, February 17, Jeffrey Card, twenty-one, ran screaming into the Santa Cruz police station. After the desk officer calmed him down, he babbled that he had found his brother and three other boys dead in a shack in Cowell State Park. Since the location was not in the city, the police called the sheriff's office.

Detectives Howard Sanderson and Terry Medina drove to the police department. Sergeant Arbsland was already there.

"The kids were camping up near the Garden of Eden Overlook," he reported. "Jeff said he hadn't seen them for a week, so he hitchhiked over from Boulder Creek to see what they were up to."

Medina looked at the stricken brother, who was hunched over in a chair, his fists pressed against his closed eyes. "Any idea how they died?" he asked Arbsland in a low voice.

"All he could say was that they were all covered with blood. He didn't stick around long."

While Medina and Arbsland left to drive young Card to the campsite, Sanderson telephoned technician Seibel and a pathologist and asked them to meet him at the police station. The three arrived at the turnout on Highway 9 just before twilight and walked up the muddy fire road to the lean-to. The others were waiting for them, their faces grim. Silently, Medina lifted the flap so Sanderson could look inside. A sickly sweet stench assailed him as the beam from his flashlight darted around the enclosure.

"My God," the detective implored, "what's going on around here?"

It was the next day before the doctor could determine that the four youths had been shot, apparently with a .22-caliber gun. Because it had been nearly sunset by the time he reached the scene, the area had been sealed off, guards had been posted, and the bodies had been left where they lay overnight.

"There's blood all over the place," the undersheriff had told the reporters who waited in the cramped shelter of their cars on the highway during the night. "We don't know how they were killed, or who killed them. There appears to have been some kind of scuffle, but it was impossible at first glance to estimate how long they had been dead. One victim had mold on his hand."

After the corpses were taken away in black rubber bags in the morning, the detectives removed the plastic covering from the structure. Jeff Card was brought up from Santa Cruz.

"It looks as if the money was stolen from their wallets. The motive could have been robbery. Does it appear that anything is missing?"

Card walked around the skeleton of the rude cabin he had helped to build six months earlier, peering into boxes and under tarps.

"There was a .22 rifle in the corner last week," he said. "I don't see it around anywhere now."

When Lieutenant Pittenger heard about the missing rifle, he thought immediately about the Perez murder. He also had just learned from the pathologist how the four boys had been killed. He dialed the telephone number of the crime laboratory.

"Mullin," he muttered to himself. "It's got to be Mullin."

On Tuesday, February 20, Chang added four more murder counts to the six charges already pending against Mullin. Ballistics tests had revealed that the four campers had been shot with his revolver. An eleventh count of murder, for the slaying of Father Tomei, was in abeyance in Santa Clara County awaiting the outcome of the case in Santa Cruz.

In Alameda County, coroner's investigator Roland Prahl definitely identified the bodies of the two women found the previous Thursday by a road crew as those of Alice Liu and Rosalind Thorpe, the two missing university students. Even though both had been decapitated, and the hands of Miss Liu also had been severed, Prahl was able to compare X-rays taken when the two were alive with those he made at the morgue.

In Santa Cruz, Sheriff Douglas James told a press conference that Mullin had been "a one-man crime wave" and hinted that he might have been responsible for several other murders. He refused to be specific.

At dawn that Tuesday Lieutenant Pittenger had led a posse of mounted deputies into the hills around the city, ostensibly searching the trails and back country for the bodies of other people who had been reported missing but never were found. He didn't say so to the newspapers, but they also were looking for the rifle stolen during the murders in Cowell Park. Jeff Card had not been able to identify positively the one discovered in Mullin's car as the gun he had seen in the shelter.

What bothered the police and sheriff's investigators most was that at least eleven other killings, some involving rape and butchery, remained officially unsolved. The San Francisco newspapers were suggesting openly that more than one mass murderer was at work in Santa Cruz, leading to further alarm in the already jittery community. The largest gun store in town reported record sales, and one police patrolman told a reporter that he and his fellow officers were nervous about responding to calls after dark. "Somebody might mistakenly shoot one of us as a trespasser," he explained.

Many of the older residents blamed the outbreak of violence on the university, pointing out that there had been hardly any crime in the county before the thousands of young students began migrating there from all over the United States. But in an interview Lieutenant Scherer attributed it instead to the young transients who moved into vacant summer cabins and turned them into communes or drug factories.

"The hills are a hot spot for dope and trouble," he said.

The counterculture types were equally afraid, but they no longer believed the murders had anything to do with drugs. At the Catalyst, a popular gathering place for hippies, the manager, a muscular immigrant from San Francisco, blamed Governor Reagan.

"He shut down the nuthouses and all the crazies came to our town," he complained.

At the university, the chancellor's office issued another stern directive to all students telling them not to hitchhike. Still, the warnings were largely ignored.

"It won't happen to me," an eighteen-year-old girl told a staff writer for a San Francisco newspaper who picked her up on the highway from Santa Cruz to San Jose.

"Famous last words," exploded Scherer, chewing on a cigar. "That's what they all say. We see them occasionally looking face up in the morgue."

On the morning of March 1, Mullin appeared again before Judge May, this time wearing the bright orange uniform of an inmate in the San Mateo County Jail. He had been transferred to the larger prison because it afforded tighter security than the jail in Santa Cruz. Jim Jackson, the public defender, stood beside him. Mullin had just fired Richard Pease as his attorney, and it was apparent that his family would not be able to afford the cost of a long criminal trial.

After the new counts were read, Mullin sat down at the counsel table and wrote silently in a legal tablet. He ripped off the page and handed it to the court clerk, who gave it to the judge.

"The defendant pleads *nolo contendre* to the offenses charged. March 1, 1973, Thursday," May read aloud.

"Were you aware of this?" he asked Jackson.

"I'm afraid Mr. Mullin insists he wants to represent himself," the attorney said. "I don't agree with the plea."

"I'm sorry, Mr. Mullin, but I can't accept this," the judge said.

His lips pursed, Mullin scribbled again. He passed a second piece of paper up the bench. "The defendant pleads that he is guilty to the offenses charged. March 1, 1973, Thursday," it said.

"I can't take that either," the judge said. He turned to Jackson and prosecutor Chang. "We have no proof that Mr. Mullin is capable mentally of representing himself, nor that he is acting on advice of counsel," he said. "Shall we set a new date for a preliminary hearing, gentlemen?"

"Your honor, we plan to submit this matter to the grand jury for an indictment," Chang said. "That would move the case directly to superior court, and no further proceedings in municipal court would be required."

"I appreciate that," the judge said, "but we have to follow normal procedure until that happens. I'll schedule a preliminary hearing for March 13. If you can get an indictment before then, we can always cancel it."

Mullin was led from the crowded courtroom. He had not said a word.

18
Our Client

THE AFTERNOON following Mullin's second arraignment, Jackson called me at my office at Stanford. He did not sound pleased.

"You're not gonna believe this," Jackson said, "but we've got another one. Only this time I don't think he was trying to protect the environment. How does that grab you?"

"You must mean Mullin."

"Give the man a cigar."

"How many people has he allegedly . . ."

"Eleven and counting. They think he may have murdered at least a few others, but he's only charged with ten so far. What I'm afraid of is that the cops will try to use him to clean up the books."

"The papers are treating him like Jack the Ripper," I remarked.

"That's fair. He supposedly killed more people."

"I imagine he's showing some signs of irrational behavior?"

Jackson laughed harshly. "I've only talked to him a little, or tried to talk to him. He's very uncommunicative. Most of the preliminaries were handled by a family attorney. They just called us in.

"To answer your question, using purely clinical terms, you understand, I'd say he's as nutty as a tree full of fish."

"The media's been acting as if he were already convicted," I said, trying to avoid the direction I knew the conversation was taking. "What do you think?"

"Wait'll you see the news tonight," Jackson said. "The bastard tried to plead guilty on me today. Fortunately, the judge wasn't having any."

"Any chance he's innocent?"

Jackson's voice became more serious. "I'm pretty sure he killed some of them. As I said, he won't talk to me yet. That's why I'm calling you."

Here it comes, I thought.

"We want to hire you as a defense psychiatrist."

I stifled a groan. I was incredibly busy. In addition to my classes in both the medical and law schools at the university, I was writing an extensive revision of a book, and I had been trying to avoid court appointments. Unlike many forensic psychiatrists, I feel strongly that valid diagnoses cannot be made without hours of analysis and exhaustive investigation of a defendant's past life. For me, a case such as this would probably turn into a temporary career, as had happened with Frazier. I also was keenly aware that only about 2 percent of murderers were ever found insane in American courts.

Sensing my reluctance, Jackson marshaled his argument. "It looks like this guy may have been bounced in and out of at least a couple of state hospitals," he said, aware, from several barroom conversations, of my concern about the state of public mental health treatment. "This may turn out to be another case of society screwing itself by failing to take care of its crazies."

"Well, I won't promise anything, but I'll take a look at him. Where is he?"

"They moved him to the San Mateo County Jail over on your side of the hills." Jackson chuckled. "They say it's for his own protection, which is bullshit, naturally. I'll send you a letter assigning you to the defense."

On Friday, March 9, Harold Cartwright picked me up at the university in Palo Alto and drove me to the jail in Redwood City. Armed with my credentials from the public defender, I had attempted to visit Mullin five days earlier, but the deputies told me that he refused to see anyone. A guard took Jackson's letter to Mullin, but returned and said he wouldn't talk to any psychiatrist without his attorney present. The jailer declined to let me go to Mullin's cell to try to convince him he should be interviewed.

As he drove north on the Bayshore Freeway, Cartwright brought me up to date on the case. The investigator had a lot of friends in the police department, sheriff's office, and district attorney's office and knew about most of the evidence they had gathered.

Cartwright was a former marine who had enlisted in the corps out of high school. He joined the Ventura Police Department after his discharge and worked up to the rank of lieutenant before deciding to resign and move his family to the less hectic milieu of the central coast. Now, in his early thirties, he was working seven days a week as a private detective and taking a full load of courses in law school at night in San Jose.

"When do you find time to study?" I asked.

"Oh, between about five and nine in the morning."

"You ought to see an analyst," I said. "That kind of schedule is bound to drive you nuts."

Mullin had agreed to talk with me as long as Cartwright was there representing the defense team. I studied him closely as he was brought into the interview room. His dark hair was plastered down, and his thin mustache had been shaved, giving him a somewhat less sinister appearance than the booking photographs I had seen. Mullin did not shake hands when Cartwright introduced us. He was guarded and suspicious.

"How are things going, Herb?" Cartwright asked.

"The conditions here are terrible," Mullin complained. "They have the television set on twenty hours a day for the other inmates. It interferes with my ability to meditate.

"Radio and television are psychological warfare," he added.

"We need to take your medical and personal history," I informed him. "Would you mind if we used this tape recorder?"

"I refuse to speak to you if you turn that on," Mullin said.

"Fine," I replied, putting the machine back in my briefcase. "Is it all right if I take notes?"

"Go ahead."

"All right, then, perhaps you could tell me about yourself."

"You know I was a conscientious objector," Mullin said. "I was taken in by the peace advocates. I wanted to join the military and go to Vietnam, but I was brainwashed into becoming a conscientious objector. I was tricked by the peace advocates who played with my mind."

"Did you do any alternative service?"

"I went down to San Luis Obispo and worked for Goodwill Industries," Mullin said.

"How long were you there?"

"I had a mental breakdown in San Luis Obispo."

"What happened?" I asked.

Mullin didn't answer. He was staring into space. I was almost certain he was hallucinating. After a few minutes of silence, I changed the subject.

"What did you do after you left San Luis Obispo?"

"I moved around a lot. I lived in a lot of different places and had a lot of different jobs. In San Francisco I was a boxer. I worked out every day for seven months in a gym. The whole thing was crazy. I must have been insane."

"Were you successful as a boxer?"

"I always had trouble getting along financially. I donated money to UNICEF and Save the Children and CARE. I'm not sure why, because I wasn't earning a salary. I was also a regular donor at the blood and plasma bank."

"Did you live anywhere else?"

"I went to Hawaii with Pat, and I spent a couple of weeks at the Krishna Temple on Maui. I ended up in a mental hospital and came home two weeks later."

"Why were you hospitalized?" I inquired.

"That's none of your business."

I made a note to check state hospital records in California and Hawaii. "Why did you buy the gun?" I asked.

"I bought a pistol in December," Mullin said. "That was after I realized I could hear people's thoughts."

Cartwright and I looked at each other. "Do you mean you can read people's minds?" I asked.

Mullin had the hint of a smile. "If you and Mr. Cartwright stopped talking, I could probably hear your thoughts, yes."

"You never said why you bought the gun."

"It's important that everyone be armed. In Switzerland all men belong to the militia. They're issued a gun which they keep in their homes."

"What happened in January?"

"By January I realized that the peace advocates and flower children had played tricks on my mind, and I had to reap vengence. By January 23 or 24, I guess, I reached my breaking point."

"Did you kill the Gianeras and the Francises?" I asked.

"You see, you can deduce what happened from the evidence, so there is no need for me to tell you."

Harold and I were silent as we walked back to the car. We had spent nearly two hours with Mullin but had been unable to obtain any information about the murders. His answers to questions had been unresponsive and hostile. I leaned back against the seat as Cartwright backed out of the visitors' parking area and turned toward Palo Alto.

"What do you think, Don?"

I gazed through the windshield. At this point I was reacting mostly to intuition. "It's possible he may be the craziest sonofabitch I've ever met."

Cartwright grinned. "Legally insane?"

"As far as I'm concerned he probably is. I'll have to spend a lot more time with him, though, before I can form a solid opinion. I'll have to get him to trust me."

"Do you think we could convince a jury?"

"It's hard to say. He shows symptoms of paranoid schizophrenia, the same illness Frazier had. You remember how that came out. Juries are reluctant to send murderers to state hospitals no matter how crazy they are because they're afraid they'll get out."

"Sometimes they're right," Cartwright observed.

I was, frankly, woolgathering. "We might be able to make a case for legal insanity under the M'Naghten Rule," I mused. "If he's guilty, that is."

Cartwright stared at me. Then his eyes snapped back to the road as he wrenched the steering wheel and the car swerved off the shoulder where it had drifted.

"Aw, come *on,* Don," he said. "You've got to be joking. They have enough on him to send him up until the twenty-fifth century. He tried to plead guilty, for chrissake."

"That's one of the things that bothers me," I said. "One of the symptoms of paranoid schizophrenia is grandiosity, the delusion that he's more important than he really is. Right now, Mullin is the most important man in Santa Cruz. When you were a cop, did you ever have some crank come in and confess to a highly publicized crime that he didn't commit?"

"Sure, but you can't compare that to a case like this. Ten people were killed by the two guns found in his car, nine of them with his pistol and Perez with the rifle he stole from those kids he blasted in the woods."

"Persuasive, but circumstantial. Besides, you told me yourself the sheriff isn't sure that was the same rifle those boys had. Look, I'm not saying he didn't kill anybody, it's just that there aren't any real witnesses."

"Bullshit. That woman saw him kill Perez."

"She saw someone sitting in a car similar to his. She couldn't pick him out of a lineup. And the other two, Clarke and Houts, couldn't identify him either."

"How about the fact he knew Gianera?"

"Several hundred people went to high school with Gianera, I imagine. That doesn't mean any of them murdered him."

"They found his fingerprint on the confessional in Los Gatos."

"He's not charged with killing the priest yet," I said. "Let's not borrow trouble. But, for the sake of argument, he was raised as a Catholic. That church isn't far from his home. There could have been any number of reasons why he might have gone there for confession sometime before the murder."

Cartwright shook his head. "Doc, you're the one who needs a shrink."

"Listen, Harold, I repeat I'm not saying he didn't kill anybody. All I'm trying to point out is that we have to know who he may have murdered, and why. We can't even begin to explore an insanity defense until we have the answers to those questions.

"You and I both know the authorities are likely to try and use Mullin to wrap up as many unsolved murders as they can, but even so, nobody has suggested seriously that he's responsible for all the ones you've had down there lately. That means there's at least one other killer loose in Santa Cruz, and I'm just afraid that Mullin, in his present mental condition, might cop out to things he didn't commit."

Cartwright thought for a minute. "This is all highly unlikely," he said finally. "But, what the hell. Where do you want to start?"

"We'll have to re-create his life in minute detail from the day he was born until he was arrested, and I'll have to figure out a way to get him to talk to me." I was anxious to get back to the office. I have a quirk about not smoking in cars, including those that belong to other people, and I suddenly wanted a cigarette.

"I'm afraid the detective work is just starting for both of us," I said.

19
An Ordinary Childhood

BEFORE MY first visit with Mullin in jail, Jackson and Cartwright had given me all the information they had about him from all sources, including his parents. Externally, at least, Herb's early life had been archetypically normal.

After Harold dropped me off at Stanford, I drove home with the material in my briefcase. Marilynn made me a gin and tonic and then went into the kitchen to do something about the staggering nutritional requirements of the five boys. I sat down and read a transcript of Harold's conversation with Mr. and Mrs. Mullin.

Herb was born April 18, 1947, in Salinas, a farming community in Monterey County south of Santa Cruz. His father, Martin William Mullin, worked in a furniture store there following his discharge from the army after World War II. Herb's older sister, now married and living with her husband on their Christmas tree farm near Sebastopol north of San Francisco, was born just before her father enlisted.

According to Cartwright, the parents seemed ordinary and uncomplicated. Herb's father had grown up in Oregon and had graduated from college there. His mother, a Californian a few years younger than her husband, had gone to college for a year.

Before Herb was a year old, the family moved to Walnut Creek, one of the postwar suburbs that mushroomed east of Oakland, where Bill Mullin got a job with a larger furniture store. Not long before the boy's fifth birthday they moved again, this time to San Francisco, where they lived until Herb finished his second year in high school.

The parents told Cartwright their son had been well adjusted and an able student. His record of deportment and grades was good during his eight years at Saint Stephen's Grammar School and during his freshman and sophomore years at a parochial high school.

Herb's aunt and uncle owned a summer house at Boulder Creek, and the family used it often for vacations. During the summer of 1963, the Mullins moved to the Santa Cruz area permanently and lived in the cabin until finding their present home in Felton. Herb enrolled in the public San Lorenzo Valley High School. His sister, Patricia, had stayed in San Francisco to finish college. Their father, who had been employed as a traveling salesman for a furniture company since 1952, eventually went to work for the post office in Santa Cruz.

The parents recalled that Herb had made friends easily after winning a place on the football varsity. He had occasional dates and in the fall of his senior year began to go steady with one girl, Loretta Ricketts. In June of 1965, he graduated forty-third in a class of 134.

That August, while Herb held a summer job in a service station in Santa Cruz, his best friend was killed in an automobile accident. The parents said the tragedy affected their son deeply, and that he cried for weeks. He appeared to recover from his grief, however, by the time he enrolled that fall at Cabrillo College as an engineering student in the school's highway technology department.

He graduated from the junior college in the summer of 1967 with a two-year degree in road engineering. For the second summer in a row, he worked full-time for the county public works department, waiting for the fall term to begin at San Jose State College. Earlier that year he and Loretta patched up a six-month-long separation and became engaged.

Bill and Jean Mullin had been proud of both their children, proud of Herb's scholastic achievements and confident in his stability.

But by the fall of 1967, their son began to change. The parents suspected he had been experimenting with marijuana and perhaps LSD, although they had no tangible evidence. Now he showed a growing interest in eastern religions, questioning the faith in which he had been raised. A year earlier, he had told his father he wanted to join the Army Corps of Engineers when he finished college. In September of 1967 he instead became active in demonstrations against the war in Vietnam, and vowed to register as a conscientious objector. According to the transcript, that decision dismayed Bill Mullin, who not only had been an army captain during the war in the Pacific but had also served an enlistment in the fleet marines in China in the 1930s. At San Jose Herb changed his major from engineering to philosophy, but his growing passion for the study of exotic religions led him to withdraw from classes six weeks later.

For the next several months he seemed to drift. His mother and father were concerned about the profound change in his goals but, reluctantly, Bill Mullin finally agreed to write a letter to his son's draft board supporting his appeal for conscientious-objector status.

In March of 1968, Herb and Loretta broke their engagement. The following month Herb was arrested for possession of marijuana. He was allowed to plead guilty to a lesser offense and was sentenced only to probation.

His parents were encouraged when Herb got a job at Goodwill Industries. After a brief stint as a trainee, he was assigned to manage the vocational rehabilitation organization's thrift store in San Luis Obispo, about 100 miles down the coast from Santa Cruz. After he was granted his CO classification in October of 1968, the Selective Service board credited his time employed by Goodwill toward his required alternative service.

But Bill and Jean Mullin became apprehensive again in February of 1969 when their by now unpredictable son abruptly quit his job and announced he was going to India to study yoga. Instead, he moved to Sebastopol and lived in a trailer on the ranch owned by his sister and her husband, Albert Bocca. There, during a family dinner at his sister's house on March 28, he manifested his first clearly defined symptoms of psychosis. As his family watched with confusion and then alarm, he began imitating every move his brother-in-law made. When Al Bocca picked up a fork, so did Herb. When Al ate a mouthful of food, Herb aped him. He seemed to be in a trance, unable to communicate. This behavior, the parroting of the actions of another person, is known as *echopraxia,* and it is one indication of schizophrenia. The following day, after his father drove to San Rafael and consulted a priest who was a family friend, Herb agreed to a voluntary commitment at Mendocino State Hospital near Ukiah not far north of Sebastopol. There he was diagnosed as schizophrenic, his condition apparently aggravated by drug abuse.

Herb had stayed in the hospital about six weeks, visiting his sister on weekend furloughs. Released in May at his own request, he went to Lake Tahoe with another former patient and worked for several months as a dishwasher for a hotel-casino. In September he returned to Santa Cruz and, to the relief of his parents, moved into the community's drug rehabilitation center. They both believed that drug use was the sole cause of Herb's mental condition. Here at last, they thought, he would receive meaningful treatment.

But Herb soon drifted away from the center. He moved into a house with friends from Cabrillo College, supporting himself by working in a service station. His mother and father saw little of him, and they were shocked in early November to get a letter from him saying he had been forcibly committed to the psychiatric ward at San Luis Obispo General Hospital. When they drove down to visit him, he told them he was a homosexual. He had been admitted to the hospital by a local physician after he had made advances to the doctor's nephew. He also had shaved his head and had burned his penis with a cigarette.

Herb's confession appeared to be particularly galling to his father, whose views on sexual morality were as straightforward as his opinions about the antiwar movement. Nonetheless, Bill Mullin agreed a month later to bring him home after he was released contingent upon his becoming an outpatient at the Santa Cruz Mental Health Clinic. Again, Herb's condition had been diagnosed as paranoid schizophrenia. His parents still believed his problem was drug abuse.

For the next six months his behavior was erratic. He moved out of the house, having qualified for welfare payments because of mental disability. He got a job as a dishwasher and lived in a cheap hotel near the beach. By now prepared for disappointment where Herb was concerned, the parents were nevertheless appalled when he suddenly quit his job, dropped out of group therapy at the clinic, and said he was going to Hawaii with a woman in her forties, an addict he apparently had met in a commune. A short time after his hasty departure, they received a letter from him saying he was in another mental hospital, on the island of Maui. A month later he wrote for money to fly home. His mother and father drove to San Francisco to pick him up, but on the way home he began ranting angrily, reciting gibberish, to the point that they became frightened. Bill Mullin stopped at a telephone booth along the way and called the local police. He tried to convince two patrolmen that his son should be hospitalized, but they told him they were powerless to force Herb to do anything if he had not committed a crime. The three returned to Felton, and the parents were heartened a little when Herb reentered the outpatient program at the clinic. He also reapplied for welfare.

On July 30, 1970, Herb was arrested for being under the influence of drugs. When he appeared in court, his shouted demands for the legalization of marijuana and LSD caused the judge to order him into the psychiatric ward at the county hospital. The charges were dropped a few days later when it was learned the drugs Herb had been carrying were antipsychotic medication prescribed at the clinic. He was released shortly after and returned to group therapy.

By now Herb was twenty-three. Gradually his parents had become acclimated to his weird behavior. They faced each day with resignation. He moved in and out of the house and held desultory jobs. His father was in a hospital recovering from surgery when Herb was arrested again on March 28, 1971, for being drunk in public and resisting an officer. The drunk charge was dismissed, but he spent ten days in jail for the latter offense. In April his case was closed at the mental health clinic because of his failure to keep group therapy appointments, and in May he left Santa Cruz and moved to San Francisco.

For the next year and a half Herb's life was more or less a mystery to Mr. and Mrs. Mullin. His letters, sometimes rational, sometimes not, came from a succession of seedy hotels in the city's Tenderloin. Once he told his parents he had been training at a boxing gymnasium. But for the most part they didn't know where he was or what he was doing.

Then, in mid-September 1972 Herb moved back home. By now he had replaced the aging Volkswagen he had driven for a number of years with an equally decrepit Chevrolet station wagon. He told his parents he had decided it was time for him to make something of his life. He would join the Coast Guard, he said.

In October he went to the recruiting station in San Jose and filled out an application. Later that month he got a job as a busboy in a restaurant. In November, after driving to the Armed Forces Induction Center in Oakland for preenlistment tests, he was rejected by the Coast Guard for failing the psychological examination. He began visiting the marine recruiter in Santa Cruz. At first the sergeant discouraged him, but he persisted. Eventually, the recruiter approved his enlistment papers. He was elated, and for the first time in years, Bill and Jean Mullin dared to be optimistic. Although a little strained, Christmas dinner that year at the Boccas was not unpleasant.

On January 15 he passed the physical and, oddly enough, mental examinations for the Marine Corps. The only step that remained was for him to sign a copy of his criminal record, which the corps had agreed to waive. But he insisted it was incorrect, that it should have reflected the fact that the officer who had arrested him on drug charges in July of 1970 had been reprimanded for making a mistake. When he refused to sign, his application was turned down.

In the months since he had returned to Felton, Herb had argued periodically with his parents, implying that his troubles had been caused by the way he had been reared. Now upset by his latest failure, his criticism became more strident. His father finally told him he would have to get a place of his own, and on January 19, 1973, he moved into the Pacific View Apartments on Front Street. He visited his parents home often, and told them he would try to enlist in the army. At the same time he applied for a variety of jobs.

On February 13 his mother expected him to deliver a load of firewood he had promised.

Instead, she was visited by the police, who told her that her son had been arrested for mass murder.

It was obvious from the account Mr. and Mrs. Mullin gave Cartwright that Herb had suffered from pronounced symptoms of mental illness. I asked Harold to try to get all of his medical records from the hospitals and clinics that had treated him since 1969, knowing that it would probably be a long and difficult task because of the chaotic state of the files in California's crumbling mental health system. I also asked him to arrange a meeting for me with Mr. and

Mrs. Mullin, to allow me to get their firsthand impressions of their son's symptoms.

In the meantime, I said, we still had the problem of finding out who Herb might have killed, and why.

"If I recall correctly," Harold observed, "the purpose of this little exercise is to prove he did it because he's bananas."

"No matter how insane a person is, he doesn't go around killing people without a reason," I said. "It may be a crazy reason, but it's still a reason." Then I asked if he could finagle an early look at the autopsy reports for me.

"We'll get them on discovery eventually anyway," he said. "You think one of those people isn't dead or something?"

"Try to get them sooner," I said. "Sometimes they tell a lot more about a victim than just cause of death, like what he ate and drank before he died, his lifetime habits, health, that sort of thing. I want to know everything I possibly can about the victims as well as Mullin."

We knew the police had been busy in the days since Herb's arrest, and that the district attorney probably was aware of everything the parents had told Cartwright. We also knew they were trying hard to find evidence that would tie him to other murders, and they were way ahead of us.

Although the investigators had been unable to connect the rifle found in Herb's car with the one missing from the tent where the four boys had been shot, they did manage to retrace its whereabouts up to a few months before his arrest.

After poring over their sales records, U.S. Treasury agents finally reported that the rifle had been sold December 4, 1970, to a woman in Ukiah. The store there was unable to locate a copy of the sales slip, but the Mendocino County Sheriff's Office agreed to try to find the buyer. It took the detectives a few days to learn that she had married and, under her new name, moved to Santa Cruz County. When the police located her, she told them she had sold the gun to the owner of a furniture store in Felton.

Lieutenant Scherer called Medina at the sheriff's office. "Check and see if you've got a report of a burglary at Trusty's Furniture in Felton," he suggested. "I think we got a line on Herbie's rifle."

"Yeah, he reported it," Medina said, after finding the record. "It seems that three young men came in to the store just before it closed last November 15 and tried to sell Tom Trusty a banjo. They saw he had the rifle for sale and asked how much it was. When he told them fifty-five bucks they said they didn't have that much and left. By an amazing coincidence, a window was jimmied and the gun was missing when he opened the next morning."

"That's the rifle we took out of Mullin's car," Scherer said, "the one that killed Perez. We found the original owner, and she said she sold it to Trusty some time in October to buy shoes for her kids."

"So you think the Card brothers and the Dreibelbis kid lifted it to use around camp, and Herb relieved them of it after killing them with his own gun. That would nail it all down perfectly."

"Where is Jeff Card?" Scherer asked.

"Last we knew he was staying with some people in Boulder Creek. Maybe we ought to pay him a visit."

20
The Main Victim

BEFORE HE WITHDREW as Herb's attorney, Dick Pease went to see Lieutenant Scherer at his office. At the detective's request, he had prepared a list of the names of about two dozen of Herb's relatives and acquaintances. Scherer wanted to compare it with a roster of potential witnesses already questioned by his investigators and the sheriff's office.

"Is his ex-girlfriend on here?" Scherer asked, tapping the paper.

"I'm afraid I don't know her name," Pease said noncommittally. "She got married sometime after they broke up and has a different one now anyway."

Scherer knew he would be on shaky ground if he pressed a defense attorney for information about his client. He tried to think of a diplomatic way of framing the obvious question, of pointing out that the parents surely knew the woman's name, but Pease spoke first.

"I don't think it makes much difference in any case," he said. "Mullin apparently is bisexual. At different times he's lived in a homosexual relationship with fellows."

"Oh?"

"This one particular fellow, whose name I don't know, was made the beneficiary in Herb's will."

This time Scherer did ask the obvious question. "Didn't you draw it up?"

"Oh, no. I guess it was just something he wrote himself. I do know who his life insurance agent is over in San Jose. He probably changed the beneficiary on his policy, too."

"I guess the family is taking all this pretty hard," Scherer observed.

"Yeah." Before he left, Pease wrote down the name of the insurance agent.

The same day Pease went to see Scherer, another police officer, Don Larson, found Loretta Ricketts purely by accident. Her married name was Falkner, and she worked as a waitress in a restaurant on the Municipal Wharf.

Larson had gone to the restaurant in search of another employee who, it turned out, wasn't working that day. He had been tipped that the other woman might have some information about Mullin, a lead that later turned out to be false. After Loretta Falkner gave the officer the absent waitress's address and telephone number, he routinely showed her a photograph of Mullin and asked if she had ever seen him in the restaurant. She seemed hesitant.

"Yeah, I knew him," she said finally.

"Very well?"

"I went with him about four years ago."

"No kidding? Hey, would you mind if I asked you a few questions?"

"No, but I'd like to have my lawyer present."

"No problem. What's his name? I'll try to set it up for this afternoon."

Robert Darrow, an attorney who represented Loretta Falkner, shook hands with Larson as he ushered him into his office. The young woman was seated near his desk.

"The reason my client wanted me to sit in is because of her concern about adverse publicity," he explained. "A number of recent newspaper articles have indicated that Mullin had an unidentified girl friend who possibly may have jilted him, and they speculated that it might have driven him crazy and caused him to commit the murders.

"She's perfectly willing to answer any questions, and I certainly have no objections."

"Don't worry," Larson said. "I understand there's going to be a gag order preventing us from making any statements to the press anyway." He turned to Loretta. "When did you first meet Mullin?" he inquired.

"When I was in high school. I went to Holy Cross and he went to San Lorenzo Valley. He was a year ahead of me. He was popular and a good athlete. We went steady for about two and a half years while I was in high school."

"Were you ever engaged?"

"Later we were. At that time we talked sometimes about getting married someday, but after he graduated we broke up and didn't see each other for awhile."

"Did he know Jim Gianera?" Larson asked.

"They were fairly good friends," she said. "He was one of the first guys at San Lorenzo Valley High to go the hip drug route. Herb stayed friends with him when they went to Cabrillo, and it seemed to change him. That's why we broke up."

"How did he change?"

"Well, for one thing, he went through a real bad mental strain when his best friend, Dean Richardson, was killed in a crash during the summer of 1965. It really freaked him out."

"You said that you later got engaged?"

"Yeah. Sometime after I got out of high school we began dating again. Then Herb bought me a ring, and we were planning to get married. We never set a date, though."

"Why was that?"

"Our relationship wasn't very good the second time we went together. For one thing, Herb told me he was using drugs, and I didn't like that at all. Sometimes I was afraid he was potentially violent. Sometimes my mother and I were scared of him."

"Did he ever hit you?"

"Yeah. He never really hurt me. He'd just slap me with his open hand on the legs. He didn't like me to make decisions, and if I ever tried he'd get mad."

"Did you ever talk about raising a family or what to name your first baby?"

She laughed scornfully. "No, and I don't know where the papers got that story."

"Did Herb have any special places in the mountains where he'd like to go, or where he took you?" Larson was thinking of the possibility of undiscovered bodies.

"Yes," she said. "He had one very special place. As far as I know I was the only one he ever took there. I think I could find it, but I doubt if I could find it on a map. It's above the university on Empire Grade. There's a little road off to the right just before you get to Ice Cream Grade."

"Anyplace else?"

"Somewhere called Frog Rock in Boulder Creek. He used to talk about it, but he never took me there."

"Was Mullin in the habit of picking up hitchhikers?"

"He most definitely did pick them up, and it scared me to death. He'd pick up men or women, it didn't matter, while I was in the car. When I complained, he'd get mad."

"What kind of car did he drive in those days?"

"It was a black Volkswagen, license number HNB 413."

Larson's face registered surprise. "It's funny you'd remember that after all these years."

"My mother and I both memorized the number in March of 1968, while we were finally breaking up for good. He was doing weird things by then, and we were afraid of him. We wanted to be able to give it to the police if he tried anything."

"Did anything ever happen regarding his picking up hitchhikers?"

"Once, in late '67 I think, Herb disappeared for three days. His folks and mine got worried, and we filed a missing person's report with the sheriff. But he showed up, and we canceled the report." She looked down. "He told me he'd picked up some blond girl hitchhiking around Santa Cruz, and when she said she was on her way to Los Angeles, he drove her there."

"Did he tell you what she looked like, or what he did during those three days?"

"No." Larson made a mental note to check with the authorities along the coast route to Los Angeles for any five- or six-year-old unsolved murders of blond females.

"What finally caused you to break up?" he asked. He thought Loretta looked uncomfortable.

"It was a mutual thing," she said. "I . . . I became very disinterested in him when he told me he was queer, that he had a homosexual thing with a guy."

"Do you know who it was?"

"Not his name. I think I met him once before Herb told me about it. He was real hip.

"It was a combination of things, though," she added. "Herb's homosexual tendencies, his downward slide because of drugs, his fits and violent temper. In the end I was really scared of him, so I gave him back the ring."

"We understand he was an antiwar activist."

"I guess in a minor way. He went to San Jose State for a little while and got interested in Indian religions and applied for conscientious objector. I never did know how all that came out."

"When was the last time you saw him?"

"Summer of '72. I was in a laundromat in Santa Cruz with my three-year-old daughter, and Herb came in. He walked up to me and I introduced my daughter, but he didn't say anything. He just stared at me in an eerie way. I got really scared and took the baby and left right away."

Larson stood. "OK, I guess that's all for now. Would you be willing to help us locate Herb's secret spot on Empire Grade?"

"More than willing."

On the morning of March 12, Detective Medina kept an appointment with Mr. and Mrs. Mullin at their home. When he arrived, the father asked him to follow him to a small plot of freshly turned ground about two by five feet at the extreme rear of the back yard. He carried a spade.

"I've been thinking about something," Bill Mullin said. "Not long ago Herb said he was going to plant some carrots back here. I felt sure that's what he did, but in view of what's happened, I think it should be dug up."

"Let me help you with that," Medina offered.

"No," the father said grimly. "I'll do it."

Medina watched as he hefted shovels full of heavy, rich soil out of the bed. He felt sorry for Mullin, but he couldn't think of anything to say. They found the dirt had been cultivated to a depth of only six inches. Nothing was buried there.

Medina accompanied Mullin back to the house. He had some questions for both parents that had been given to him by the Santa

Clara County district attorney's office, which was still wrapping up its investigation of the slaying of Father Tomei.

"Did Herb have any friends or relatives in Los Gatos?" he began.

Jean Mullin glanced at her husband. "No, not that we know of," she said.

"Did he ever go to a seminary or anything like that?"

"No, the father answered. "He was in the Newman Club for a while about three years ago. He got interested in it because there was a young priest in Capitola working with the club who seemed to help young people that were going astray."

Medina asked whether Herb owned a black leather jacket, which was what Mrs. Reed recalled that Father Tomei's assailant was wearing. They said that if he did, they never saw it.

"Did either of you, or Herb, know Father Henri Tomei, the pastor of the Catholic church in Los Gatos?"

They both shook their heads. "Do you know where Herb was last November 2?" He paused. "I guess you know that's the day the priest was murdered."

"Yes," Mullin replied. "We know." He walked to a wall calendar and flipped back through the pages to the previous year. "That was All Souls Day," he said. "It's a day when the dearly departed are remembered in prayer."

"Was it an important religious day for your family?"

"Not particularly," the father said. "Every Sunday was a church day for us."

He sat down again. "I remember Herb came down from San Francisco early in September for three Sundays in a row, and he went to mass with me. I generally take communion every Sunday, and one time Herb asked me if he should too. I told him I didn't know if he could make that kind of act of contrition."

"Did he say anything?"

"No. He just looked sort of embarrassed, and blushed," Mullin said. "Another time I remember, when I took communion, I was walking back from the rail, and Herb just kind of looked at me, shaking his head."

On March 14, I went by myself to the San Mateo County Jail for my second session with Herb. By now, I knew a lot more about him than when we first met. I was hopeful I could get him to tell me about his past psychiatric treatment, but it became obvious a few minutes after he was brought to the interview room that he was still hostile and suspicious.

"How are you doing?" I asked.

"They still won't turn off the television set in the cell block," he seethed. "It's driving me crazy. Last Sunday I went into a rage and demanded they turn it off so I could meditate. They put me on two weeks restriction, which means I don't get commissary privileges. I can't buy paper to write."

"Have you seen your parents lately?"

"They visited me last Sunday. I told them I didn't think they should come anymore."

"I should probably remind you that the visitors' telephones are bugged," I remarked. He suddenly looked alarmed.

"Do you think this room is bugged?" he asked.

"Not as far as I know."

I attempted to continue my history taking and had a little success, although it was extremely difficult. At times he simply was uncooperative. He was especially sensitive about answering a question twice. Several times, after I had asked him about a date or medical detail, he screamed, "You asked me that when you were here before! I won't answer it again!" I decided to leave his history alone for a time.

"Is there anything you want to tell me about the murders?"

"There's nothing I can tell you that you don't already know."

"We don't know why any of these people were killed," I said.

"I imagine the main victim was James Ralph Gianera," he replied after a short silence. I restrained myself from asking him why. This was the first time he had indicated any knowledge of the murders.

"When did you meet Gianera?"

"In September of 1963, when I went to San Lorenzo Valley High School. He was someone I looked up to."

"In what way?"

"When we went to Cabrillo College in 1965, I fell under the influence of James Ralph Gianera," he said. "He converted me into a conscientious objector by playing tricks and playing games with my mind."

"Did Gianera get you involved in drugs?" I asked.

"That's none of your business."

"What makes you think he was the primary victim?"

"I began to think a lot about it after the turn of the year," he said. "I was very bitter about being refused induction into the Marine Corps. I rented an apartment, but I didn't plan to stay there very long because I was hoping to get a job and move back to San Francisco."

"Had you tried for anything?"

"Everywhere. I applied to the U.S. Civil Service Commission at the federal building in San Francisco, and at the California Department of Employment, Kaiser Engineers, the Dream Inn."

"What's that?"

"A hotel by the beach with a big restaurant. I had experience. I also tried the flower growers and nurseries around Santa Cruz, but nobody would hire me."

"Do you have any idea why?"

"Sure. It was because I had been a conscientious objector, and they all knew I was an ex-mental patient with an arrest record. And that was caused by the peace advocates who played with my mind. James Ralph Gianera was the most important peace advocate." He was becoming agitated as he described his frustrations of January. I turned to another murder.

"What about the four boys at the campsite?" I asked.

"I already told you about that."

"I'm sorry," I said, "but if you did, I've forgotten."

"Well, when you see the evidence you will be able to figure out what happened."

"Can you tell me how you got the rifle they found in your car?"

"They shouldn't have had it in the park," he said. "They were flower children. I was able to relate to flower children because there's a connection between conscientious objectors and flower children."

"Do you have any idea why Mr. Perez was killed?"

"I have no explanation for why he died," he said.

"Do you feel that at that point, at least subconsciously, you might have wanted to get caught, and that's why you might have committed that crime without any particular effort at concealment?"

He reflected for a moment. "That could be a possibility," he said finally. Then he asked me a question.

"Do you know what the penalty is for what I'm charged with?"

"Well, the penalty for first-degree murder is a life sentence. If you were convicted of ten or eleven murders . . ."

"Eleven?" he interrupted. "What was the eleventh murder?" He seemed sincerely distressed.

"There is the possibility of your being charged with the murder of a priest in Los Gatos," I told him.

"I don't remember having anything to do with that," he said. "I remember vaguely hearing about it on the news when it happened, but I don't even know when it was."

I looked at my watch. I had been there for about an hour and a half. Herb was showing signs of irritation again, so I decided to postpone further questions. I told him I would be back in a week.

"Could you bring me some paper when you come next time?" he asked while we waited for the guard to come and open the door. "I want to continue with my notes."

"I'd be happy to," I said. "Perhaps you might share some of them with me."

"I have another request," he said stiffly.

"Oh? What's that?"

"I want both you and Mr. Jackson to get shorter haircuts before the trial."

Herb's case had moved through the legal process with the deliberate pace that led Hamlet to despair about the law's delay. On February 20, after he had learned that Mullin would be charged with the additional murders of the four youths found dead a few days earlier, Judge May had revoked his bail. On February 23, when the counts had been filed, he issued a sweeping gag order prohibiting anyone connected with the case from making public statements of any kind.

On March 14, the county grand jury indicted Herb on ten counts of murder, and the charges in municipal court were dismissed the following day. On March 16 he was arraigned before Superior Court Judge Charles S. Franich, who reissued Judge May's order of secrecy and also sealed the transcript of the grand jury hearings. Franich set March 27 to hear Mullin's plea.

21
The Parents

ON MONDAY, March 20, Mr. and Mrs. Mullin came to my office at the Stanford Medical School. After reading the transcript of Harold Cartwright's earlier conversation with them, I had decided to interview them separately. They had disagreed occasionally in their responses to questions, though not contentiously. Still, I thought they might be more open if I talked with each of them alone.

My first impression of the couple when they walked through the door was that Herb bore a stronger resemblance to his father than his mother. Bill Mullin was about the same height as his son, perhaps an inch taller, with a slightly broader face and lighter brown hair, graying and receding slightly. He was wearing glasses and was dressed casually in slacks, a sports shirt, and a brown jacket. He wore heavy-soled shoes, the kind favored by people who spend a lot of time on their feet.

His wife, though a few years younger, actually looked somewhat older than her husband. Her gray hair was pulled back and she wore a simple dress and little makeup. She was almost as tall as he. Her features seemed more mobile than his as we exchanged the awkward, routine pleasantries. His face was virtually expressionless.

I suggested that Mullin go to the hospital cafeteria nearby and get a cup of coffee, and that Mrs. Mullin could come and get him after we were finished. They both accepted the idea, and he left.

In addition to the transcripts, Harold Cartwright and Jim Jackson had provided me with copies of some of the letters and papers they had been given by the parents, either directly or through Dick Pease. I had just reviewed them again in preparation for the interviews. They formed a poignant record of a family in torment.

On the night of February 19, just after it had been disclosed that the gun registered to Herb had been used to kill the four boys, the emotionally drained mother sat down and wrote a grieving declaration on the back of a piece of stiff paper used to punch Braille characters. I had learned that she worked sometimes as a translator for the blind.

> After hearing the news this evening I think the only thing to do for our son, Herb, is to declare him guilty and ask the court for mercy.
>
> No mere man or group of men can judge these inhuman actions. Only a Creator who gave him life and hope—and then for His own divine providence let these horrible events of the last few weeks, and suffering of the last few years occur—can judge him. May the Good Lord and His Darling Mother help our son and us in our hour of need.
>
> Our son, Herb, is not competent at this time to instruct his attorney, Richard Pease, and so, as his mother, I give my consent for him to proceed as he sees fit. His father can make his own statement.

A couple of days later Mrs. Mullin gave a letter to Dick Pease and asked him to deliver it to Herb, who had refused to see her.

> Herb Darling:
> It's all over now, darling, all your suffering and agony of the past years. Now, please help us try to help you once more.
> You are safe now. No one can hurt you and you can't hurt anyone else.
> Now you must be very, very strong and try to cooperate with everyone who is trying so desperately to resolve this whole terrible tragedy.
> It's the only way. Then we will all be able to go on living each day, knowing only our Good Lord, Jesus, will know what is in our hearts and minds, and be our ultimate judge.
> We all must be very truthful in all respects so the process of a just

society can go forward.

All the men that have been associated with your case have been very kind and gentle with your Dad and I, and we have tried to cooperate with them in every way.

I pray every moment of the day for your strength to do the right thing and know the Good Lord and His Darling Blessed Mother will continue to help us all through this ordeal.

Dad and your many, many friends join me in sending our love and constant prayers. Lovingly—Mother."

On March 2, the day after he tried to plead guilty, Herb wrote a chatty letter to his parents. It showed little concern for his plight. He described his routine in jail and asked them to tell the other members of the family not to try to visit him until the proceedings were concluded.

Following his arraignment on March 16, Herb wrote to his parents again. The letter was more somber.

Dear Dad and Mom,

As you know I appeared in Santa Cruz Superior Court today. My attorney waived formal reading of the indictment. We asked for an extension until the Grand Jury's investigation is typed and we have a copy of it. My next day in court will be March 27th, 1973. I will enter a plea at that time.

I appreciate your willingness to attend the trial proceedings, but the reporters and spectators are so cruel, and I wouldn't get to visit you before the trial or after. I hope you agree with me that the attorneys can inform you about what's going on without having to subject you to the cameras and questions.

I hope the trial won't take too long. I don't like our name being used under such circumstances.

Thank you.

Good-bye.

Herbert William.

I began the interview by apologizing to Mrs. Mullin for making her go over the same ground again, explaining that I was interested in different facts from those the investigators wanted.

Again, I began by taking Herb's medical history. His mother told me there had been no epilepsy or insanity in the family. She had no trouble during pregnancy. The baby had to stay in the hospital in

Salinas for ten days because of a diarrhea epidemic, but as he grew up he suffered only the ordinary childhood illnesses.

"He get good grades in grade school?" I asked.

"Yes, and then he went to Riordan High School. It was a Catholic school, and he did resent the attitude of the brothers, so he was quite happy when we decided to move when he went into his junior year."

"What did he resent about the brothers?"

"Well, he'd always been brought up to respect the teachers and respect the authority, you know, and I guess some of the brothers were a little pushy about how they would get order . . . just his remarks about the way they kind of pushed some of the big guys around, and the guys would just have to stand there and not hit back."

"Was he physically punished much at home?"

"No."

"Ever?"

"Oh, yeah. His father . . . and then I would have to give him a good whack now and then, because his dad was on the road, you know."

In answer to a question as to how Herb got along with girls, Mrs. Mullin launched into a long, rambling account of her son's life. It was obvious that she had been looking back a lot lately, and I didn't interrupt her, even though I already knew most of what she was telling me. Toward the end, she talked about his brief enrollment as a junior at San Jose State College.

"He came back and said that he had taken a leave of absence," she recalled, "and that he wanted to give up his student deferment and apply for conscientious objector. Well, that was the first time we'd really had strong words in our house. We were trying to convince him that the best way would be through the medical corps but, no, he'd definitely made up his mind that he was against the system, he was against the army, he was against the war on religious grounds. And he'd been a deeply religious child, you know, altar boy in the Catholic religion."

She went on to describe his difficulties with the draft board and concluded that the burden of his responsibilities, along with the prospect of marriage, was too much for him. I used the reference to his former fiancée to get back to where we had started.

"What do you think were the reasons they broke up? Did she

break it up, or did he?"

"No, I think it was a combination of the two . . . she was a very sweet girl, and she stuck by him, too, for quite a while, when the drugs came into the picture. She could see the change in him, but I think she was having pressure at home. In fact, I know her father called Herb a coward regarding the draft, because he's an ex-service-man like Herb's father."

We went back over the episode that led up to Herb's first hospitalization. I was particularly interested in learning whether, in addition to echophraxia, mimicking the movements of his brother-in-law, he had shown any signs of echolalia, the parroting of what others say, another classic symptom of schizophrenia. She couldn't recall him speaking: "He was just sitting there with a blank stare on his face and almost baring his teeth, you know, like an animal does when an animal is vicious."

She told me that Herb was put to bed, and then in the morning his father drove to San Rafael to seek advice from John O'Connor, a priest they had known in San Francisco. He suggested self-commitment to a hospital.

"I was out walking with the kids in the morning and Herb was perfectly all right. He went in and showered and everything else. I guess Al had talked to him, and he was willing to go to Mendocino. He said he was scared to death of brain damage because of the marijuana. Whether it was more than marijuana or not, we didn't know at that stage . . ."

"Herb said that?" I asked, surprised.

"Afraid of brain damage? Yes. That was why he was willing to admit himself. But he's held it against us ever since. He keeps bringing it up the last few months, that we should never have tried to talk him into going to Mendocino."

"Later on there was an episode in San Luis Obispo. Do you recall the conversation when you took him to Morro Bay?"

She sighed. "About being a homosexual? Yes."

"What did he say?"

"Well, we were walking up and down the beach picking up some rocks, and he said, 'I want to tell you something.' So we stopped. He said 'There seems to be some homosexual tendencies that I have right now that I'm trying to control.' Of course, his father practically flipped . . . To me it's like any other abnormality that has to be tended to. To this day that bothers Bill."

"Was there ever any suspicion of that when he was younger?"

"No. And, like I said, he was never a violent person. That was why I was so completely shocked. He has more my temperament than Bill's. His sister is very much like her father in mannerisms and quickness to get mad. Herb and I both have a tendency to keep things in ourselves."

Mrs. Mullin said she was alarmed by Herb's sudden decision to drop everything and go to Hawaii. At the time he was in outpatient therapy in Santa Cruz, was taking antipsychotic medication, was working hard as a busboy at the Holiday Inn, and had saved $500.

"Well, next we heard that he was in the hospital. Then he needed money to get home."

"He was actually in a mental hospital there," I said. "I guess you know that."

"Yeah. Well, he said he'd gone to the mental hospital. Then, he always had enough sense most of the times to know when he needed this help, I guess."

She told me about her son's time as a resident of the drug abuse center, which she described as a successful community program. "But it didn't seem to work for Herb," she observed sadly.

"Wait a minute," I said. "Did it occur to you at any point that maybe Herb's problem was not so much drugs as it was mental illness?"

"No, we thought it was the drugs, whenever things got too bad for him, and the association with these people . . ."

"How about now? Can you . . ."

"Oh, definitely now, yes . . . but we thought we were doing the right thing in the different places we were going."

"I mean," I asked, "does it seem that you can accept the fact now that perhaps he was mentally ill and that drugs were maybe a sidelight?"

"Oh, definitely. I can see that now, but I always thought that he just had a nervous breakdown after trying to go through this business of the conscientious objectors. I mean, just taking so much abuse over such a long period of time. Not many human beings can take that much. But we always thought it was the drugs that were making him go off."

"It was the more obvious thing," I agreed.

"Yes."

"Actually, as near as I can tell so far, the drugs that were taken were not strong enough and weren't the sort that would account for his behavior."

"Has he told you what he'd been taking?"

"No, I'm just getting it . . ."

"We don't know the names of all of them, but I know he's experimented with a lot of them."

"I understand that," I said. "You know, having seen so many young people who have experimented with the same ones in much greater quantities, it's not enough to account for what's happened to him. On the other hand his behavior does seem to fit, well, what he'd been diagnosed as—you've been told this before—a schizophrenic. It's a mental illness which is not caused by drugs. It may be aggravated . . ."

"Well, a combination of the two is just dynamite," she interjected.

"Yeah, but I think that . . ."

She broke in again. "You see, he could fool us, with his unimpaired intelligence, I mean."

"Well, that's one of the things about schizophrenia, it's one of the hallmarks. Intellectual functions are not particularly impaired, and that's why it can be so deceptive."

She repeated that whenever Herb appeared to be "normal," they assumed it was because he was not taking drugs.

"But you really had no way of knowing that he was on or off drugs, did you?"

"No, except by his attitude."

"Yeah, but could you really tell, at least looking back on it, whether his strange attitude or behavior was caused by drugs or mental illness?"

"No."

"Would you be able to tell the difference?"

"No, I don't think so. But I'd say that we could tell when he . . . when he was ever home with us, trying to get back into the right stream of life."

Mrs. Mullin told me she didn't remember James Gianera from Herb's high school days. She said his best friend had been Dean Richardson.

"Dean was a tremendous personality," she continued, "a kind of diamond-in-the-rough type person. He'd had a heck of a lot of life he'd lived, and he was practically keeping the whole family together. So Herb took over a lot of the responsibility, for the funeral and everything else when Dean died, and he helped Dean's mother."

I wanted to learn more about his behavior and symptoms during the period of the murders, starting in November when Father Tomei died.

Although Herb was not yet charged with the priest's murder, it was more than likely that he would be eventually, and that I probably would be summoned to testify. In order for him to be found not guilty by reason of insanity, he would have had to have been insane at the time of each crime. In addition, I had been impressed with Herb's denial that he had killed Father Tomei.

"What was he like last fall?" I asked. "Was he different, or was anything unusual about his behavior?"

"He was more withdrawn and started constantly telling me we should have done this, we should have done the other thing, that we shouldn't have talked him into going into Mendocino and the medical center and drug abuse and all those different places, that those places didn't do him any good. And, that we should have started telling him about sex when he was in the sixth grade.

"Bill got on the phone and talked to the Santa Cruz mental facility and told them we had a boy that was home and was disturbed, and he'd been down there before. Bill wanted to line up an appointment, but Herb absolutely, positively refused. He would not go down. He said he'd had enough of psychiatry and all the games."

22

"God, I Loved the Kid"

I TOLD MRS. MULLIN that I thought I had put her through enough for the time being and asked her to summon her husband. I suggested she get a cup of coffee herself, promising I would try to make his interview brief.

I watched her as she left the office—a plain, strong woman whose life had not prepared her for these obscene events. Yet obviously she was learning to cope with them.

During our conversation she had mentioned the letter her husband had written to Herb's draft board supporting his petition for CO status. Clearly, it had been one of the most difficult things Bill Mullin had ever done and it had been a watershed in their family relationships. While I waited for him, I found it in the file and reread it. They had given it to Cartwright along with the other papers. A series of handwritten drafts stapled to the carbon of the finished version showed the writer had agonized over the language for a long time. It was dated February 5, 1968.

It is not an easy task for a parent with a background such as mine . . . to make a written and sworn statement for public record of the fact that his son is a sincere conscientious objector.

My son . . . very definitely is now living a mental, physical, and religious life of a conscientious objector.

Herbert has been raised in the normal manner of the average middle-class family boy. . . . The summer after Herbert's graduation from high school he lost a classmate, with whom he was very closely tied in friendship, to a tragic automobile accident. The death of this very close friend was traumatic to Herbert; his mother and I became very concerned that he could not shake the loss and the resultant change in friendship patterns for a long period of time. After the fall college term started he seemed to bear down harder than ever. . . . At the same time he was studying his Bible more than ever before. After Cabrillo he started San Jose State College but, although he was registered in engineering, he started concentrating on philosophical studies. . . . Mother and I were so upset about the trend that at those times when Herbert was visiting home, the occasion became heated sessions of parental objection and attempted direction. We have been through a long siege of biblical and philosophical quotation; we have seen this boy grow into a person whose life seems to be regulated by Christian Doctrine, whose conduct is now morally virtuous, though socially is quite companionable with all walks of social strata. Mother and I, as parents, after these long months are convinced that son Herbert is committed to God in such a manner that he feels impelled never to carry arms against any other human being, even though his own country is engaged in War. . . .

I slipped the flimsy copy into a desk drawer when Bill Mullin knocked on my office door. He was not unfriendly, nor did he appear wary when I let him in. During the preliminary conversation, however, he was not particularly outgoing. It struck me later that during the next hour the only time he showed any noticeable animation was when he talked about his varied military career.

Mullin told me he had graduated from Oregon State College in 1933 with a bachelor's degree in business and an ROTC commission in the army reserve. He had to resign from the reserve when he enlisted in the marines two years later.

He said he joined up because jobs were hard to find during the Depression and also, in part, to break away from the family home in Portland. He mentioned a stepfather with whom he didn't get along.

"What were some of the kinds of things you wouldn't see eye to eye on?" I asked. "Can you give me an example?"

"Oh, yeah. As a kid I liked to box and work out, and I remember one time he told my mother, 'That kid is learning to fight just so he can handle me.' Well, there wasn't any truth whatever in that."

"Was there any truth in terms of your fantasies, of wanting to beat up on him?"

"No." He thought for a second and repeated it. "No."

He said he had been twenty-five when he enlisted in the marines, emerging after four years as a sergeant. Following basic training in San Diego, he was shipped to Shanghai and joined the old Fourth Marines. Up to this point in our conversation his speech had been precise, almost stilted. Now he spoke with the fluency of pleasant reminiscence. He had started out in China as a company clerk.

"After a year there the flagship, Asiatic Fleet, came in. It had about a sixty-man marine guard on board, and I applied for transfer to the flagship and was turned down because of my height. They wanted six-footers. Three days later the pigiron madhouse of the Asiatic Fleet comes steaming into Whangpoo." He chuckled. "And they drop three or four marines off for the local complement, and I had no choice, having put in for sea duty . . . I spent one year in and out of every major port in China."

He recalled that after getting his sergeant's chevrons, he was shipped back to Camp Pendleton at San Diego to await discharge. While he was there he applied for a job with the Oregon state police, but ended up as an oil company warehouseman in Alameda, starting in February of 1939.

"Were you disappointed not to get a police job?"

"I don't know. Yes, I guess I was. I think I've even mentioned it a few times."

"What was the reason? Was it your height again, or do you know why you didn't get a police job?"

"Well, there wasn't an opening at the time." He added that he had asked his former coach at Oregon State for a letter of recommendation, ". . . and I'll be goddamned, excuse me, if he didn't place two of his All-Americans on that police force before I got paid off in the Marine Corps, so help me, and I put the idea in his mind, I know I did."

He said that he met his future wife in March of 1939, just before he was transferred by the oil company to Chico, a ranching town in the northern Sacramento Valley. He commuted by train and ferry to San Francisco every other weekend to see her. They were married the next year, and he was transferred as a tank truck driver to Colusa, another valley town not far from Chico. It was there that Patricia was born in 1942.

Shortly after Pearl Harbor he applied for his old reserve commission at the Presidio of San Francisco, but it was nine months before he was called to duty. He went to an antiaircraft training center, joined an automatic weapons batallion, and eventually became a company commander in the Solomon Islands campaign. In 1945 he was discharged as a captain.

Just before he left the army, he said, he wrote to Jean and told her that since they had a family started, he would try to find a job that required fewer transfers than he could expect driving a tank truck. He worked for the small furniture store in Salinas for two years, then joined Jackson's, a larger store in Oakland, and stayed until 1951, when he became a traveling salesman for a furniture distributor. It was the following year that the family, now numbering four, moved to San Francisco from Walnut Creek. From that time until he went to work in the post office in Santa Cruz, he was usually on the road from Monday through Thursday nights.

I asked him about his religious background. He said he was baptized a Lutheran and attended a Methodist Church as a child in Portland.

"Did you ever convert to the Catholic faith?"

"At Walnut Creek. I'd been a black Irish Mason down in Salinas, and I ran into an incident of dreadful prejudice one night down there on the part of a man in a pretty lofty position. He was making one joke after another, and it did not set well with me."

"Was there any reason then why you chose or didn't choose to have more children? Was that a time when it would have been your feeling that you should have a large family?"

"Well, you see Jean had lost twins in a miscarriage in Chico, prior to Patricia's birth. Whenever she was pregnant, she spent nine months vomiting." He glanced at me, then looked away. "Uh, number two, I wasn't the best provider, I wasn't making a million."

"Did you think when Herb was growing up you had any special feelings one way or another? Was he like a favorite child as far as you were concerned? Does anything stand out about him as a child in terms of your attitude toward him?"

"God, I loved the kid. I loved the kid very, very dearly." He said it with little passion in his voice.

"Was he a lovable child?" I asked.

"Yeah. I tried to . . . well, I even got mixed up with the Boy Scouts when he became a scout." I looked up from my notebook. He sounded faintly annoyed. "I became the assistant scoutmaster, and I didn't want to be the assistant scoutmaster because I traveled, I was away from home.

"When he was about eight we got the troop mixed up in the West of Twin Peaks baseball league, and I wound up as a coach in the darn thing for four years, fighting all the mothers and fathers who thought they all had All-Americans as sons."

"Eighth grade, or sometime around then, he went through puberty. Do you recall if he ever had any problems with or asked questions about sex?"

"He had a girl in the eighth grade," the father said, not answering the question directly.

"Did he have many girlfriends? In high school?"

"Well, his first two years he was in a boys' school. Then he transferred down to Felton. About the time he got out of Cabrillo College and went to San Jose State for that one miserable term he bought Loretta Ricketts a ring. It was all set and then that blew up."

"What happened?"

"Well, see, this was just about the same time that he decided that his approach to the Vietnam military program was going to be as a conscientious objector, and I think he ran into a little trouble with her father and family over this and was called a coward.

"And, I suppose he was from many different angles, now that I think about it . . ." His voice trailed off.

"You said that her family probably said that he was a coward. You said that maybe he was in some ways . . ."

"He related conversations of what Mr. Ricketts had accused him of: he was a coward, he was not going to war because he was a coward." He became brisk. "So, to what extent it went, I don't know."

"Did you ever have that feeling yourself, or express it to him?"

Bill Mullin looked uncomfortable. "I wrote him a letter of recommendation," he said.

We went back over the years from the time Herb graduated from high school until he went to work for Goodwill Industries. Suddenly, he looked at me sharply and demanded, "Are you implying that something rather traumatic happened in Herb's life back then that I might have missed or might not know of?"

"No, I'm just looking for something that might mean something to me, in terms of his childhood, but it wouldn't be surprising that there was nothing remarkable."

"The two traumatic things that stand out in my mind are the loss of that very deep boyhood friendship of his with Dean Richardson and then the split-up with Loretta Ricketts."

"After his friend was killed, he apparently would stay in his room for periods, was pretty withdrawn," I said. "Was he anything like that after he broke up with Loretta?"

"I don't think so . . . not much."

"He wasn't as upset?"

"Uh uh. Not until he got into this damned Oriental religion thing . . . and I think that's where initially he really got on pot."

"That's about the first time you suspected he was using pot, or anything?"

"Right."

A few questions later, we reached the point of Herb's second hospitalization, the one in San Luis Obispo.

"What did he tell you then?" I asked, studying him.

"He said, to quote him, 'They tell me that the last couple of years I've been living the life of a homosexual.'"

"'They' meaning the doctors?"

"I guess that's what he meant."

"Did he say anything else?"

"And I said, 'Well Herb, I'm quoting the doctor, I asked him about it, and he said when the boy gets over this traumatic kick of the drugs and the split personality that he has right now, this will also go. He says that it's kind of tied together, and he says he will become more normal again.' And I told Herb this, and I said, 'You're going to have to work on that drug bit.'"

"Do you have any knowledge of any drugs he took besides pot?"

"Acid."

"Anything else?"

"Well, he mentioned once that he had taken heroin and he didn't like it. That was in Santa Cruz."

"When do you think he quit using drugs?"

"God, how can you tell?" he cried. "I mean, how can you tell?"

"Did he ever tell you, for instance, that he'd quit?"

"Yes! I think every time he'd come home, 'I'm off, haven't used them for a year and a half, haven't used them for two years.' "

He said that he suspected that during the time Herb lived in San Francisco, he might have had a number of homosexual relationships, although he had no compelling evidence of it. After he came home in September, he occupied himself drawing, reading, and gathering firewood. To help pay for his board, he volunteered to panel his parents' recreation room.

"Did you know that he'd bought a gun in December?" I asked.

"No."

"Had he ever had a gun before? Been around one?"

"The police asked me where he picked up his markmanship, because evidently he's a pretty good marksman." His eyes fell. "They . . . they felt he was, anyway."

He then said that Herb had learned to use a rifle at Boy Scout camp, and that he later joined a National Rifle Association chapter in San Francisco. I shifted the conversation back to the previous December.

"Did he ever say he was hearing voices, or did you think he was hearing voices or seeing things that weren't there?"

"No."

"Was he very suspicious of people? Did he worry that somebody might be looking for him, or was after him?"

"No."

"Did he ever threaten anybody that you know of?"

"He scared me once. You see, I had taught him to box, to block and parry and so on, and ever since he was a tot we've sparred open-handed, say in the kitchen when we're just waiting for dinner or something like that. About the time he came home I did this, and he closed. He closed right now. And he'd picked up a few moves, you know, in his professional training, and he hit me a couple of times right smack on the jaw, just boom, boom. And he says, 'Come on, let's go . . . it won't last long, it won't hurt long,' just like that. And that's the last time I sparred with him, believe me.

"He . . . he scared me," the father said. "It was such a departure from what we had normally done all our lives, see, that it scared me." He suddenly acted as though he wanted to make sure I knew what had frightened him. "His manner. Did I make myself clear?"

"Oh, yes, very," I said. "In January, did you see him much, or at all?"

"Oh, hell! We couldn't keep him away."

"From coming home?"

There was an edge of annoyance in his voice, which rose slightly. "Kept coming home! Every other day! For an hour, two hours, for this reason or for that reason. Inventive. Sometimes they were sound, like he wanted to borrow the typewriter to type out applications.

"I tried to talk him into moving into the Oakland area, San Leandro area, Alameda area, in order to look for employment, where industry is, rather than down in our tourist haven."

"Did you see him around the time of the first killings . . . in January?"

"God, I don't know, doc." He seemed to be getting tired. "Honest to God, I don't know."

"Let's put it this way," I said. "You undoubtedly heard or read in the papers about the Gianera and Francis killings, right?"

"Yes."

"Now, do you recall if you saw him . . ."

"Oh, yes, I saw him after that, and I remembered the name Gianera from his high school days."

"What do you remember about him?"

"Gianera was on the football team with him, and the rest of those kids."

"Was he ever around the house? Was he a close friend of . . ."

"I met him at our house, once."

"When would that have been?" I asked. "A long time ago?"

"Senior year in high school."

"Never saw him since?"

"Uh uh."

"Did you know that Herb was seeing him? At Cabrillo?"

"No."

"He didn't ever talk about it?"

"No. I don't think the kid was that close to Gianera."

"OK, you said when you read about it in the paper, you recognized the name, and then did you see Herb?"

"I recognized the name . . . and I remember talking about it, and Herb said, 'Yeah, I remember Gianera.' And that was about it. He didn't add another thing."

23
Classic Symptoms

"WELL WHAT DO you think?" Jackson asked on the telephone.

"I have a better idea now what the family was like," I said. "I don't think his childhood was deliriously happy, but I don't think it was unusually unhappy either. The word that comes to mind is average."

"What do you make of the parents themselves?"

"It's hard to pinpoint exactly what family tensions there might have been before he began acting strange. His father may have intimated to him that he thought he was a coward when he became a CO. They both, the father especially, wanted to blame his condition entirely on drugs, as if they're afraid if they admitted he was mentally ill, someone would have blamed it on them."

"Well?"

"Oh, bullshit, Jim. If I could prove exactly what causes schizophrenia, I could retire to the Riviera with my Nobel Prize and wouldn't have to screw around with lawyers and murderers."

Jackson told me that Harold Cartwright had some new help, a young man named Steve Wright, a student at the university who was working for the public defender as a sort of intern while he gathered material for his major thesis. I asked him to have one of them go to Sebastopol and interview Herb's sister. It was possible she might remember incidents or details the parents forgot or were reluctant to disclose. A major thrust of the defense would have to be to prove that Herb had been insane for a long time before the murders, which themselves appeared to have been senseless—except for the death of Gianera.

The killing of a man he knew and obviously despised did not preclude insanity, but unless it fitted into the pattern of his mental illness the prosecution would have a strong argument that he had rational motives for the five murders he apparently committed January 25—hatred and then the need to eliminate witnesses.

It was raining and cold when I drove from Palo Alto to the jail in Redwood City the next day. A wet, dismal fog obscured the hills of the Peninsula, and the atmosphere inside the car was almost oppresive, even with the defroster on. The newspapers and television news that morning had been full of reports about the siege against a group of Indian militants at Wounded Knee and rumors about the Watergate scandal. I didn't have the radio on in the car. The weather was depressing enough without listening to the news.

In contrast, Herb was almost cheerful when he was brought into the interview room. He seemed to be relaxed and in a more cooperative mood and was pleased to get the pencils and legal tablets I had brought for him.

I asked if he had thought any further about the question I had asked him before, if he might have wanted to get caught. "Did you look ahead at the possible legal consequences of your actions?" I asked. "Specifically, did you think you might be subject to the death penalty?"

"Absolutely not," he said. "In fact, I didn't know what the penalty for murder was until you told me."

I asked him about Gianera. His responses revealed classic symptoms of paranoia.

"James Ralph Gianera had plotted against me," he said. "He had been belittling me behind my back for years. He also sold me the drugs that harmed by mind."

"Do you recall buying the gun?" I asked. "The .22 revolver?"

"Yes. I got it at Western Auto in Felton in December." He paused. "At the time I was hoping they wouldn't sell me the gun. I shouldn't have been sold that gun."

"Really?"

"Why would they sell me a gun when I have a record of arrests and being in mental hospitals?"

I didn't have an answer for him. The federal gun control act of 1968 and California's ostensibly stricter regulations are virtually unenforceable. Although the state law prohibits the sale of guns to convicted felons and drug addicts, and the form does ask potential buyers if they have ever been in a mental hospital, anyone can do what Herb did, simply check the boxes indicating "no." Even with the five-day waiting period for picking up a weapon, it's not surprising that state officials didn't find his hospital records. He had been in jail five weeks already, and they still hadn't located them for us.

There may be as many as 200 million firearms in the hands of civilians in the United States, just short of one for every man, woman, and child, a number so staggering as to make any scheme to disarm the population totally unworkable. In the meantime the per capita homicide rate involving guns in this country runs about 3,500 percent higher than it does in the United Kingdom.

"Why did you buy the pistol?" I asked.

"In November or December, I read a book about Albert Einstein called *Einstein on Peace*. It said that in Switzerland every adult male was in the militia and kept a gun in his house for protection. I needed it for that purpose because I am one-third Scandinavian."

"I see," I agreed without understanding. "Did you have any other guns?"

"I had a .30-.30 that was my grandfather's," he said. "James Gianera made me sell it."

"Did he tell you to sell it?"

"Yes. By telepathy."

"Tell me more about why Gianera had to die," I suggested.

"About the turn of the year, I really began thinking about my life and my life's mission. I woke up on the morning of January 25, 1973, and knew that I had to kill Gianera."

"What was your life's mission?"

"It had been made clear to me by voices and messages I received through telepathy."

"What about the others, Mrs. Gianera, Mrs. Francis, the two children?"

"They just happened to be present when I went looking for and then found James Ralph Gianera," he said.

Although he was reluctant to tell me about his so-called mission, he was talking more freely now. I decided to find out what I could about the later murders.

"I came on the campsite while I was out walking one day," he explained.

"Were you armed? Were you thinking of killing anyone?"

"No. When I came back I found these four hippies. They had a rifle, which I had to take from them, and I told them they had to clean up the place and leave because they were on state property. They argued with me and said they wanted to stay a few more days. I was going to turn them in to the ranger. Instead, I went berserk and killed them."

"What happened then?" I asked.

"I . . . I don't know. Most of the rest of the time until I was arrested is like a blank."

"Do you recall the day you were arrested? What did you do that day?"

"I got up, and I was going to deliver a load of wood to my parents' house. But I got a telepathic message that I had to kill someone first," he said. "That old man, Mr. Perez, was the first person I came across when I left my apartment that day."

"Were you taking any drugs then?"

"No. I smoked dope and dropped acid when I was at Cabrillo, and later right up into 1972, but I wasn't on anything in February or January."

"How about the preceding months, October, November, and December?"

"No. I was trying to present myself as a candidate for the armed forces then. In September, I petitioned to get my draft status changed back to 1-A. It was December before it finally came through."

"Could you tell me a little about your religious beliefs?" I asked.

"I was raised a Roman Catholic, but I started to backslide in my junior year in high school. I haven't really gone to church much since then."

Although he didn't appear to be fatigued, he wasn't as talkative as he had been earlier. "I think this might be a good place to stop for now," I said. "Next time I'd like to talk a little more about what you finally realized in January, about what you had to do."

"All right," he said helpfully.

"Would you mind if I brought a tape recorder next time?"

"I'll think about it," he said.

"You've got one hell of a job on your hands," I told Jackson that afternoon. "There's no doubt that he murdered at least the ten people he's accused of killing.

"Actually," I added, "I think it's possible that if those four kids had done what he told them to do and hadn't given him any lip, he might not have shot them."

"But is he legally insane?"

I replied that although I was a little hazy yet about his motives, I believed he thought he was committing moral acts. That being the case, he may not have known the difference between right and wrong. And unlike Frazier, who had never been treated by a psychiatrist, Herb had a long history of hospitalizations and diagnoses of paranoid schizophrenia.

Jackson reminded me again that courts and juries are reluctant to hospitalize murderers, no matter what's wrong with them.

"Jim, it makes about as much sense for a jury to put this sonofabitch in prison as it would if he'd been arrested for disturbing the peace because he coughed in a theater and it turned out he had tuberculosis. I know that jurors are afraid if they let a murderer go to a mental hospital he'll be out day after tomorrow, but that's not the case, certainly not with somebody who's in the condition he is.

"The taxpayers are probably going to have to support him for the rest of his life either way, and he's young and physically healthy and likely to live a long time. How the hell is society protecting itself better by sticking him in a penitentiary where he won't get any treatment? At least in a mental hospital he might end up being of some use to himself."

Although California's mental health system had largely been dismantled, one facility that undoubtedly will always remain funded is the state hospital at Atascadero, which provides maximum security for defendants who have been found legally insane. During the summer of 1968 I had worked as a replacement psychiatrist there and had a chance to become familiar with the programs for people popularly termed "criminally insane."

There also was a practical side to my conviction that Herb should go to Atascadero. Under constant psychiatric supervision, with proper medication available, he would be far less dangerous. Denied treatment, which he would be in the penitentiary, it would be impossible to predict what he might do, to himself, a guard or another prisoner.

It was tragic and ironic, I thought, that after the system had failed repeatedly to help Mullin and, by extension, the public, it could be given one last chance—but only because he had taken ten lives.

24
Two Detectives

HAROLD CARTWRIGHT had spent quite a bit of time with Herb on his own. Mullin had made the amazingly sane suggestion that we put together a chronology of his life, something that would be invaluable to me in tracing the history of his psychosis. From conversations with the client, his parents and some of his acquaintances, the private detective had begun an outline of events from Herb's birth until his arrest nearly twenty-six years later.

By the time he drove north to interview Herb's sister and her husband, Harold knew that Herb had visited them several times in the past few years. The couple had two children, a daughter, Jennifer, and a son, Al, Jr. The family's Christmas tree farm was just outside Sebastopol, a community better known for its apple orchards. The last time Herb had been there was the previous Christmas, with his mother and father. In September, a couple of days before he moved back into the house in Felton, he had spent a night with the Boccas, doing little but reading a Bible. Two years earlier, in September of 1970, he had visited them with his parents. At that time, the family said, he was on a macrobiotic diet, had shaved his head, and was wearing a goatee. On that trip the Boccas had told his parents that a few months earlier he had shown up dressed as a bracero and affecting a Mexican accent. Later, he had arrived with a friend from Santa Cruz. Mrs. Bocca had told her mother that both Herb and the friend had done something "strange" but did not elaborate.

Cartwright had tape-recorded his interview, but while a transcript was being typed, he telephoned to tell me about it.

"She didn't have much to add that we didn't already know," he said. "She did remember a time Herb visited the ranch in 1970 with a friend from Santa Cruz, a guy named Ed Lawrence."

"What happened?" I asked.

"Apparently he inhaled a whole joint in a single puff, then he and Lawrence took their clothes off, sat cross-legged on the living room floor, and pounded their chests rhythmically until they were exhausted and fell asleep."

"Where the hell was everyone else while this was going on?"

"It happened after the family had gone to bed," Cartwright said. "Apparently her father-in-law was visiting too, and was sleeping on the couch. It woke him up. She said it scared him, and he pretended to be asleep."

About Herb's childhood, all Mrs. Bocca could remember was that Herb had told her he was disappointed when the family moved to San Francisco from Walnut Creek because it had meant he wouldn't get a chance to take a bus to school when he entered kindergarten. She also recalled that Herb thought none of the children in the neighborhood liked him. Since she had stayed in San Francisco to attend college when the Mullins moved to Felton, she had not seen much of her brother after 1963.

In the late summer of 1965, she told Cartwright, she went home for a visit. She was perplexed when she found what appeared to be a shrine in Herb's room, a photograph flanked by burning votive candles.

"Let me guess," I interrupted. "It was a picture of Dean Richardson."

"Yep. She said she never knew their friendship was that strong."

Although it had meant nothing to her at the time, she said, Herb once told her that he had been approached by homosexuals on the Cabrillo campus, and that it upset him. This led Cartwright to ask whether there had been any sex education in the home when she and Herb were growing up. She replied that it had been "an uptight subject around the house." Then he inquired about Herb's furlough visits to Sebastopol from Mendocino State Hospital.

"He just seemed relieved, like he was starting to get it together," Cartwright quoted her as saying. "He seemed happier. He was told to ask questions whenever he questioned things. He asked if I wanted to sleep with him, and I said no. He asked me if I thought Al wanted to sleep with him, and I said no, I'm pretty sure he didn't. He said well, I have to be sure, so he asked Al and Al said no."

"Did you ever have any idea that he was physically attracted to you before that time?" Cartwright had asked.

"No. In fact I didn't think so after that."

"Did you think maybe he thought you were?"

"I don't know. . . ." She added that in retrospect, it seemed to her that Herb had acted "restless" during visits when she and her husband went to bed for the night.

Mrs. Bocca said that after Herb had been released from Mendocino he told her there had been several times when he thought she was communicating with him telepathically.

"Did he ever tell her he was actually hearing her voice?" I asked Cartwright.

"No. She said, and I quote, 'I think it was more emotional feelings, vibrations, things like that.' "

"Anything else?" I asked.

"There is one other thing. She volunteered that a pair of detectives from Alameda dropped by not too long ago and questioned her for an hour about Herb's background."

"Alameda?" I asked, surprised. "What the hell are they trying to pin on him now?"

"I don't know, but I think we'd better find out."

In late March, the defense investigation intensified. Jim Jackson had obtained a brief postponement, but he had to be ready by April 5 to enter a plea to the indictment. We knew the authorities had talked to literally scores of people, including Herb's friends from high school, college, and the local drug culture. Eventually, Jackson would be able to get those names through pretrial discovery.

The big gap in Mullin's life appeared to be the year and a half he lived in San Francisco, from May 1971 until he returned to his parents' home in September of 1972. From my point of view this was a critical time. It was the longest period since he was twenty that Herb had gone without any psychiatric treatment at all, so there were no professional records of his symptoms and behavior. To complete a record of his insanity, we needed witnesses. It was essential that we find out from the people who knew him then what he had been doing and how he had acted.

About all Harold Cartwright and his young assistant, Steve Wright, had to go on were the return addresses on the letters his parents had saved. Herb's own recollections were fairly vague, although he was able to provide the names of some of his acquaintances in the city. Others came from his notes and address books.

On Wednesday, March 28, Cartwright drove to San Francisco and parked in front of the Elwoods Hotel, a rundown building on Bush Street in a district peopled to a great extent by homosexuals and former mental patients turned out of institutions. He tried to interview the landlady, but she spoke very little English. She summoned her assistant, a man named Slim Obitz, who acted as her translator.

"When did Herb live here?" he asked Obitz, who had brought the registration book.

"From May 4 to July 4, 1972. For about three months after he checked out, he'd pick up his mail on the first or second of each month."

"What did you think of him?"

"He seemed introverted," Obitz said. "He was a loner type, sort of defensive."

"Did he look like he had mental problems?"

"Definitely. It was impossible to understand him sometimes. I thought he must be mentally retarded."

"He did pretty well in college."

"It's hard to believe he ever went to college. He hardly ever started a conversation himself, and about the only thing I ever talked to him about that got any reaction was art."

"Do you know where he lived after he left here?"

"In his car, as far as we know. He had it fixed up with a bedroll, and he didn't give us a change of address for a long time."

"Did any of the other tenants know him very well?"

"There were a couple, I think. Rick Barton knew him. He still lives here."

"What room?"

"210."

"He home?"

"Far as I know."

Cartwright climbed the stairs to the second floor and knocked on Barton's door. There was no answer, but he could hear voices inside. He tried the knob. It was unlocked. With instinct born of experience, he nudged the door open with his foot without stepping over the threshold.

"Hey man, come on in," a thick voice invited. "Join the party."

Cartwright found two men in the room, one supine on the floor and the other lying on a disheveled bed. A nearly empty gallon bottle of cheap red wine sat between them.

"Which one of you is Rick Barton?" he asked.

"What can I do for you?" the man on the bed slurred cheerfully.

"I'm trying to find out a few things about Herb Mullin."

The man peered up at him with the curious myopia of drunkenness. "You a cop?"

"A private investigator. I'm working on his murder defense."

"Yeah, I heard about that. Never thought old Herbie had it in him. Have a seat, Sherlock." Cartwright sat down gingerly. The third man had not spoken.

"We found some letters in his effects from someone named Rick," he began. "That you?"

"I never met Mullin before he moved in here," Barton said. He belched. "As far as I know, I never wrote him any fucking letters."

"Was he a homosexual or bisexual?"

"How the hell would I know. It never came up."

"Did you see much of each other?" Cartwright asked.

"He'd come here sometimes at night, 'cause I have a light and drawing table and he didn't. He'd sit there all night, drawing, while I slept."

"What kind of shape do you think he was in mentally?"

"He was incompetent to function in society," Barton said. "He should have been in a hospital. I told him so. I told him he should go to the mental health clinic down the street, but he never did.

"It's closed now," he said. "They're all fucking closed."

"Did you ever see any bizarre behavior?"

"Just once. He came in here and asked very politely if I minded if he hit the floor. I didn't know what he meant, so I just said, 'Shit

man, go ahead,' and he slugged the floor with his fist as hard as he
could. It scared me. I told him never to do anything like that again."

"Anything else?"

"Herb took me to dinner once at Arnie's in Cedar Alley. Real nice
place, Arnie's. When Arnie came to wait on us, Herb was so spaced
out he could hardly give his order."

"Was he on drugs?"

"Not as far as I know. I never saw him drop anything." Barton's
mind seemed to be wandering a little. "He was a nice kid. Likable.
He just really had mental problems. I could tell."

"Any other symptoms?"

"Sometimes it was impossible to understand what he was talking
about. He'd jump from one subject to another with every sentence.
The only times he ever stuck to the point were when he talked about
art."

"What were some of the other subjects?"

"I don't remember, man. He did tell me once he donated a lot of
money to charity. He even showed me some receipts." He took a long
pull on the wine jug, spilling some of the dark liquid on his chest.
"You know, when he hit the floor that time, I asked him what was
freaking him out. He wouldn't give me an answer."

"He have any other friends?"

"He knew a few people."

"You know any names?"

"Let me think a minute, man. It's hard to remember."

While Cartwright was questioning Barton, Sheriff's Detective
Terry Medina parked his car outside the Mullin house in Felton. He
recently had been promoted to sergeant and was assigned to the
murder case full-time. On the back seat were several boxes and
envelopes containing evidence seized by the police, sheriff's officers,
and DA's inspectors. He wanted the parents to identify Herb's personal possessions, to sift out any items that might have belonged to
one of the victims. He also had a number of questions posed by the
prosecutors.

As they had promised on the telephone, both parents were at home
when he arrived. The father helped him carry the boxes into the
living room.

Medina asked whether Herb had ever used any car other than his own station wagon, in particular the green Datsun sedan owned by Mr. and Mrs. Mullin. He had walked around it on the way into the house, looking for college or university decals or parking stickers, but saw none.

"He asked to use it a few times," Bill Mullin said, "but we turned him down."

"Did he have an extra set of keys for it?"

"No. He used the other car, the '62 Chevrolet, a couple of times while he was paneling the family room, but only to go to the hardware store."

"As you know, we picked up a lot of his letters and personal papers," Medina said. "We found one from you mentioning a ranch in Monterey County."

"Yeah, Herb wanted to try and get a job there," the father explained. "His grandfather in Carmel used to be friends with one of the foremen. I wrote and told him I didn't think Jean's father could help him.

"Besides," he added, "the job would have been too close to the relatives in Carmel. Herb made them nervous."

Medine held up a makeup kit and asked the parents whether they recognized it. The investigators had speculated that Herb might have used it to disguise himself while stalking his victims.

"I never saw it before," the mother said.

"It might have something to do with his try to get a door-to-door selling job," Mullin offered. "He applied at the Fuller Brush Company, but he never followed through with it."

The parents identified several items of clothing, a tape recorder, and Herb's razor. Then Medina pulled a wooden walking cane out of one of the boxes.

"Did Herb ever have to use a cane?" he asked.

Bill Mullin snorted. "When he first came home from San Francisco, he sometimes went downtown wearing a long overcoat and a beatup hat and walking with that cane. After a while we got into an argument about it. I asked him why he was using a cane when he didn't need one, and warned him it would hurt his chances of getting a job.

"Herb asked me if I ever read the San Francisco *Chronicle*. I told him he knew I had, and then he asked me if I'd ever read the column by Herb Caen. I said of course I had, and then he said something like, 'Well, my name's Herb, and I use a cane. Herb Cane, get it?' It was crazy."

"In one of the letters we found a reference to a family named Koch," Medina said. "Would you know who they are?"

"Dr. Richard A. Koch and his family lived across the street from us in San Francisco," Mrs. Mullin said.

"They had three sons," her husband added. "The youngest is a medical student, and the one in the middle was apparently having some kind of emotional problems about the same time Herb was having problems.

"When Herb flew home from that trip to Hawaii, the youngest son drove to the airport and met him. We picked him up at the Kochs' house. Apparently, the two of them had a long talk, and Herb told the youngest son, the one studying to be a doctor, about some shock treatment he had received."

"Did he ever live with them or stay there for any extended periods?"

"Not as far as we know."

Medina showed them a string of rosary beads. They said they had never seen it before, nor a black silk pouch that had been found with it in Herb's apartment.

After reloading the boxes and envelopes into his car and bidding good-bye to the Mullins, Medina drove to Saint John's Catholic Church in Felton and found the parish priest, Father Patrick MucHugh, in his office. The pastor told him that Father Tomei had never visited his church. The detective showed him the pouch.

"That looks like something a priest might have," Father McHugh said.

"Is it part of the required attire?"

"No, but priests of the old school sometimes use pouches like that to hold their stoles."

"You mean the confessional vestment?"

"Yes. Something like this would be a fairly common item for a priest of the old school, to carry a stole, or use it as a coin purse."

"Thanks a lot, Father," Medina said. "You've been a big help."

25
A Sweet, Tender Person

CARTWRIGHT WALKED the three blocks from the Elwoods Hotel to the rooming house on Geary Street. He pulled up the collar of his raincoat against the cold wind blowing off the bay and wondered idly whether the two young men walking ahead of him wearing skin-tight jeans and T-shirts were chilly. A derelict huddled in the doorway of a boarded-up building stared at him with wild, mad eyes as he passed. The neighborhood gave him the creeps.

The detective was glancing down the list of names on the mailboxes when a man pushed through the front door. "Looking for somebody?" he asked.

"Yeah. Does a Mike Roberts live here?"

The man looked at him for a moment warily. "Yes, I do," he said finally. Cartwright identified himself and asked if Roberts had a few minutes to talk about Herb Mullin.

"I'm just on my way out," he said. "What do you want to know?"

"When did you meet him?"

"Last summer, while he was living at the Elwoods Hotel. He was really crazy."

"How so?"

"A little while after I met him, I invited him out to the beach. When we got there, I had to stay with Mullin all the time because he was acting so erratic and insane I didn't dare leave him alone."

"What was he doing?"

"It wasn't so much what he did, but what he didn't do. You couldn't communicate with him. I had to persuade him to get out of the car and then persuade him to get back in it when the time came to leave. He really wasn't competent to take care of himself. I dropped him off at the hotel and later in the day I was driving over in North Beach and I saw him on the sidewalk. I was amazed he could function well enough to live alone, much less get around San Francisco."

"Did he have any close friends that you know of?"

"He was pretty much a loner. He only seemed interested in painting. He had an old station wagon, but he didn't drive it much because he couldn't afford the gas."

"You ever see him take drugs?"

"I saw him smoke a joint once, and after just a little bit, he just stood in one place and wouldn't talk. He couldn't speak."

"You don't seem surprised that I'm asking you about him."

"I read about it in the papers," Roberts said. "I just couldn't comprehend him killing one person, much less ten."

"Why's that?"

"He was a very unmotivated person. I don't think he was capable mentally of getting it together enough to kill anyone. At least not when I knew him."

"Do you think he was a . . ." Cartwright corrected himself. "Was he gay, do you know?"

"He never talked about sex one way or the other," Roberts said. "I got the impression he was capable mentally of making it with a guy, but I don't believe he could ever physically go through with it. He would have freaked out."

"What about a woman?"

"I don't think he was capable of enough passion to make it with a girl either. He was really sensitive to people's feelings, especially about not being wanted. Maybe a little too sensitive." He shrugged. "Anyway, he seemed to be able to handle it without any hard feelings."

Cartwright elected to let the subject drop. "When was the last time you saw him?" he asked.

"He was going to move in here," Roberts recalled. "He even did a lot of work on a room. But then the owner wouldn't let the manager rent to him because Herb said something strange, or she saw him do something crazy. I don't really know.

"Later, a bunch of us convinced the manager he should be allowed to move in. He shouldn't have been alone. The manager supposedly wrote and told him he could move in, but never got an answer."

Roberts looked anxiously at his watch. "Look, I really gotta go."

"Sorry I held you up. Would you be willing to talk to me some more, in depth, if I came back at a more convenient time?"

"Sure. If you think it'll help."

Cartwright let himself in the building, found room number 23, and knocked. The door was opened by a woman in her early forties.

"Jean Carlisle?" he asked.

"Yes."

He produced a card. "My name's Cartwright. I'm an investigator for the Santa Cruz County public defender. We're working on the Herb Mullin case. Some people said you knew him."

"He was such a sweet, tender person," she said soulfully.

"Mind if I come in?"

"Not at all."

Cartwright began by asking her occupation.

"I'm a professional photographer," she said. "I also draw Aid to the Totally Disabled."

"What for?"

"Psychiatric problems. Herb was on welfare, too."

"How'd you meet him?" Cartwright inquired.

"Through Mike Roberts. He's a photographer too, and he lives here."

"I met him. You said Herb was a sweet person?"

"Yeah. He helped me a lot by taking me places, helping me do my shopping and like that. He even baby-sat for my four-year-old son."

"What did you think of his mental state?"

"He certainly had mental problems." She lowered her voice conspiratorially. "I didn't think he was as far out as some of the other people in this building.

"He was real proud of his heritage," she said, "and talked a lot about his ancestors. But I think he may have been alienated from his family.

"He was deluded, there's no doubt about that. But he wasn't as strange as some of the others."

"Did he take drugs?"

"I don't go along with drugs or grass," she asserted properly, "so I never saw him smoke or take anything. But I remember Mike telling me once Herb shouldn't do grass because he acted pretty crazy when he was high."

"Did you and Herb ever go anywhere together?"

"Sometime in July or August, I can't remember when, I was planning to go stay with a friend overnight in San Jose. I was getting ready to take the bus to the train station, and Herb volunteered to take me. He was real sweet that way.

"Anyway, he drove me all the way down there, and he took me to the rest home so I could visit my ex-mother-in-law, and then he took me to my friend's house. He slept in his station wagon all night in the driveway. He was very neat, and his car was always arranged just so. I think he lived in it after he left the Elwoods Hotel."

"Did he ever stay here?" Cartwright asked carefully.

"I think he may have crashed here a few times after he left the hotel."

"What I'm getting at . . ."

She laughed. "Forget it," she said. "He never made any sexual advances to me or showed any interest in me that way."

"Did you ever wonder why?"

"He knew I had a regular boyfriend. Besides, I was so much older than he was, I think I may have been more of a mother figure."

"Did he ever get excited, or seem to be violent?"

"No, he was very gentle and peaceful. That's why this is all so hard to believe. The only time I ever saw him upset at all was the last time I saw him."

"When was that?"

"He wanted to move in here where he had some friends. Angelo, he's the manager, promised him a room. The room was a mess, and Herb came over and cleaned it up and was getting ready to paint it when the lessee of the building came by. She asked Herb to carry some stuff upstairs for her, and he did. After that she told Angelo not to rent to Herb because he was strange. Hell, everybody here is strange.

"Anyway, when Angelo told Herb that, Herb got real upset and depressed. He said something that made me afraid he was going to commit suicide."

"What was that?"

"I can't remember exactly. I haven't seen him since that day."

"Who's the lessee of the building?"

Jean Carlisle was rummaging through a drawer. "Mrs. Walker," she said. "Angelo can tell you how to get hold of her. Ah, here they are." She withdrew a photo development envelope. "These are some pictures I took of Herb. I thought maybe you'd want them."

Cartwright looked at the slightly blurry snapshots. He recognized Mullin. He was playing chess with another man. "Who's that?" he asked.

"Max Butler. He lives here too."

Harold thanked the woman and left. There was no answer at Butler's door, nor could he get any response from the manager.

He hurried back to his car. It was getting late, and he had a law class that night in San Jose.

He was glad to be leaving San Francisco.

26
Conversations

THE NEXT MORNING, Cartwright received a telephone call from Ralph Johnson, a fifty-three-year-old man who lived with his three dogs at the Oregon Hotel, a battered place on Valencia Street in San Francisco's Mission District. Herb had lived there for three months before moving to the Elwoods Hotel, and someone had recalled his meeting Johnson. Cartwright had stopped by the Oregon before going to the Elwoods the day before, but he was not at home. He had left his card with a note asking Johnson to call collect.

The caller said he had talked to Herb a few times, and that Mullin had become acquainted with Johnson's nephew, who had been working in San Jose but living in San Francisco. He actually didn't get to know Herb well himself until May, he said, when he was laid off from his job.

"Somebody mentioned that he used to come over to your place and watch television," Cartwright said, doodling on the corner of a notepad.

"Not really," Johnson said. "He came down and borrowed my typewriter once. He wasn't watching television. He saw my typewriter, and he was talking about art. I'm not interested at all in art. It was just one of those things, but I didn't want to be impolite to him."

"How did he appear to be mentally?"

"Mentally? Well, I'll tell you the truth. I thought he was . . . I was stunned when I read this in the paper. I thought he was very well mannered and very well balanced."

"You felt he was competent?" the detective asked incredulously. "You didn't suspect that there was anything mentally wrong with him?"

"Definitely not. I never would have gotten around him if I'd even thought that."

"What did he like to talk about besides art?"

"Well, he was actually quiet. He didn't talk too much. He would come down and borrow something, and I'd go talk to him for a little, just to make conversation. I had nothing in common with him. After all, he's a young fellow, and I was working and he wasn't working. From what I gather they were on welfare."

"They?" Cartwright inquired sharply. "He was on welfare. Was there anybody else around?"

"Well, when I say 'they,' I mean the building. The building is practically a welfare hangout. The reason I was living here is because of the dogs. I can't get in anywhere else with three dogs."

"I can understand. Who else did he hang around with?"

"Gee, I don't know . . . I didn't really talk to him much, oh, not more than two or three times. He was down to see my nephew about the possibility of a job maybe three or four times, and they were talking like a couple of young guys will about chicks and stuff. But it was nothing serious. He would always leave, and my nephew would go out to work on his car or something. I don't believe they ever went anywhere together."

"OK, very good, Mr. Johnson. I sure appreciate your calling me."

"Could I ask you a question?"

"Sure, go right ahead," Cartwright said.

"Do they think he's insane?"

"That's a possibility. That's a definite posibility. He's certainly not normal."

"There'd have to be something wrong with you at the time you done something like that, anyway."

"I don't know how he was in May. That's the reason I'm trying to talk to people. I don't know how he was then. He's definitely in bad shape now."

"Gee, I was really sorry to hear that."

"Yes, apparently he had a lot going for him at one time in his life."

"Yes, so the papers say."

"OK, Mr. Johnson. Thanks again."

Just about the same time Harold was hanging up the telephone, Dr. David Marlowe, a psychologist on the faculty of the University of California at Santa Cruz, was at the jail in Redwood City. Herb had agreed to take the Minnesota Multiphasic Personality Inventory, the most widely used test of its kind. The examination then consisted of 550 true and false questions aimed at measuring, on a scale of 1 to 120, depression, hypochondria, paranoia, hysteria, social introversion, and so forth. A score of seventy or more on any one of ten scales is considered abnormal. The overall pattern of the scales is then used to determine the so-called personality profile.

Herb scored over seventy in six out of the ten subgroups. Dr. Marlowe concluded he was suffering from "schizophrenic reaction, paranoid type."

"I think you're going to see an interesting phenomenon here," I told Jackson after he gave me the test results. "I don't believe we're going to find any psychiatrist or psychologist who has or ever will see this kid who doesn't agree on the diagnosis."

"That would be interesting," he said. "Unanimity in your racket isn't that common."

About 8:00 A.M. the next day, Friday, March 30, Sergeant Medina and another sheriff's officer picked up Mullin at the jail in Redwood City to drive him to Santa Cruz for a meeting with his attorney. It was raining heavily, and even though it was well past sunrise, the detective had to drive with his headlights on.

Herb was silent for most of the trip, until they reached the long straight stretch of Highway 17 on the southwest side of the pass near Scott's Valley. They were running late, and Medina was indulging a little in the luxury of driving a black and white patrol car by ignoring the speed limit.

"Waves of fear come over me when you drive like this," Mullin said suddenly. "What would happen if we hit that." He pointed toward an oncoming cement truck. "I'd go to hell for sure."

Medina slowed down. "I didn't want to make you late for your appointment," he said. Then he asked, "What makes you think you'd go to hell?"

Herb didn't answer. About five minutes later, just before Medina turned into the parking lot at the sheriff's office, his prisoner spoke again. "What's a sophisticated word for feeling sorry for yourself?" he asked.

"Do you feel sorry for yourself?"

"I think so."

"Do you feel sorry for yourself, or sorry for what you did?" Medina inquired offhandedly. Mullin didn't reply right away. "Do you think the word 'remorseful' fits?"

"I don't think so," Herb said slowly. Medina drove through the lot and into an alley where there was a guarded entrance to the building. "I feel sorry for the way my life changed and what happened in January," Mullin said. "Maybe I should have got some money and bought a house."

After escorting Mullin inside, putting him in a locked conference room and taking off his handcuffs, Medina returned with an office dictionary. "Maybe together we can find a word about feeling sorry for yourself," he offered. They leafed through the pages for a couple of minutes. Medina glanced up at the clock on the wall. "I've got to go now," he told Mullin. "Let me know if you find a word that fits your feelings."

Steve Wright sat that same day in a small office at Jackson's law firm, going over his notes. He was a dark, athletic-looking young man whose mustache fit in well with his large, even features. His part-time student project, working as an investigator for the public defender, had turned into a compelling vocation, demanding many more hours than he had bargained for. His major, broadly called community studies, allowed him more time than most for work outside the classroom. Still, the frustrations and late nights sometimes got him down. His hectic schedule didn't leave time for another job, and this one only paid expenses. Luckily his wife, Rita, not only had the ability to put up with his moods after days spent engrossed with insanity and violent death; she willingly worked a full-time job every day that made his education possible. He often wondered if it would be fair to her for him to go to law school.

Since Wright and Mullin were close in age, Jackson and Cart-wright had Steve sit in on several conversations with their client, and he also had talked with Herb alone. This Friday, Wright had finally run down a man named Allan Hanson, whom Herb said had be-friended him not long after he had first moved to San Francisco. It had taken him a while to find his new address and telephone number.

When Hanson answered the telephone, Wright identified himself and said that Herb had brought his name up several times.

"Well, I was his roommate for a month," Hanson said. "We lived together in San Francisco."

Steve reacted wordlessly. Herb had not said anything about that. "Where was this?" he asked conversationally.

"605 Juniper Street. The building since then has been torn down, I think. Actually, when I met him, he was a member of some kind of church or something."

"Yeah?"

"I was a member of a different group then. I'd gotten kicked out of it, and I was pretty much bored and just looking around for something to do on weekends. I'd been invited to this place and I met him there. It was about a month later I met him on the streets, and then a couple of weeks later he moved into the apartment that I was staying at." Hanson paused. Wright waited. "It was sort of . . . he wasn't like he was living there. It was sort of like . . . he was a guest of the house."

Wright decided not to pursue the living arrangement.

Hanson told Wright that Herb had moved in sometime in September or October of 1971. The young investigator explained that although Herb was now so paranoid that he blamed almost everyone he had ever known for his troubles, he remembered Hanson warmly. He asked him what he had thought of Herb mentally.

"This is very difficult," Hanson said slowly, "because . . . it's very difficult to say. For one thing, I know why he's in the situation he's in, and why he did what he did."

"You do?"

"Yes. And see, this is . . . if Herbert really likes me—I called him John, by the way—if he really likes me it's because I knew him. God, this is really strange. He wanted to save the world. He wanted to make the world a better place and, um, he hasn't done anything worse than Richard Nixon. He hasn't done anything worse than anyone, as far as I'm concerned. He just did something that pretty much is not a very nice thing to do."

That, thought Wright, is the understatement of the century. Aloud he asked, "Did he say something to that effect to you at all?"

"No. I was totally shocked. I did tell him that he was going off the deep end, and that he was getting to the point where he was not only daydreaming, but he was living out his daydreams, which of course the whole world is right now."

Hanson hypothesized that the murders might have been the result of suicidal tendencies on Herb's part, a desire to be caught and executed. I had not discarded the idea entirely myself. "In other words," he explained, "you set yourself up to be killed or destroyed somehow.

"I did feel, though, that he had destroyed himself, a certain part of himself," Hanson continued. "He had given up, he had quit out on his life. He told me that he hated me for saying that."

Wright decided to encourage him. "Maybe you did really know him and really did convince him that you knew him, because of the way he speaks about you now. It's out of character for him to talk nice about anybody now.

"Did he ever discuss with you anything like mental telepathy?"

"Yes. I told him mental telepathy was something that was not available to ordinary beings on the planet earth, and that only when someone made tremendous efforts in their life and had evolved psychologically to a certain point could that kind of thing be possible. And then it wasn't really what's called mental telepathy, it's a situation where you know the truth about yourself, you know the truth about someone else.

"I mean, I'm talking to you and I don't know you, so it's hard for me to talk in a way I know you will understand me. And that was something I could do with Herb—Herbert, or John. He couldn't have a conversation with anyone else on this whole planet like he had with me, because when he would say something I would tell him in a way that made sense to him that that was either impossible or not available."

"Did you worry that he was going to explode, or do something violent?"

"No. I didn't believe he was capable of doing that. He was extremely calm, very, very quiet—uh, actually I could even say shy."

"Did you ever talk about reincarnation?"

"Right, and I told him that reincarnation was not necessarily a desirable thing, it only happened to people that had not done what it was they had to do this particular time, and that they were given three chances each lifetime. In other words, it is the theory of eternal recurrence, people make the same mistakes over and over again and they're born, they die and they're born.

"We discussed the Book of the Dead and I explained it to him—this must really sound weird, me talking to you like this. . . ." Hanson paused, but Wright didn't comment. "I explained to him that reincarnation, like coming back as animals and things like that, did happen, and that at one time, for instance, horses were beings that were capable of doing for this planet what we're doing as human beings now, only somehow they blew it and they had to live a lower life . . .

"I explained it to him how it existed as I understood it, and it apparently made sense to him because he thought it was very interesting. He was the kind of person who would go out and tell other people to listen to me."

Hanson's theories also made some sense to Wright, in a totally different way. He and Harold Cartwright had talked with Herb several times in recent days, and Mullin was confiding more. They told me he had tried to explain an elaborate theory involving reincarnation. It was obvious he didn't yet trust all of us completely, and he had not disclosed all of his beliefs. I had not had an opportunity to discuss them with him, but I intended to as soon as possible.

The most important fact we learned was that Herb may have been trying to work out a theory of reincarnation as long as seventeen months before his arrest. Although Wright had not been able to understand him fully, Herb had said certain useful acts, such as preventing earthquakes, would assure a person of a better life in his next existence.

And he had hinted that one way of preventing earthquakes was to murder.

In the afternoon, Sergeant Medina and the other deputy put Mullin in the rear of the patrol car for the trip back to the jail in Redwood

City. This time Medina didn't drive. He wanted to be free to chat, if Herb felt like it.

"That was a good dictionary you gave me," Mullin remarked.

"Did you find a word for feeling sorry for yourself?"

"Kind of. 'Self-pity.' "

"Does that describe how you feel?"

"It was as close as I could find, but not exactly." He sat quietly for several miles. "I'm having trouble with Mr. Jackson," he said unexpectedly.

"That so?"

"He and the others want me to trust them without question. I'm not that type of person. I asked Jackson to give me an outline of what he has done so far on the case. I asked him to communicate with me in writing, but he won't." Herb gazed out the window. "Maybe I should change my approach. Maybe I should just give in."

Medina held his breath. He knew that if he pressed for a confession under the circumstances, the defense would shred it in court.

"What do you think will happen to me?" Herb asked.

"What would you like to have happen?"

"I'd like to go to a hospital so I could have a halfway decent life, so I could get help and get rehabilitated. I don't want to spend the rest of my life in a nine-by-sixteen-foot cell."

Mullin fixed Medina with his eyes through the wire mesh that separated them. "I'd like to go to a hospital some day so I can say, 'I, Herbert Mullin, did the willful destruction of ten human lives.' " The other deputy stole a look at Medina, who was taking notes. "I know what I've said," Mullin added. "I've told you. I know anything I say can be used. I know you will use it. I said it out loud. I don't care if you use it."

He stopped for a minute, reflecting. "They told me not to say anything to you guys. I don't want to talk to you about my case anymore."

"What would you like to talk about?" Medina asked.

Mullin didn't answer.

27

A Promising Boxer

THE PUBLIC PRESSURE on the authorities to prove that Mullin was guilty of additional murders was mounting by the end of March. Although he had been in custody for more than six weeks, nearly a dozen known slayings and suspicious disappearances remained unsolved. It was decided the investigators would have to sift again through all the minutiae collected with search warrants.

On Tuesday morning, April 3, Police Sergeant Chuck Gilbert set out with a handful of sales tags from local stores recovered from Herb's car. It was the kind of dull routine much unloved by detectives, especially on a day that showed the first promise of spring.

Gilbert drove first to a small grocery store in the west end of Santa Cruz, not far from the house in which the Gianeras had died. The owner recognized a slip dated February 9, 1973, but he couldn't recall Mullin's being in the store. The next stop was a variety store, where Gilbert showed the manager a receipt for thirty-one cents plus tax dated February 8. The manager consulted his schedule and said the clerk who had rung up the purchase was working now.

Gilbert showed the tag to Irene Conner, who was summoned from her cash register.

"I can't remember who bought something that far back," she complained. Then Gilbert produced a photograph of Mullin. "Oh," she said, "yes, I know him."

"How well?"

"He came in here on a Thursday, I think, between 9:00 and 11:00 in the morning. I think he bought one of those little screwdrivers over there." She pointed to a display. "Yeah, they're still the same price, thirty-one cents."

"How do you happen to remember what he bought?"

"We talked a little. I put the screwdriver and the sales slip in a little bag . . ."

"Yeah, we found that."

". . . and he said he needed it to tune a new guitar he just got. He asked me if he could come over to my place and play the guitar for me. He was really friendly."

"What did you say?"

"I told him some other time."

"Did he give you his name?" the detective asked.

"He introduced himself as Herb." She gestured toward the picture. "Is that this guy's name?"

"Uh, yeah." Gilbert was taken aback by the fact she apparently did not know who Mullin was.

"Well, that's him all right."

"What was he wearing?"

"A pea coat and a blue knit watch cap. I thought he might be a fisherman or a merchant seaman."

"You ever see him again?"

"He came in the next day, Friday, and asked one of the other girls where I was. Then he came up to me and asked me again if he could come over and play his guitar. I turned him down."

It was a good thing you did, Gilbert thought. That was the day before he killed the four boys in Cowell Park.

On Wednesday morning, April 4, Cartwright drove back to San Francisco. That same morning, at the parents' home, he had picked up a large envelope full of Herb's papers and drawings that had been overlooked by the police. Among the documents he found a receipt for workouts at the Newman-Herman Gym, a boxing hangout in the city. After finding the address on Leavenworth Street, he looked up Vic Grupico, a trainer.

"Yeah, I remember him," Grupico said. "I liked him, felt sorry for him. I even gave him a seventy-dollar suit once while he was working out here."

"How long was that?" Cartwright asked.

"Four, maybe five months in late '71, early '72. Just a minute." He went to get a record book from the office. "Yeah, he paid from September to March. I guess he was here over six months. Don Stewart was the other trainer who worked with him."

"Was he any good?"

"He was a tough kid, a kid who would go into the center of the ring and plant his feet and trade punches with anybody. He never developed a lotta skill or technique, but he could sure as hell take a lot of punishment, and he punched hard."

The trainer flipped a towel to a dripping boxer as he clambered through the ropes and then turned back to Cartwright.

"The biggest problem we had with him was he always questioned what we told him. If you told him to punch a certain way, he'd say, 'Why?' or he'd tell me, 'Don told me to do it this way.' Then when he was working out with Don, he'd say, 'Well, Vic told me to do it that way!' "

"What did you think of him mentally?"

"To tell you the truth, I was surprised when the State Athletic Commission gave him a permit to box in the Golden Gloves in 1972. Mullin told me he had a dope arrest, and in this state that's usually good enough to get you disqualified. Also, I didn't think he'd pass the medical because he obviously had mental or emotional problems."

"What did he do to make you think that?"

"Well, he was all right as long as we were telling him what to do, or if you just put him on the heavy bag. He'd stand there and punch the bag until you stopped him. But if you weren't paying attention to him for a minute, you'd find him standing in the corner with his hands folded, talking to himself."

"Anything else?"

"Whenever he couldn't keep a training day, he'd write a letter, almost like a kid getting an excuse for being absent from school."

"Did he have any bouts?" Cartwright asked. "Outside of sparring, I mean?"

"Yeah. He fought a kid in the Golden Gloves some time early in '72. The other kid went on to win the championship, but Herb was only beaten out by a few points." He laughed. "I remember when I was getting him ready for the fight, I noticed he had a tattoo just below his belly button that said something like 'Legalize acid.' I thought that was a little funny, because he hated hippies."

"How do you know that?"

"There was a guy who used to train here, and we got to be friends. He'd come back now and then, and he let his hair grow, like most young kids nowadays, I guess. Anyway, he came in one day and walked up to Mullin. Herb shoved him and told him he didn't like hippies and to beat it."

"How long after his Golden Gloves bout did he stop coming?"

"A week maybe. He just came in one day and said he was quitting."

"Did you ever think he was dangerous?"

"Not outside of the ring. He was weird, all right, but I never thought he was dangerous."

Cartwright talked with Don Stewart, the other trainer, and Joe Herman, the co-owner of the gymnasium. Stewart told him Mullin had never been injured in the ring, beyond suffering a puffy eye on one occasion.

"I remember once I had him sparring with another kid who had a lot of experience, and he was punishing Herb pretty bad. We told him to take it easy on him. The next day they boxed again, and Mullin knocked him down twice."

"You recall anything else about him?"

"He read the Bible a lot. Talked about being a priest sometimes. Other times he talked about gurus."

The only thing Herman could add was that when Mullin would write a letter explaining why he couldn't keep an appointment, it would be three or four pages long.

"We all knew he was a little strange," he said.

Before leaving, Cartwright borrowed a telephone and called the State Athletic Commission office in the city. The clerk who answered said Mullin had a card on file indicating that he was issued a temporary license for the Golden Gloves in 1972, and that he had fought only once, losing a decision on March 6.

"You have anything there about his arrest record, or the results of his physical?" Cartwright asked.

"You'd have to get all that stuff from Sacramento," the clerk said.

Jackson and I had met several times to discuss the strategy of entering a plea. Although I had no doubt that Herb was legally insane, Jim agreed with me that we should postpone an insanity plea and, if possible, avoid a pretrial competency hearing.

As a practical matter, a defendant is found incompetent to stand trial only if he is unable to cooperate in his own defense. That was not the case with Herb. More important, the psychiatrists appointed by judges to determine competency often are prosecution-oriented. As long as we didn't allege that Herb was incompetent or insane, the DA would not be able to have him examined. For that reason it was Chang, not Jackson, who pushed for a competency hearing. It was obvious from Herb's earlier conduct that we were likely to plead him insane eventually, and Peter was anxious to get psychiatric opinions as soon as he could.

On Thursday, April 5, Herb appeared before Santa Cruz County Superior Court Judge Charles S. Franich. He walked into the crowded, heavily guarded courtroom wearing a suit. He was clean-shaven and had a neat haircut.

"Your honor," Mullin said, "I move the charges against me be reduced to second-degree murder."

"Mr. Mullin, you have a lawyer present," the judge pointed out.

Jackson shrugged helplessly. "He's decided again that he wants to represent himself," he said.

"The answer is the same as it was in the lower court," the judge told Mullin. "I don't believe you're capable of defending yourself without counsel."

Mullin pointed to Jackson's bushy red hair and walrus mustache. "I don't care to be defended by a longhair," he asserted sharply.

"I just can't understand what a man's appearance has to do with his ability," Franich said. "Mr. Jackson may wear his hair long, but I don't think you can call him a 'longhair.' Besides, he's the ablest criminal defense lawyer I've ever known." In view of the attorney's florid complexion, it was impossible to tell whether he blushed.

"In that case," Mullin declared in a clear voice, "I plead guilty to ten counts of first-degree murder."

"Again, I can't accept that," the judge said. "First I've got to determine if you are able to stand trial. Until that's realized, I can't accept a plea of guilty from you forthright." He turned to Jackson. "Do you have a plea prepared?" he asked.

"Yes, your honor. The defendant pleads not guilty to all counts, but specifically reserves the right to enter a plea of not guilty by reason of insanity at a later date."

"Very well," the judge said. "In view of my own rising doubts about the defendant's sanity, I am setting April 16 for a hearing to review that issue and possibly appoint psychiatric witnesses to determine if he is competent to stand trial."

Sergeant Medina had watched Mullin's performance in court. After locking him in the back of the patrol car for the trip back to his cell in Redwood City, he started north on coastal Highway 1, the longest route back to the San Mateo County Jail via a winding road over the mountains. He wanted to give Herb plenty of time to talk. His earlier, offhand confession to Medina had been his only self-incriminating statement to the authorities. They knew nothing of what he had told us.

When Medina turned east at Pescadero Creek and the car began climbing toward the ridge, Herb said abruptly, "I wish that I had run into someone that could have straightened out my life, so I would not have taken those peoples' lives."

"Who might have done that?" Medina asked.

"If I was allowed to go into the Coast Guard or the Marine Corps, I would not have taken all those peoples' lives."

Mullin lapsed into silence. They had almost reached the jail before he spoke again. "About four or five times, I had two choices to make and I would stand there and think about it, and then usually make the wrong choice."

Medina said nothing, but his mind was racing. Four or five times, Mullin had said. The ten victims he was accused of killing died on there separate days. Even if he had murdered the priest, that was only four.

Four or *five* times?

28
The Die Song

MY NEXT INTERVIEW with Herb was on April 10. I took along a tape recorder, hopeful that he would allow me to use it if he began to explain his reasons for the killings. From what the investigators had told me about their own recent conversations with him, it was clear that he was in the grip of a remarkable delusional system.

Paranoid schizophrenia is a psychosis characterized by hallucinations, such as hearing voices; delusions, which may include grandiosity, persecution, or highly personal, bizarre religious beliefs, and feelings of suspicion, hostility, or aggression. Full-blown symptoms rarely manifest themselves before the twenties, although early indications sometimes appear in the late teens.

The imaginary voices a paranoid schizophrenic hears rarely command him to do anything, and even less often do they dictate violent acts, although it does happen occasionally. A delusion, on the other hand, may be such that murder is a perfectly logical consequence of a patently illogical idea.

For example, Daniel M'Naghten, who unwittingly gave his name to the infamous generalization that has made a shambles of insanity defenses throughout the English-speaking world for over a century, was a paranoid schizophrenic who suffered from the delusion that the prime minister of England, Sir Robert Peel, was in conspiracy against him. His conviction that he was important enough for Sir Robert to plot against revealed classic symptoms: delusions of grandeur and persecution. The delusion, of course, was illogical, but everything he did as a result of it was logical, or at least would have been were the delusion true.

At first M'Naghten sought to escape the fancied tormentors shadowing him by traveling in England and Europe. When that didn't work, he finally concluded—logically—he would get no peace until he eliminated his chief persecutor. On January 20, 1843, after waiting outside 10 Downing Street for about an hour, M'Naghten pulled a pistol from his belt and fired at the back of a man he thought was Sir Robert. In fact, he wounded Edward Drummond, the prime minister's private secretary, who was returning from an errand at a bank. When Drummond died five days later, M'Naghten was charged with capital murder.

M'Naghten was acquitted because everybody, including the crown prosecutor, agreed after two days of testimony that he was insane. The jury didn't even leave the box to deliberate. Unfortunately, public outrage led in part by Queen Victoria resulted in the judge and his colleagues being hauled before the House of Lords to explain themselves, and the result was the so-called M'Naghten Rule. It is ironic that prosecutors have been using it ever since to prove that paranoid schizophrenics are legally sane since they usually can differentiate between right and wrong.

Mass murderers are almost always insane. A number of studies of mentally ill killers in the United States and Canada have found that about half of them are paranoid schizophrenics or suffer from some symptoms of paranoia or schizophrenia. We already knew that Herb was a paranoid schizophrenic. To understand his acts, I had to know what delusions they flowed from. He had already mentioned reincarnation to the other members of the defense team and had hinted that murder, or violent death, might have something to do with preventing earthquakes.

I didn't take the tape recorder out right away. I wanted to gauge Herb's emotional state first. To my dismay, he was somewhat more paranoid than he had been on my previous visit.

"I can't understand why they won't let me represent myself," he fumed. "It's my life and my future, but Mr. Jackson won't take my suggestions."

"The court is simply concerned that your rights be protected," I told him. "The judge has to be sure that you're mentally competent to stand trial, much less defend yourself."

"I must be declared competent," he said heatedly, "because I am competent. I want you to declare me competent."

"I'm afraid I'm not in a position to do that."

"Why not?" he demanded. "Do you think I'm insane?"

"That's not what I meant at all," I assured him hastily. "What I mean is that the court will probably appoint other impartial psychiatrists to determine your competency to stand trial. I'm retained by the defense. In that sense, I work for you."

"I don't see how they can keep me from pleading guilty. I should be allowed to plead guilty."

"There are several other avenues that should be explored first," I began.

"I understand the laws," he interrupted. "I understand the charges against me, and I understand the various defenses available to me."

"It's a moot point right now, I'm afraid. We have no control over the situation. Even if Mr. Jackson did agree to withdraw and let you represent yourself, you've seen yourself that the judge won't allow it." I decided to try to change the subject. "Last time you said we might go into the reasons for the murders, what you finally realized was your mission in life."

"I've already tried to explain it to Mr. Jackson, so he would know I was competent and would let me defend myself."

"Well, he's only told me a little bit. I'd like to hear it from you so that I get it straight. Now, you said something about reincarnation . . ."

"That's only part of it. It's very complicated."

"Was part of it revenge?" I asked. "I mean, was that why Gianera had to die?"

"Maybe in the beginning, but the main reason, you know, was to avoid the great earthquake that was coming earlier this year. And it was prevented."

OK, I thought, it's now or never. "During my last visit, you said you would think about letting me record some of your more important thoughts," I said. "I think it would be a good idea, to make sure that your very important thoughts are taken down correctly."

"All right," he agreed.

I took the little machine from my briefcase and positioned it on the table so that it would not be in his line of vision as we talked.

"You say that it started with revenge, but that it also had to do with preventing earthquakes, which I guess other people had been doing. Other people were killing other people, which was keeping the earth quiet. In particular the San Andreas fault? Or in general? Or what?"

"All faults," he explained. "We human beings, through the history of the world, have protected our continents from cataclysmic earthquakes by murder. In other words, a minor natural disaster avoids a major natural disaster."

"But if murder is a natural disaster, then why should you be locked up for it, if it's natural and has a good effect?"

"Your laws," he said. "You see, the thing is, people get together, say, in the White House. People like to sing the die song, you know, people like to sing the die song.

"If I am president of my class when I graduate from high school, I can tell two, possibly three young male Homo sapiens to die. I can sing that song to them and they'll have to kill themselves or be killed —an automobile accident, a knifing, a gunshot wound. You ask me why this is? And I say, well, they have to do that in order to protect the ground from an earthquake, because all of the other people in the community had been dying all year long, and my class, we have to chip in so to speak to the darkness, we have to die also. And people would rather sing the die song than murder."

"What is the die song?"

"Just that. I'm telling you to die. I'm telling you to kill yourself, or be killed so that my continent will not fall off into the ocean . . . see, it's all based on reincarnation, this dies to protect my strata."

In contrast to his manner when I arrived, Herb was talking easily now, although his speech was deliberate and precise. He seldom looked at me, which gave me a chance to study him without interfering with his discourse. There was no emotion in his voice whatsoever, and he rarely gestured. For the most part he kept his hands folded in his lap. I almost had the impression of a student explaining a scientific theory during an oral examination.

He told me that if I would prepare a chronology of the world's wars and famines and compare it with a list of major earthquakes throughout history, I would see that when the death rate goes up, the number of earthquakes and other natural disasters goes down. He added that when the death rate drops below about 5 percent of the population, mankind has to protect itself by helping it along. "Therefore," he concluded, "we will always murder."

"You mean not just earthquakes but also floods, tornadoes, hurricanes?"

"Yeah, all of those things. You read in the Bible about Jonah. There were twelve men in the boat, Jonah was in the boat, you know, it was just like Jesus. And Jonah stood up and said, 'God darn, man! If somebody doesn't die, all thirteen of us are going to die.' And he jumped overboard, and he was drowned.

"And the sea, God of the sea, uh . . . well, he died all right, and in about half an hour or so it calmed down, half-hour or hour. I mean, it doesn't happen right away.

"Picture two guys standing together in the bilge after Jonah jumps over, after the storm's all over. Two guys are standing there smoking their pipes after the danger has passed and they say, 'You know, I bet if Jonah hadn't of killed himself, God would have killed all of us.' And they get to town and they go to a bar and they tell the people at the bar about Jonah, and they say, 'We think Jonah saved our life by committing suicide.' And the people at the bar say, 'Well, maybe that will help us,' so they go out and get somebody." He sighed. "So the story goes on."

"According to the story, though, Jonah didn't die," I said. "He was cast up on land by the whale and was still alive, so doesn't that contradict your theory?"

"Well, OK, you're asking me to explain what this means, the swallowing of Jonah. I'm asking you to believe. I'm the typical, how would you say, scapegoat. I'm a scapegoat. I'm asking you to swallow this Jonah story and believe that a minor natural disaster will prevent a major natural disaster. And if you believe it, then you will live, you know, *you,* Homo sapien. I'm not talking to one man, I'm talking to everybody. I'm writing this story so everybody can read it . . . and say, 'Well, here's some guy wrote about Jonah. That sounds like a good one, you know, mankind, Jonah, twelve people, twelve signs, twelve months . . .' "

Twelve plus one, I thought. Twelve apostles plus Jesus made thirteen. Twelve men in the boat plus Jonah added up to thirteen. The mystic number. The last murder occurred on February 13, and Herb had surrendered peacefully. But he had killed only ten people. Or had he? Aloud I started to ask, "Are you writing it out so that . . ."

"No, I'm not going to write anymore. I can't write anymore. You can use stuff like this, but don't use any of my uh . . ." He halted abruptly. "Will this tape be heard by the district attorney?" he asked.

"No, absolutely not. This is not for Mr. Chang, that's for sure."

"Is it for Mr. Chang?"

"I said it is *not,* definitely not. No, Mr. Chang gets nothing from me. In fact, I haven't even seen him for a couple of years. As I said, this is strictly for the defense. I thought you were saying that you wanted a certain part of this story widely known to the people."

"No, I'm telling you about Jonah, the guy who wrote Jonah."

"Oh."

"No, I don't want my story told throughout the world. I don't like the publicity. I don't like what happened to me."

Paranoid schizophrenics often are ambivalent, as Herb was about publishing his theories. In fact, ambivalence is a symptom of the disorder, especially in relationships between the patient and others —love accompanied by hate, trust combined with fear. He continued to talk.

"I wish I had had the self-control to say, 'Well, I'll play the role of the masochist, rather than the role of the sadist.' A sadist gets revenge. A masochist doesn't. A masochist says, 'Well, I see you guys took me for a ride, you put me through *dementia praecox.* I'm just going to let you do it. I'm not going to get revenge.' I wish I did, you know, I wish I would have said, 'Well, I'll just get a job, and a wife and children, and barbecues on the weekend . . .' "

". . . crabgrass on your lawn . . ."

"Yeah, the whole thing."

I had been startled by his use of the term *dementia praecox,* an early term for schizophrenia. Taken from the Latin it means literally "precocious insanity," and was once applied to patients showing signs of melancholia, withdrawal, hallucinations, delusions, and so forth in late adolescence or early adulthood. He obviously had heard the term "paranoid schizophrenia" from other psychiatrists. He must have looked up a synonym in an old dictionary.

"How did they lay *dementia praecox* on you?" I asked. "Was that done through drugs, or how?"

"Well, yeah, you know . . ."

"Do you mean marijuana?"

"Yeah, marijuana. Marijuana induces *dementia praecox,* you know. It furthers *dementia praecox,* is what it does. If Jim Gianera had given me some of the Benzedrine that he was using, if he had sold me Benzedrine while he was using it, then I wouldn't have had this trouble because Benzedrine, I have found as I look back on my experience, causes one to talk and to act . . . as a matter of fact, you become an artist, so to speak, you want to paint, and draw, and carve, and sculpt, you know.

"Benny Bufano?" he continued, invoking the name of one of California's beloved carvers. "Well, he used to take Benzedrine in the morning, and look at the sculptures he had. Right down on San Francisco Wharf he's got a sculpture that I bet is one of the nicest sculptures I've seen. Yeah. Some guy standing there with big long sleeves that you can put things in and stuff."

"That's right, I've seen it."

"Yeah . . . he didn't sell me the Benzedrine, Gianera, because he'd rather have that picture of me for five years in *dementia praecox.* "

I confess it was the first time I had ever heard anyone suggest that Benzedrine was an antidote for schizophrenia, or the effects of marijuana, for that matter. I wondered where he picked up that misconception.

"He would just sell you a lid, but no bennies?" I asked.

"Yeah, and he wouldn't even tell me about the bennies."

"Why do you think he had it in for you, to do that to you?"

"Because I'm a better sadist."

"You mean he was jealous?"

"Yeah."

A long silence followed. I hoped that he would break it himself. After about a minute, I asked, "In terms of reincarnation, do you expect that Gianera will be reincarnated, or already is maybe?"

"I don't know. I'm just saying that everybody I've ever met subconsciously believes in reincarnation, although they won't ever talk about it."

He looked at me with a trace of a smile. "I appreciate your situation. You think you have me going. 'I got him talking now,' this is your position. I'm trying to mimic your subconscious force as it talks to itself: 'The only thing I want to do is to get Herbert Mullin to continue talking and explaining his mind, so that I can have material that I can use to psychoanalyze him, to find out exactly how he works.'"

"That's very good," I said. "That's very close to the truth."

"Yes."

"Are you also getting the vibrations in terms of what I think of what you said?"

"No," he said. "I'd like to hear it."

"Well, I will tell you fairly bluntly, because it's better that you should hear this now than in court where it might come as a surprise. I think that if you get up, or if I get up, or if the attorney gets up and says that you killed people in order to prevent earthquakes, the judge is going to think you're crazy, and he will declare you incompetent, because most people don't believe that killing prevents earthquakes. Most people would raise the question, 'What evidence do you have for this?'

"So I guess that's my next question," I added. "What evidence is there? I'm not aware there is any correlation in 1905 and 1906 of a drop in the murder rate in San Francisco. Are you sure of that? Can you tell me during World War I there were no earthquakes or natural disasters in the world? In World War II?"

"I'm telling you that *you,* as a male Homo sapien, should get yourself a list of the earthquakes that have happened. You should get yourself a list of the death rate per day, you should get yourself a list of the natural disasters like typhoons and things, you know, a chronology . . ."

"Have you ever made such a list?"

". . . from the beginning of written history. That's what you should do, and then we could talk about this."

"We can only talk about it if you have prepared any lists."

"I have begun," he said. "I wrote the United Nations. I went to a library. I started studying the demographic data. They have a yearbook."

"You mean here?" I asked, indicating the jail.

"No, I did it in Santa Cruz."

"Oh, before you were here?"

"When I did it was in December, while I was going through the process of becoming a United States marine."

Here, for the first time, was the possibility of proof that his delusion preceded the murders, that it was not a notion that he had formulated after his arrest to explain his crimes. If we could provide evidence that he had evolved his bizarre beliefs prior to the killings, it would go a long way toward proving he was insane.

"Which library did you get that from?" I asked.

"The main library."

"The main library in Santa Cruz?"

"Uh huh."

"Did you check out the book?"

"Ah, no, you don't check it out. It has to stay with the girl."

"Do they have a record? Did you sign anything?"

"No, nothing."

"You did write to the United Nations at that time roughly? Did you get a reply? Did they answer your letter?"

"Yeah. They said to check the library, the demographic records."

"Oh, I see." What I hadn't seen was the alleged letter from the U.N. It had not been among the papers Jackson had given me. We knew that Herb kept most of his correspondence. I wondered whether the letter was in the hands of the DA. As I was musing over this, he asked me a question.

"Do you believe in reincarnation?"

"In the sense that people come back as . . ."

"People?"

". . . or, some people believe that people come back as animals. Which version are you talking about?"

"Well, I'd just like to know what your interpretation of reincarnation is, and whether you believe in it."

"Well, my general interpretation would be that it is a view that personalities return in other generations in the form of other bodies," I said. "My own view is that I have no evidence to believe or disbelieve that. You certainly see what appear to be striking similarities from time to time between, say, a young person and some deceased person that you might have known or might have known about. I don't know how to account for that. On the other hand, I've never met anybody who seemed to be consciously aware of previous lives. Are you?"

"No, I don't ever recall ever being here before, or being here afterwards. I know that I go to sleep and I wake up, and I don't remember anything in a dream, so when I'm sleeping maybe that's the other life."

"I've heard that idea," I said, "and who knows what happens when you sleep?"

Actually, a great deal is known about what happens during sleep. I was very interested in his remark that he didn't ever remember dreaming. A sleep researcher at Stanford, Bill Dement, has a theory that the hallucinations of schizophrenics may be a dreamlike phenomenon occurring in a waking state. There are two bits of evidence that support this hypothesis. First, studies have shown that schizophrenics seldom experience REM (rapid eye movement) sleep, that period when most dreams occur, so they dream much less than normal people. Second, it is known that if anyone is deprived of sleep long enough, he or she is likely to start hallucinating after a few days.

Although no one claims to know exactly what causes schizophrenia—whether its roots are organic or environmental—research has revealed a number of common denominators. Dement's work has led him to believe there may be something wrong with the sleep mechanisms of schizophrenics, so that dreams occur when they are awake. Since they know they aren't sleeping, logic tells them they can't be dreaming, and they conclude their hallucinations must be real.

We talked for a while about what he was doing to occupy himself in jail, and he promised to give me some of his writings, which he said further detailed his beliefs. I noticed the tattoo on his ankle that said "Kriya Yoga" and asked him about it, but he only replied, "If reincarnation is true, and I hope it is, I hope I will be able to find my way to a situation where I can understand Kriya Yoga perfectly."

He added, however, that he still regarded himself as a Catholic and that he would like to make a confession and receive communion.

"As far as what you've said today goes, the thing that puzzles me is that if you really had in mind preventing a greater natural disaster, then how do you construe this as murder with malice aforethought and so on, if your intention is helpful, to prevent disaster?" I asked.

"Well, I understand the law, you know, I've read the history of the United States. I know that laws are instituted among men. People got together and decided it's against the law to commit murder. And the reason it's against the law is because when a man starts taking other lives, he becomes strong in the next life.

"You know, after I die I'm going to have to be conceived again," he continued. "I believe man has believed in reincarnation, consciously, verbally, for 10,000 years. They believed—they *knew*—this minor natural disaster averts a major natural disaster. Well, they'd let a guy go kill-crazy, you know, he'd go kill-crazy, kill maybe twenty or thirty people. Then they'd lynch him, or they'd have some other kill-crazy person kill him, because they don't want him to get too powerful in the next life. That's what I mean about being a scapegoat for my generation.

"They don't do anything. All they do is sing the die song, you know, 'Go kill something for me.' They don't kill for themselves, the people that make the laws."

"But they also make distinctions between some killers who are murderers and some killers who are not," I argued, "which is the point I was bringing up before. By what you're saying now, that anybody who kills is a murderer, then all the armed forces should be convicted of murder."

"You would have to study military science and police science and the story of Jonah in order to answer those questions," he said impatiently, and added, "Listen, doctor, I think that we've gone far enough today. I'd really like to cut the interview short if we could. I don't want to put any more of my thoughts down."

29
Another Killer

SHORTLY BEFORE midnight on April 23, the desk officer at the Santa Cruz Police Department answered a call from a man who identified himself as Ed Kemper and who said he was in a telephone booth in Pueblo, Colorado. He demanded to speak to Lieutenant Scherer about the "coed murders." When he was informed that Scherer was not on duty, he ordered the officer to summon him and said that he would call back later.

After hanging up, the officer concluded that the caller was drunk and forgot about it.

An hour and a half later, after the shift had changed, another officer refused to accept a collect call from an obvious crackpot in Colorado. He told the operator that if Kemper wanted to talk with Scherer, he would have to call back at 9:00 A.M.

Finally, at 5:00 A.M., a third policeman agreed to listen to Kemper, who said he had been camped in a rented car near the telephone booth for six hours. He was exhausted but highly agitated. He disclosed to the incredulous officer and a colleague listening on an extension that he had murdered six coeds. Further, he said, they would find the bodies of his mother and a friend of hers in her apartment in Aptos. At the officer's suggestion, Kemper obligingly walked from the booth to a nearby intersection, looked at the street signs, came back to the telephone, and recited his location. While the policeman tried to soothe him and keep him talking, his partner telephoned the police in Pueblo and told them to take him into custody.

Kemper was arrested at gunpoint as he stood in the booth, telephone in hand, enthusiastically describing how he had killed eight people and disposed of their bodies. The Pueblo police found three guns and 200 rounds of ammunition in the automobile parked at the curb.

A short time later, Sheriff's Sergeant Mike Aluffi and another detective broke into the apartment at 609A Ord Drive where Kemper said he had lived with his mother, Mrs. Clarnell Strandberg. Since Aptos was unincorporated, it lay within the sheriff's jurisdiction. In one closet they found the nude, beheaded body of Mrs. Strandberg. In another they discovered the corpse of Sara Taylor Hallet, a fellow office worker with Mrs. Strandberg at the University of California. Mrs. Hallet had been strangled, and a plastic bag was tied over her head.

Within a few hours Allufi, Lieutenant Scherer, District Attorney Peter Chang, and an inspector from his office, Dick Verbrugge, had flown to Pueblo to interrogate Kemper. The tale that unfolded during the next few hours was unbelievably grotesque.

Kemper was not unknown to the law enforcement apparatus of Santa Cruz County. He was a shambling giant of a man, six feet nine inches tall and 285 pounds. His brown hair and mustache were always neatly trimmed, and his wire-rimmed glasses gave his hazel eyes an owlish look. He had a reputation as a gentle, soft-spoken guy who enjoyed the company of cops, telling them often he would have sought the same career for himself if his size had not prevented it. He liked to hang out in the Jury Room, a saloon not far from the county courthouse frequented by off-duty policemen, sheriff's officers, and lawyers from the DA's office.

Among other things, the investigators soon learned that the eight murders Kemper had committed in the previous year had not been his first.

The product of a stormy marriage that broke up when he was seven, Kemper, who was two years younger than Mullin, saw little of his father after the separation. He grew quickly and was bedeviled by both the physical and social awkwardness brought on by his size. He began arguing with his mother at an early age, and she tended to punish him by ridicule. He told the investigators he began fantasizing about killing her when he was only a boy.

When he was fourteen, Kemper was shipped from Montana, where he had been living with his mother and two sisters, to stay with his father's parents on their ranch in California. Not long after, because he felt rejected, he shot both his grandparents to death.

Since he was a minor, Kemper was turned over to the California Youth Authority. Owing to the seriousness of his crime, he was transferred to the state hospital at Atascadero, not because he had been found insane but because it provided maximum security. He received little in the way of treatment during the next five years and was sent back to the CYA after his twenty-first birthday. He was subsequently paroled to the custody of his mother.

Mrs. Strandberg, herself a strapping six-footer who was particularly quarrelsome when she had been drinking, had moved to California and had a job at the university in Santa Cruz. He went to work as a road crew flagman, and she never told anyone where her son had been before he came to live with her.

Between May 7, 1972, and February 5, 1973, Kemper picked up six young female hitchhikers and killed them. They included Cynthia Schall, the Cabrillo College student who disappeared on her way to school on January 8, and Alice Liu and Rosalind Thorpe, the two University of California coeds who vanished while hitchhiking on the Santa Cruz campus and whose bodies had been discovered in Alameda County.

As the investigators gathered at the police station in Pueblo listened, speechless, Kemper described how he dissected each of his victims and committed acts of necrophilia.

Early on the morning of April 21, 1973, the day before Easter Sunday, Kemper stole into his mother's bedroom and bludgeoned her to death with a hammer as she slept. Later in the day he invited the friend of hers, Sara Hallet, to the apartment and strangled her immediately after she walked through the door. The purpose for the second murder, he told the authorities, was to make it appear Mrs. Strandberg had gone somewhere for the holiday weekend with her friend.

On Easter morning, Kemper took the cash and credit cards from the purses of the two dead women, wrote an anonymous note taunting the police, loaded his guns and ammunition into Mrs. Hallet's car, and drove off, expecting a nationwide manhunt for the "coed killer." In Reno, he abandoned the car and rented another before continuing his flight eastward, constantly listening to the radio and wondering why no bulletin had been broadcast for his arrest. At one point he thought he had been apprehended, when he was stopped for speeding in Colorado, but the highway patrolman, unaware that he was a mass murderer, let him go.

Finally, when he realized that once again he had concealed his grisly triumphs too well, he called the police in Santa Cruz.

Kemper was returned to California and meekly led a posse of flabbergasted lawmen on a gory hunt for the remains of those of his victims who had not already been found. Because he didn't have the resources to hire an attorney, the task of representing him fell on the hapless Santa Cruz County public defender.

Jim Jackson hired me to examine Kemper, even though I told him that he seemed to fit the profile of a sexual sadist and probably was not insane in the legal sense.

"You know," I added, "Peter Chang may be right. You might be living in the murder capital of the world."

"Maybe it's something in the water," Jackson said.

"No," I told him, "but it has to be one of the goddamndest coincidences in history."

Although it would be some time before any one took the time to figure it out statistically, Chang's offhand remark contained a great deal of truth. During the period that Kemper and Mullin were on their rampages, the murder rate per 100,000 population (the measurement used by the FBI) quintupled in Santa Cruz County. It attained the dubious honor of leading the nation in homicide.

I had seen Herb once in the time between his explanation to me of the "Jonah Theory" and the day of Kemper's return to Santa Cruz. He went into detail about his belief in reincarnation and provided me with more of his writings. During the same period, the defense investigators talked to more of his acquaintances and other members of his family. Gradually, a picture of his life emerged that provided a context for his psychosis, including his delusions and hallucinations. The pieces of the puzzle were finally falling into place.

Herb's twenty-sixth birthday, April 18, 1973, came and went without any particular notice, other than a couple of cards. Although we didn't know it at the time, the date had great significance for him.

As mentioned earlier, there are a number of hypotheses about the causes of schizophrenia, including organic imbalances or genetic defects. The fact remains that no single cause has been identified for what is the most common mental illness known to man, affecting one in a hundred human beings. In Herb's case, though, we eventually were able to chronicle his symptoms in remarkable detail and to identify some of the influences that shaped his beliefs.

His parents had no way of knowing during his childhood that Herb was tortured by sexual tensions, religious doubts, and ambivalent feelings toward them, especially his father. There's a perfectly good reason for this—Herb didn't know it himself until he was an adult and began to brood about it. For example, the remark his sister made to Harold about his disappointment when his family moved to San Francisco and he was unable to take the school bus to kindergarten was based on something Herb told her years later. He doubtless experienced no conscious feelings of persecution when he was five or six, but in retrospect he genuinely was convinced that the move was part of a sadistic attempt by his parents to "retard my social and sexual awareness."

Bill Mullin was a strict disciplinarian who loved his children but revealed little warmth to them. He was a man whose high point of achievement had come when he served as an army captain. After that, he held a succession of fairly dull jobs, providing a livelihood that assured his family of a stable but ordinary middle-class existence. Both at home and in parochial schools, Herb was taught an almost absolutist moral code.

In San Francisco the boy was separated from the children in his neighborhood because he did not attend the local public school. As a result, he had no close friends and, to a degree, suffered from loneliness and alienation. It was not until he transferred to the high school in Felton in 1963 that he found close companions his own age and began dating.

Even in the freer environment of San Lorenzo Valley High, his father expected rigid obedience. In November 1963, Herb cut his afternoon classes with some of his newfound friends. It was a couple of weeks before his parents were routinely notified of his unauthorized absence by school officials. That same night Bill Mullin wrote a letter to the principal: "Believe me, both Mrs. Mullin and I are shocked to learn of this infraction of the rules . . . I have taken a measure of discipline as a parent . . . I understand that Herbert must compose a thousand-word thesis and spend brunch periods in your office until the lost time in school is made up. I am in agreement with this as just and proper. . . ."

The theme Herb was assigned was "Justice." In his essay, the sixteen-year-old youth revealed a lot about his training:

The laws are the regulations designed to help protect the people. . . . Justice is the quality of being right or correct. . . . Thus we can see that if one has the quality of being fair and correct and right, then he certainly will obey the laws.

The true honest man will not lie, cheat or steal. In other words, he is completely truthful and trustworthy.

Justice is the foundation of a good country, good state, good family and good man. . . . Along with justice comes honesty. . . . Under honesty we discussed cheating and all the possibilities that are open to people today who may want to cheat. This is a bad thing and surely the work of the Devil. . . .

Nonetheless, Herb was happier than he had ever been. He scored high in his achievement tests in Felton, and his grades generally improved over those he earned at the Catholic high school in San Francisco. Even after he began dating Loretta, his most intimate friend remained Dean Richardson, a handsome, self-assured young man who was the valley's premier athlete. In contrast to his years in San Francisco, Herb was now part of the top group in the teen-age caste system. Even his father's harsh reaction when he and a group of his buddies were picked up for having beer in their car didn't tarnish the pleasure of being envied by underclassmen for having had a dangerous adventure.

In addition to football, Herb played basketball and baseball, and he was vice president of the Varsity Club in his senior year. He was also a member of the honorary Key Club and was elected chairman of his twelfth-grade "Sneak Day." During the summers he worked part-time at Johnnie's Super, a market in Boulder Creek, and at Vic and Bill's Service Station in Santa Cruz. In the spring of 1965 he showed an almost cocky self-confidence when he filled out his pre-graduation questionnaire: "I pride myself on my ability to work hard and efficiently. My employers have always respected my ability. . . . They have also enjoyed my personality, with them and their customers."

After getting his high school diploma, Herb went back to work that summer at the service station. One day Jeff Alongi, a life insurance agent from San Jose, drove in and approached him as a prospect. Herb told him he didn't need insurance and refused to make an appointment to talk about it.

In August, a month before they were to start classes together at Cabrillo, Dean died in the automobile accident. Herb was desolate. He felt he had been betrayed. The most important person in his life had been taken from him. It was as if a promise had been broken by God. Neither had expressed any homosexual feelings toward one another; in fact they had double-dated and bragged about imaginary feats of heterosexual prowess. But Herb had suffered his first loss of someone he loved. He was unable to accept the cliché that death is God's will. Earlier in the year, in the spring before commencement, Herb had asked for his parents' permission to live that summer with Dean at "Baker's Rest," his uncle's cabin, but they had refused. For years he was haunted by the belief that if they had been allowed to stay together, Dean would not have been in the car the night of the accident.

No one had any reason to see his despondency and ritualistic grief as early symptoms of schizophrenia, which many psychiatrists believe can be triggered by a deep disappointment.

A short time after the accident, Alongi looked up Herb again. Now keenly aware of mortality, he agreed to buy a $10,000 life insurance policy.

Many members of Herb's high school class also attended Cabrillo that fall, and he began to pal around with those who had known Dean, including Jim Gianera. The following March, in 1966, Herb went to the beach with Jim. Jim produced a marijuana cigarette and lighted it. He offered one to Herb, who refused at first but finally accepted it. It was a month before he tried marijuana again. After that, he used it occasionally with friends, more often than not buying his supply from Gianera.

Jim told Herb he believed the war in Vietnam was corrupt. The previous summer, United States forces began their first all-out offensive as combatants rather than "advisers," and President Johnson had announced that draft calls would be doubled to augment the 125,000 American troops already there. Antiwar rallies were becoming larger and more frequent, and in spite of a wavering consensus backing the administration in the House and Senate, the first congressional critics, led by Senator Fulbright, were beginning to be heard.

Gianera's view by no means yet represented the unanimous opinion of Herb's contemporaries. Some of them submitted willingly to conscription, while others joined the armed forces. Herb himself planned to enlist in the Army Corps of Engineers when he finished college. But Gianera insisted the only honorable path was to resist, either by leaving the country or becoming a conscientious objector. Herb disagreed, but he began to doubt.

In June Herb finished his first year of college with a B average in civil highway technology, and he got a summer job with the county road crew. He also broke up with Loretta, but he did not date other girls. Instead he occupied himself with his work and scuba diving lessons.

In October, a month after starting his sophomore year, Herb had his first experience with LSD at a friend's cabin in the mountains. He found it unpleasant and frightening. That fall and winter he worked hard in school, at the same time holding down a part-time service station job. In January of 1967 he and Loretta started dating again, and a short time later they became engaged.

By that spring Herb's friends had noticed subtle changes in his character. He had widened his circle of acquaintances to include a number of young men who had not been classmates of his in high school, among them Ed Lawrence and Ernie Keller. He shared marijuana and LSD with them and was exposed for the first time to some of the spiritual values that grew out of the flower generation. He was still mourning the loss of Dean Richardson. He began to look for answers by reading about eastern religions, especially those that embraced reincarnation.

After graduating from Cabrillo and putting in another summer with the road crew, Herb moved into a boardinghouse in San Jose, enrolled as student at the state college there, and got a job as a dishwasher in a neighborhood dive near the campus. For some time he had been afraid he was a homosexual. He knew he had ambivalent feelings about women and found himself occasionally attracted to men, but homosexuality was a sin, and he feared for his immortal soul. He looked for more forgiving alternatives to Catholicism, and he withdrew from college to devote himself full-time to the study of Hinduism, specifically the disciplines of yoga. But his roots in Christianity were too deep for him to turn his back altogether. He began to try to rationalize a common ground for the two faiths.

Herb's preoccupation with Richardson's death and his study of religions gradually brought him to the belief that war was immoral after all. In January of 1968, after returning home from the month spent working for his brother-in-law at the Christmas tree lot in San Francisco, he decided to become a conscientious objector.

That same month he made love to a man for the first time, a friend he had met in the drug culture of Santa Cruz.

His acceptance of his apparent bisexuality alternated with feelings of self-loathing generated by his years of moral conditioning. Those close to Herb blamed drugs for the evident mutation in his personality. It didn't occur to any of them, including his parents, that several of his companions were using greater quantities of the same substances with no long-term effects.

30

From Probationer
to Patient

As we continued to prepare for the trial, it became more and
more obvious that we would have to be able to give the jurors a
complete picture of Herb's life so they could understand how his
mental illness had developed and how it had led him to kill. By the
beginning of May, that portrait had been completed, with details
supplied by potential witnesses as well as Herb himself, whose confidence in us appeared to be growing.

In April of 1968, a month after he broke up with Loretta for the
last time, Herb was arrested on the marijuana charge by a sheriff's
deputy who found him asleep in the mountains. His parents were
unaware he was in custody until they received a letter from him in
jail six days later:

Bill and Jean,
    As I have mentioned in the past, someday I would meet the establish-
ment head-on. I was arrested on April 21, '68. That day the GAME
started. I requested and was appointed a public defender. I have yet to
speak with him.

The charges against me are (a) camping by the SL River; (b) possession of paraphernalia used for smoking a narcotic; (c) possession of a restricted dangerous drug without a prescription. The trial is set for May 16, 10 A.M.

As I have tried to explain, I am a student of eastern thought. But, because I was baptized a Roman Catholic, I have the gift of Christianity.

Both these philosophies agree that all things of the body and senses, and all states and activities of the mind are merely phenomena, temporary playthings.

My present imprisonment is, in an eternal sense, self-induced. A necessary event in this body's wave (birth to death). Remember the ocean. A wave is the ocean and the ocean is the wave.

Your earthly son, Herb.

His appalled father posted $625 bail and brought Herb home. On May 16 Herb was allowed to plead guilty to an amended complaint of visiting a place where narcotics were being used and was placed on a year's probation. In June he began working as a management trainee at Goodwill Industries. A month later he was transferred to San Luis Obispo as manager of the thrift store there, living in a small apartment.

His letters during this period to his parents and his sister were chatty, coherent, and full of news of his job and descriptions of the people he met. He wrote to Mrs. Bocca that he was relieved to have his ordeal with the draft board over and that he was looking forward to the next two years. Thus, they were all surprised when he returned to Felton in February of 1969 and declared that he was going to India to study religion. They persuaded him to move to the Boccas' ranch instead. A month later he was a patient at the Mendocino State Hospital.

During the next six weeks, Herb was treated with antipsychotic medication and was examined several times by different psychiatrists. He explained his episode of mimicking Al Bocca by saying, "I thought I was doing what my brother-in-law was telling me to do." He also said he heard "voices which tell me what to do," his first admission of hallucinations. One doctor noted, "At present he has a phobia about meeting gay people. His fear is that he might be over-forward. He was quite guarded when asked about homosexual experiences, and after a while gave a sigh, indicating that it was very difficult for him to talk about the subject."

When asked about his father, Herb said only that he had disliked their periodic sparring matches as a child, but now that his father was older, "I feel I can outmatch him."

The hospital records that Cartwright had finally unearthed from the archives of the State Department of Mental Hygiene showed that Herb was generally uncooperative with the treatment program at Mendocino. He did talk to some of the other patients, primarily about yoga, and at one point he told a psychiatric social worker that he "listened for cosmic emanations for guidance."

On May 9, 1969, Herb was released at his own insistence. Because he was a voluntary patient, he could not be held against his will. His discharge evaluation concluded, "Schizophrenic reaction, chronic undifferentiated type . . . prognosis is poor." He was now twenty-two years old and had been revealing some symptoms of schizophrenia for nearly four years. The best hope for schizophrenics is early—and sustained—treatment.

Herb knew that he was mentally ill but, like his parents, he believed it had been brought on by drugs. Since marijuana was the substance he used most often, he deduced that it caused "dementia praecox," the old term for what the doctors told him was his affliction.

After leaving the hospital, Herb drifted with another just-released patient to Lake Tahoe and found a job as a two-dollar-an-hour dishwasher at Harvey's Wagon Wheel, a gambling resort on the south shore. He stayed there, living with the young man, until August, when he quit and moved back to his parents' home. A few days later a forest ranger named Ron Lang came upon a lean-to near Inspiration Point in Cowell State Park. Herb was inside, sitting with his legs crossed and staring straight ahead as if in a trance.

"Did you cut down these trees?" Lang demanded, pointing to the fir saplings that had been used to make the shelter. He received no reply. "What's your name? Do you have any ID?" Still no answer.

After trying for several minutes to get Herb to move or talk, the ranger warned him that he would remove him by force if he didn't leave voluntarily. Without shifting his gaze, Herb slipped his hand slowly behind his back. Lang lunged and grabbed his arm just before his fingers reached a large hunting knife on the ground in the lean-to. The ranger summoned help with his walkie-talkie, and they took Herb to the county jail. He was released without being booked.

Still convinced that narcotics were the basis of his problems, Herb began treatment as a resident at the community drug abuse prevention center in Santa Cruz. At the same time he renewed his contacts with friends in the local counterculture. During this time he drove to Sebastopol with Ed Lawrence, and the two young men terrified Al Bocca's father by undressing and beating their chests. Herb had started to believe that Lawrence was a magician and that Ernie Keller was a powerful guru. Although they thought he was weird, Lawrence and Keller tolerated and even encouraged his antics.

After a month Herb moved out of the drug center, quit his job, and applied for welfare. In late October he packed his Volkswagen and drove south to San Luis Obispo for a brief visit with a friend, a young man who had preceded him as manager of the Goodwill store.

His host was disturbed when Herb told him he was "hearing voices" and "receiving messages." Although he had experienced hallucinations before, now the voices were commanding him to do things. When they told him to shave his head, he did. When the voices ordered him to burn his penis, he touched a lighted cigarette to it.

When he finally tried to make forceful homosexual advances, his friend called his own uncle, a physician, who came to the house. Although he was not a psychiatrist, the doctor recognized Herb's symptoms immediately. In a conversation with Cartwright later he said, "I told my nephew, 'This guy is a paranoid schizophrenic, and he's dangerous, because paranoid people go out and kill people, and we have to do something quickly.' He didn't appear to be under the influence of drugs."

With the help of sheriff's deputies, Herb was committed in the early hours of October 31 to the psychiatric ward at the San Luis Obispo County General Hospital because "as a result of a mental disorder [he] is a danger to others, a danger to himself and gravely disabled." That afternoon, he composed an amiable letter to his parents telling them where he was.

"I brought my Bible," he wrote, "and as far as I can see, everything will be all right. The staff are very good people, and the patients and I have established a good friendship. The food is average, of course. Please write when you can." He signed himself, "Your loving son, Herb." This letter led to the painful confrontation on the beach during which he professed to his parents that he was a homosexual.

Herb's stay at the psychiatric ward was slightly longer than his previous hospitalization. For the next eight weeks he was treated by Joseph Middleton, a psychiatrist who confirmed the diagnosis of paranoid schizophrenia. He showed only slight improvement when given antipsychotic drugs that usually alleviate hallucinations and delusions.

From the hospital Herb wrote letters to his doctors, parents, and several politicians and public figures who had never heard of him, detailing his religious beliefs. He carried his Bible and exhorted his fellow patients to help him change "the spiritual nature of the world." The doctor described his thinking as "paralogical, bizarre, and grandiose." In mid-November Herb wrote his parents:

> The doctors here seem to want to transfer me to a state hospital. I would appreciate it if you would write Doctor Middleton a letter telling him that you think I should still read inspirational literature by Paramahansa Yogananda. He is my spiritual guru no matter what these people say. I would appreciate your support here.

Herb pressured his father and the hospital to release him. County hospitals in California are not equipped to provide long-term psychiatric care, and beds in the remaining state hospitals were becoming scarce. They finally agreed, but only on the condition that he become an outpatient at the Santa Cruz Mental Health Clinic. He was discharged with his prognosis listed as "grave" on November 23. The following day he reported to the clinic in Santa Cruz.

For the next seven months, Herb visited the clinic intermittently. Although medication was prescribed, he didn't take it regularly, and his attendance at group therapy sessions was sporadic. He got a job as a busboy at the Holiday Inn on Ocean Street, and in March he moved into a cheap hotel near the beach. In addition to various religions, he was now reading about astrology and numerology. A social worker at the clinic later noted, "Around May of 1970 Herb began to branch out a bit and make a concerted effort at being more actively involved in life. This included dating, attendance at various peace organizations, and once again taking up his pursuit of religious perfection within the yoga discipline. I was never clear as to whether this constituted some sort of deterioration or progress."

31
Einstein's Sacrifice

WHILE HERB was in group therapy in Santa Cruz, his friend, Ed Lawrence, introduced him to a group of people living in a commune in an old house in Santa Cruz. He wanted to move in, but his weird behavior made the residents reluctant to accept him. One night he told one of the women living there, a Japanese, that she and he should have a biracial child together. When she rebuffed him, he picked up a hatchet and smashed it against the fireplace.

The one person in the commune who hit it off with Herb was Pat Brown, a woman later described as having the mentality of a child. Her conduct was even stranger than his, and they became soulmates instantly. She convinced him that he should go to Hawaii. The day after he arrived on Maui (and she had abandoned him), he sought voluntary admission to the island's mental health clinic, asking for group psychotherapy. Later a clinical psychologist there summarized the next few weeks in a letter to Cartwright:

The social work intake notes described him as a "soft-spoken, superficially gentle and friendly person. But at times, there were brief guarded

and suspicious reactions which he tried to conceal with a bland façade."
. . . His personality profile indicated strong aggressive impulses which
were tenuously controlled by denial and a passive stance. He attended
two group sessions, during the first of which he became increasingly
agitated. He was . . . admitted as a voluntary patient to the Maui Memorial Hospital on July 10, 1970. He was examined by [a psychiatrist] who
reported, ". . . He has lately had insomnia and fearful fantasies. He is not
able to accept his own hostile feelings and uses massive denial or tension
symptoms. He is passive, though impulsive. Diagnosis: schizophrenia,
schizo-affective type."

According to nursing notes, his course in hospital was marked by
several bizarre incidents such as wandering off the ward to look for work
while dressed in a hospital gown (being returned by police), repeated
requests for LSD, ingesting whatever drugs he could steal, and engaging
others in discussions of yoga and his desire to spread nonviolence. Medi-
cations included Thorazine and Stelazine. He was discharged as improved on July 17, 1970, with the diagnosis of schizophrenia, chronic
undifferentiated type. His parents were contacted about returning him to
California for continued treatment, and on July 23, 1970, he reported
receiving $101; however, he needed $10 more for the inter-island fare. He
went to an office to make a telephone call, and a frightened secretary
called the police. Lt. Cravalho, who had earlier established good relationships with Mr. Mullin, arrived and took him to the airport.

Shortly after returning from Hawaii and terrifying his parents
with his psychotic rantings on the way home from San Francisco,
Herb agreed to return to the Santa Cruz mental health clinic. Two
days later, on July 30, a police officer arrested him for being under
the influence of drugs and possession. In fact, his outlandish conduct
on the street, persistently proselytizing passersby in the name of
yoga, was a result of his psychosis, and the drugs in his pockets were
Stelazine and Thorazine, both antipsychotics prescribed by a psychiatrist. Deprived of the medication in jail, he became hyperactive and
sang loudly. When he was dragged into municipal court, demanding
the judge legalize marijuana and LSD, he was committed as an
emergency case to the county hospital psychiatric ward. In his ad-
mittance report, a physician noted, "The patient states that he has
been hospitalized . . . with a diagnosis of chronic undifferentiated
schizophrenia, which the patient describes as: 'Don't know if I want
to make love with a man, don't know if I want to make love with

a woman, don't know if I want to make love with myself. . . .' " The doctor agreed with the earlier diagnoses.

After the charges were dropped, the hospital had to release Herb under the California law that limits holding involuntary mental patients to seventy-two hours. He did begin to attend regular group therapy sessions with a psychiatric social worker, however.

Herb's realization that he was seriously ill led him to apply for readmission to Cabrillo College in August, this time to study psychology. But he failed to keep his counseling appointment.

Following his discharge from the hospital, Herb stayed in a succession of rented rooms. Then, on September 28, he wrote a conciliatory letter to his father:

Dear Dad,

I have some thoughts on my mind, and I'd like to express them to you.

My friends are working with their parents. I don't think you and I have worked with and for each other for a long time.

My conscientious objection thing was against your will. Well, that is past now. I don't know who was right or who was wrong. All I know is that I got hurt real bad because of all the confusion.

Would you let me live in your home again?

Love, Herb.

He stayed at home for a few weeks, but whatever understanding he hoped to achieve with his father failed to materialize. His hostilities began to return, and he moved out again, abruptly stopped group therapy, and changed the beneficiary of his life insurance policy from his parents to UNICEF. That same month he got a job driving a truck for Goodwill Industries. There, a casual friendship with a coworker deepened into a homosexual liaison.

In March 1971, he spent ten days in jail after an arrest for being drunk in public, one of the few times he ever drank enough to become intoxicated. In April his case was closed at the mental health clinic because he had failed to keep therapy appointments, and in May he quit his job as a truck driver and moved to San Francisco.

Herb's condition continued to deteriorate as he floated from one fifteen-dollar-a-week room to another in the city's Tenderloin. Along with most of the people he befriended there, many of them former mental patients themselves, he lived on welfare.

He began to try to codify his beliefs about birth and death and sought explanations for the hallucinations that, for him, were reality. When his new friend, Allan Hanson, confirmed his theory of reincarnation but told him that telepathy was a gift not available to ordinary mortals, he began to believe that he had been chosen by Providence to enjoy knowledge withheld from others, for he *knew* he heard telepathic voices. He haunted the library, reading about the occult, reincarnation, and astrology. He became fascinated with the works of Leonardo da Vinci and tried to ape the master by recording his own revelations in backward script. (Some historians believe that Leonardo was paranoid, and that his mirror writings were an attempt to encrypt his notes so others could not read them.)

In the fall, Herb mailed his life insurance policy to his parents for safekeeping. A short time later, they received a harsh letter:

> To Jean and Bill:
> I have made a mistake in sending you the life insurance policy . . . I would appreciate it if you would immediately send the policy to the Donnelly Hotel, 1272 Market St., San Francisco, California, c/o Herbert Mullin. I will be able to pick it up there.
> Please don't bother me with letters. I AM CERTAIN WE SHOULD NOT COMMUNICATE WITH EACH OTHER FOR A LONG TIME.
> Respectfully, HERBERT MULLIN.

Part of Herb's ambivalence centered on his feelings toward his father. Although he had begun irrationally to blame his parents for concealing the secret knowledge of reincarnation, telepathy, and homosexuality from him as a child, at the same time he wanted to prove that he was capable of accomplishing something in a man's world. He decided he would win an amateur boxing championship and took up training at the gym in San Francisco.

By the beginning of 1972, Herb fancied himself a serious artist and talked about his work with his acquaintances. In fact his sketches were crude and revealed an aberrant mentality. He filled notebooks with disjointed ruminations about Dean Richardson, birth, and death.

From the time he was a teen-ager in San Francisco, Herb had known that his birthday was the same date as the great earthquake of 1906—April 18—but he had never attached any significance to that. Now he began to wonder. At the San Francisco library he had sought out nontechnical works by and about Albert Einstein. He thought a mind that could grasp the universe must have had the power of telepathy and knowledge of reincarnation. By accident, reading the flyleaf on a posthumous anthology of essays and letters, Herb discovered that Einstein had died on his own eighth birthday, April 18, 1955. He was exhilarated. This could not be coincidence. Earthquakes, birth, death, sacrifice—somehow, the date had to be the key to the voices that haunted him, to hold the answer to the meaning of life.

As he struggled to sort out these ideas, Herb conducted his life in a relatively normal fashion. As are many schizophrenics, he was capable of handling the day-to-day chores of living. In March, he answered an ad in a Peninsula newspaper and bought the fourteen-year-old Chevrolet station wagon from a young man in Menlo Park. He raised the $200 purchase price by selling his moribund Volkswagen and borrowing the rest against his insurance policy. Although he was evicted from the Oregon Hotel in May for hitting a drunk who approached him in the lobby, he quickly found another room at the Elwoods Hotel. In June he bought a tennis racket, but he never used it.

It is not uncommon for schizophrenics to go into periods of remission, sometimes spontaneously. Throughout the history of his illness, Herb experienced such periods, which his friends and relatives misinterpreted as the result of being "off drugs." In the summer of 1972 his attitude toward his parents softened, and he exchanged friendly letters with them. Later in June he drove to Felton for a visit. His father's mother had come down from Oregon and was staying for the summer, and Herb cheerfully offered to sleep on the couch. When he returned to the city he wrote a thank-you note that amazed his parents, in view of his hostility six months earlier:

Dear Mom and Dad and Grandma,

    Hi, how are you? Thank you very much for such a nice time this past weekend. I really enjoyed seeing and talking with you. The food was just great, and I do so enjoy the mountains. The weather here in San Francisco is just fine. Foggy in the evenings but sunny and warm during the mornings and afternoons.

Again, thank you for such a pleasant weekend. We'll have to do it again someday.

Love, Herb.

From the time he left the Elwoods Hotel in July until he moved back to Felton in September, Herb tried desperately to find employment. He wrote letters to companies all over the country, from an Alaska fishing fleet to a national grocery chain. He saw an ad for a bartending school, filled out an application, and paid a seventy-five-dollar deposit, but never attended a class. Following the conversation with his cousin, Richard Watson, he registered to take an architecture course at San Francisco State College, but he was dropped when he failed to show up.

Another symptom of paranoia is projection, blaming one's failures or antisocial acts on others. Herb could not accept that his own ambivalence or lack of initiative or bizarre conduct were accountable for his inability to get a job. The fault for his condition had to lie elsewhere.

Early in September he drove to Felton, but his mother and father were away. That afternoon he purchased a fifty-five dollar tape recorder, took it to his parents' home and let himself in through an unlocked bedroom window. He stayed for the weekend, writing, drawing, and occasionally recording rambling fragments of the complicated delusion he finally had designed to explain the relationship between his birthdate, the San Francisco earthquake, and Einstein's death.

It had taken us almost four months to piece together the elements of the grandiose theory that Herb had evolved over a period of years. Now we could explain it in terms a jury could comprehend, how murder became the logical consequence of an illogical premise. Most important, it was plain that it was not an idea he had concocted after his arrest to justify his crimes.

By September of 1972 Herb *knew* that reincarnation worked both forward and backward in time, that he not only could be born again in the future, but also in the past. It had become obvious to him that Einstein had died to protect him and all beings born on April 18 from dying in the great disaster of his generation, the Vietnam war. Now Herb, as had Dean, must make a sacrifice to prevent a repeat of the earthquake that had occurred on his birthday, that was predicted for a few months hence. He considered suicide, but one life would not be enough. To prevent so great a cataclysm would require a bigger commitment, both to avert it and to guarantee his birth position in the next (or past) life. Still, he wanted empirical proof. He would write to the Department of Health, Education and Welfare, and to the United Nations for statistics on births and deaths, and compare them with historical disasters.

Why hadn't his parents explained all this to him before, he wondered? He determined they must be killjoy sadists, afraid of the power he would have in the next life if he knew the truth. Well, he did know the truth. It was so simple. But perhaps he should not confront them with it just yet.

Before his parents returned, he packed his tape recorder and drove back to San Francisco. A few days later he visited his sister and, on September 15, with the permission of his mother and father, he returned to Felton to live permanently.

The knowledge had been revealed to him that he must kill. He didn't know how to go about it. He didn't want to kill anyone, but he was the appointed scapegoat for his generation.

32
Thirteen Victims

NOT LONG AFTER he returned to Felton, Herb drove down to Carmel to visit his aunt and uncle, Bernice and Enos Fouratt, a middle-aged couple who had no children of their own. She was his mother's sister, and the elderly parents of the two women, Mr. and Mrs. Herbert C. Baker, also lived in Carmel. The Fouratts were not at home, so Herb waited beside his car.

When Bernice Fouratt pulled into the driveway that afternoon she saw the form of a man in a long black coat leaning over the fender of an old station wagon. Alarmed, she pushed down the latch buttons on the doors to her car. She was glad she had taken the two dogs with her when she went shopping.

As her automobile came parallel to the station wagon, Mrs. Fouratt recognized her nephew. She did not know he had moved home, and she was startled to see him. She braked and rolled her window down a couple of inches.

"What do you want, Herb?" she asked.

"Aunt Bernice, there are certain days during the month, . . ." he began, very seriously. "Here, I've got it all figured out that you can become pregnant."

"Herb, that's ridiculous," she said. "Please go away."

"But I have it all figured out."

"Just go away Herb."

He glared at her for a moment. She held her breath. The larger of the two dogs in the back of the car began to bark. Slowly, Herb walked back to the station wagon, backed out of the driveway, and pulled away.

Mrs. Fouratt waited a minute to make sure he was gone, then darted into the house, locked the doors, and telephoned her husband at his nearby real estate office. The Fouratts were familiar with Herb's strange conduct. Several months earlier, while he was living in San Francisco, he had visited and offered to explain yoga. His grandparents, both in their eighties, were at the Fouratt home at the time. When Herb started to take off his clothes, Fouratt hustled him outdoors and made him leave. Not long after that he had showed up at the door, walked in without being invited, and demanded of Fouratt, "Uncle, I want to know if your balls are bigger than mine."

Now, in September, the Fouratts both agreed that Herb should be in an asylum.

Bill Mullin had made inquiries about long-term psychiatric care for his son already. The results made him and his wife despair. By late 1972 most of the state hospitals that had not already been closed by the Reagan administration were in the process of shutting down. The money that had been appropriated earlier by the congress to build and staff community-based mental health centers had been cut back and, in a matter of months, would be eliminated altogether. Herb had never been in the armed forces, so the facilities of the Veterans Administration were closed to him. A private hospital at that time would have cost about $100 a day. It was obvious that the Santa Cruz outpatient clinic could not provide the kind of treatment Herb needed. Besides, he refused to go there anymore.

There was nothing they could do. The helpless family could only pray that Herb didn't hurt anybody.

On May 2, 1973, Harold Cartwright left a telephone message for me at my office. It sounded urgent.

"You're going to see Herb in the next couple of days, aren't you?" he asked, after I called him back.

"Yeah. What's up?"

"I had a talk with him today at the jail," he said. "I wired myself up with a Fargo unit so I could record the conversation without him knowing it. We're having a copy of the tape made for you now."

"Why the concealed recorder?"

"He'd been saying things recently, almost like he was dropping hints . . ."

"What did he say?"

"Well, for one thing, he killed the priest."

I whistled. "What do you mean, for one thing?"

"He says he killed Mary Guilfoyle, the girl whose skeleton they found about the same time he was arrested, and an old wino back on October 13."

"I don't suppose there's any chance he's making this up?"

"You'd get a better reading on that, but I don't think so. He gave me too many details that I doubt have ever been in the papers."

"That would make thirteen murders," I said. "I wonder . . ." I turned my desk calendar to the first page, the one containing the months of 1972. "Of course. October 13 was a Friday."

Two days later, Herb and I sat in the now-familiar interview room at the San Mateo County Jail. He had agreed to discuss the telepathic messages he had received after moving home the previous September. His hallucinations had started then to distill themselves into the voice of his father.

"When did you hear him for the first time?" I asked. "Telepathically, I mean."

"Right after I came home last fall. My father was up on the roof, working on the roof, and I heard his voice. He said, 'People have been abusing your trusting nature too long, and people who have been abusing you should be killed.'"

"Did you reply?"

"I said telepathically, 'I will not obey an order unless it is a verbal order.' He came right back at me and said, 'Goddamit, why can't you ever give me something?'"

"You couldn't see him while all of this was going on?"

"No. I was in the house."

I thought of something. "Did you hear any voices, or get any commands when you mimicked your brother-in-law that night at the dinner table, before you went to Mendocino?"

"Not that I can can remember, but I feel that I was under my father's control, like a robot."

"Are these messages always similar to spoken voices?"

"Yeah. Sometimes I couldn't tell the difference between a telepathic message and what somebody was saying to me out loud, you know."

Herb described his visits to his aunt and uncle and said that he thought he should pray for them so they would become more powerful in the next life and could have children. He had decided he would like to be reborn as their son, perhaps sometime during World War II. During my previous visit he had explained the whole family was part of the "Herbert C. Baker Dynasty," named for his maternal grandfather in Carmel.

"Enos worried that my father was more powerful than him, so he communicated with me telepathically that I should kill him."

"Kill your father?"

"Yeah."

"Why didn't you?"

"My father overheard the communication, and he told me to kill Enos instead. I refused, but my parents had been working on me since I came home, to make me kill-crazy. They wanted me to do it anyway."

"Who was the first person you killed?" I asked.

"Lawrence White."

"When?"

"October 13, 1972."

"Were you aware at the time that it was Friday the 13th?"

"I think I remember that it was," he said.

"What happened?"

"I was driving down Highway 9, and I saw this old man walking along. He was like Jonah in the Bible, he was telling me, you know, telepathically, 'Hey, man, pick me up and throw me over the boat. Kill me so that others will be saved.' "

"Saved from the coming earthquake?"

"Yeah."

He described how he beat White to death, hid his body, drove home, and cleaned the bloody baseball bat.

"How did you know his name?" I asked.

"I read it in a newspaper a few days later."

"You haven't seen the name since?"

"No."

Three days after the murder, Herb changed the beneficiary of his insurance back to his parents. A week after that, he continued, he was driving on Soquel Boulevard near Cabrillo College when he saw a teacher he had known when he went to school there. As he passed the man standing on a street corner, he heard his voice.

"He said, 'I want you to kill me somebody,' " he recalled.

"This was a telepathic message?"

"Oh, yes. I didn't have the window open."

"Did the voice say who should die?"

"No. I went home to think about it. I was reading *The Agony and the Ecstasy* by Irving Stone. It's a book about Michelangelo."

"I've read it."

"Well, it's all about how Michelangelo spent hours and hours secretly dissecting bodies so he could find out about the form of the human body for his painting and sculpture and stuff. That's why his work was so much better than anyone else's. It gave him insights others didn't have. It was like Leonardo."

"Had you been reading the book for a long time? Did you have it in San Francisco?"

"No, my mother recommended that I read it. I had read about Michelangelo before, but not this book. I think she was trying to tell me what to do, so that I could have this insight too."

"What did you do?"

"The next day I saw Mary Guilfoyle hitchhiking at Cabrillo. It was about 3:30 in the afternoon."

"Did you know her?"

"No."

"Then how did you know her name."

"I saw her picture in the paper afterwards."

"What happened?"

"I picked her up and drove her to a sidestreet and stabbed her in the chest and twice in the back with my Finn Double-X hunting knife." He went on to portray his clumsy attempt at anatomical research in the forest. He told me what she had been wearing and the condition in which he left the body. There could be no doubt that he was telling the truth.

"Who was the next to die?" I asked.

"The priest in Los Gatos." I decided not to ask why he had denied that murder earlier. According to Cartwright, Herb's account matched perfectly the reconstruction of the crime by the police, including details only the killer could have known.

"Why were you in Los Gatos that day?" I inquired instead.

"I went to San Francisco in the morning," he related. "I drove up to make a ten-dollar interest payment on the loan I took out on my insurance. I had to go to the main office because it was the last day it was due. On the way back, I stopped at the Westlake shopping center and bought a half-pint of whiskey and some beer."

"How much beer?"

"Two half-quart cans."

"Did you drink it all?"

"I drank about half the whiskey and one of the beers. When I got to Los Gatos, I got off the freeway and went to church."

"Why?"

"To pray. It was All Souls Day, uh, the day you pray for the dead."

"Had you heard voices telling you to kill that day?"

"Not up to then. My father had communicated with me earlier, telling me he was mad because I had killed for someone other than him. Father had been a Marine Corps sergeant and was used to ordering people to kill."

"You mean he was angry about the Guilfoyle murder?"

"Yeah."

"What happened when you went into the church? Were you drunk, or feeling the effects of the whiskey at all?"

"No. It had worn off. Like I said, I went to the church to pray, and then I heard the voice telling me I had to kill somebody. Only there was nobody there. Then I saw the light over the confessional, and the voice said, "That's the person I want you to kill.' "

"Why were you carrying the knife?"

"To protect myself."

After Herb's confessions to Harold and to me, I suggested to Jackson that we have him tell his story to us again in a videotaped interview. I wanted the jury to see him as he explained his reasons for the murders. The best evidence, of course, would be for him to do it in person on the witness stand, but he was acutely psychotic and therefore unpredictable. By the time of the trial anything could happen. He might refuse to testify.

Jackson finally arranged to use the television equipment at the media center on the university campus at Santa Cruz. As it turned out I was unable to leave Stanford that day, so Jackson interviewed him for the tape, in part using questions I had given him.

In the spring of 1973 I was teaching full-time. With the added burden of the Mullin case I was putting in 100-hour, seven-day weeks. Marilynn was very patient about the whole thing. I, on the other hand, had reached a point where I wanted the ordeal to end so I could return to some semblance of a normal life. I was beginning to worry that I might start calling the kids by the wrong names.

One of the courses I taught in the medical school was first-year psychiatry. It pointed up one of the problems faced by any forensic psychiatrist who has to try to explain paranoid schizophrenia to a jury. It was difficult enough to do it with medical students who already had a grounding in psychology. But I couldn't simply assign jurors 200 pages of reading and tell them I'd sort it out for them at the next class.

It was essential that the jury see and hear Herb telling it all in his own words. We made the videotape for insurance.

Following the death of Father Tomei, Herb went into at least partial remission. He had not consciously wanted to kill anyone in the first place, and the murder of a priest in his confessional was a crime so heinous that he blocked it out of his memory for long periods of time. Gradually he developed the idea that legalized killing exists, particularly that carried out by soldiers in the line of duty. He began to believe that a few people at the very top knew why killing must take place, and perhaps in the military he could carry out his mission.

In November, Herb applied to join the Coast Guard. About the same time he composed the lyrics to a song. Although the meaning of the words was never totally clear to me, I could only believe that it had something to do with Dean Richardson. He called it "The Switcheroo":

> He showed me everything, but I didn't see.
> He knew I didn't see, and he told me not to look.
> He wasn't very gentle, he wasn't very kind,

And when he wants something, he's really, really mine . . .
You're scared too, I guess,
So you light up like a horny puss,
But it probably ain't true . . .
I NEED you too, I don't know why.
It was always there, but never really jelled . . .
So it's high, high, high, singing glory on the wind,
Yes it's true in glory land, they're coming through and through,
One time only friend, happened to me too . . .
The quirk is so true, when my time is all through, the only survivor
will be,
No, not him, and not me . . ."

33
Voices

ON DECEMBER 14 Herb, who had quit a job as a busboy at the Cookbook restaurant a week earlier so that he would be ready to be sworn in, failed the psychological test for enlistment in the Coast Guard. He was badly disappointed, and the experience increased his paranoia. Two days later he bought the revolver.

About the same time, he began to frequent the office of Staff Sergeant Robert Eaton, the Marine Corps recruiter in Santa Cruz. A savvy veteran, Eaton rejected him as a candidate after their initial conversation as probably emotionally unfit. But Herb wouldn't give up. When he came back again, Eaton talked with him at length. After Herb admitted having an arrest record for narcotics, the sergeant told him that alone was enough to keep him out. Herb insisted that the drug charges against him were either dropped or reduced. When he added that his father had been a member of the prewar Fleet Marines in China, Eaton agreed at least to research his rap sheet. Just before Christmas, he called Herb and told him he thought the corps would probably waive his arrest record, if he passed all the other tests. Herb was elated.

After he and his parents came back to Felton from the holiday celebration at the Boccas' house in Sebastopol, Herb assembled a list of references for Sergeant Eaton, including two priests—Father McHugh at his own parish and Monsignor Edwin J. Kennedy, a second cousin who was pastor of Saint Raymond's Catholic Church in Menlo Park and who, coincidentally, had been a friend of Father Tomei. On the evaluation sheet Eaton sent him, Monsignor Kennedy checked the boxes indicating that Herb was above average in trustworthiness, home environment, and athletic ability. "This is a serious young man," the priest wrote, "and I am very glad that he is following his dad by entering the marines. For a while he was a conscientious objector—quite sincere about it. His present interest in the marines is quite wonderful."

Eaton made a January 15 appointment for Herb to undergo his preenlistment physical and other examinations at the military induction center in Oakland. In his cover memo attached to the processing papers, the sergeant wrote:

> Herbert William Mullin is an intelligent and highly motivated young man, with an ultrazealous eagerness to enlist in the USMC . . . because of his insistence that he can and will be the quality Marine we seek, and his father's steadfast opinion that his son will match up to our standards, I decided to conduct an analysis of Herb and his past criminal record . . . I have found that each of the allegations made were either proven erroneous or were dropped to a lesser offense (which in one case isn't even a crime any longer). Because of Herb's earnest desire to improve his lot and climb above his peers, as it were, I submit that Herbert William Mullin can, and most likely will, be a benefit to whatever unit he is assigned and a credit to the corps.

On January 14, Eaton gave Herb a government meal ticket and an overnight lodging order at a motel in Oakland and put him on a bus. Herb was in one of his states of remission, and he was cheerful and cooperative with the personnel at the induction center. When he filled out his prephysical questionnaire, he denied that he had ever seen a psychiatrist, much less the inside of a mental hospital. The physician who examined him saw no outward signs of psychosis, and his scores on the psychological and aptitude tests were acceptable. But when he refused to sign the list Eaton had compiled of his criminal arrests, insisting it was wrong, he was sent home. In the mail a couple of days later he received a curt notice from the marines: "Returned. Enlistment is not authorized."

The denial of his application was the latest in a long list of bitter disappointments. Herb began arguing with his parents, blaming them for misleading him over the years. His hallucinations returned. Finally, he moved into the Pacific View Apartments.

He applied for more jobs, always unsuccessfully. His paranoia increased, along with his frustration. He knew he was having some sort of breakdown, and he began to fix on Gianera as the cause of his troubles. The voices were becoming insistent: he must kill again. January was the crucial month for the earthquake. He had been able to avert it with the three murders so far, but it might not be enough. Now that he had been turned down by the military, the responsibility for killing rested with him alone.

On the evening of January 24, Herb ran into a neighbor in the courtyard of his rooming house, Alfred Payne, a fifty-six-year-old itinerant gardener. They had exchanged greetings a couple of times but had not become acquainted. On this occasion, however, they struck up a conversation. Herb asked whether Payne had a hotplate in his apartment, and if he could use it. The older man got the impression he had no food and invited him to dinner.

"Oh, I don't want to bother you," Herb objected.

"No, come on. I just made an oxtail stew. You're more than welcome."

"Gee, thanks."

Once inside his small quarters, Payne quickly set the table, brought a pot from the stove, and ladled out two portions. He was grateful for the company. He didn't know very many people in Santa Cruz and had little in common with the youthful surfers who were marking time for the winter in most of the other rooms in the building. This young man was different. He seemed to be polite, smart, and grown up.

"Are you in school?" he asked.

"No. I've already been to college," Herb answered.

"You have a job?"

"Not right now. I'm looking for work. In fact, I just came back from putting an application in at the Dream Inn."

"That looks like a nice place."

"Yeah."

"You from around here?" Payne inquired.

"I just moved down from San Francisco," Herb said noncommittally.

"You know, for a place that's supposed to be such a big tourist town, there sure isn't much to do in the winter," Payne observed, helping himself to another plate of stew.

"I guess not."

"That's why I joined the Episcopal church," Payne said.

"Huh?"

"I joined the church, and I joined the choir. I've gotten into something I haven't done since, well, my high school days. I enjoy it for the social life and all that." Payne paused for a moment. "What religion are you?" he asked.

"I used to be a Roman Catholic." Payne perceived his visitor was ill at ease. "I don't go anymore, though."

"Well, how come?"

"I just don't want to go," Herb said abruptly. "No reason at all." He rose. "Look, thanks a lot for the dinner. I really appreciate it, but I've got to go home to bed."

"What's your hurry? It's not even eight o'clock."

"It's too late for me," Herb said. "Good night."

When Herb woke up the next morning, he told me, he heard a clear message: "Today you must kill James Gianera."

He went to the shack near the mystery spot, which was where the couple had lived the last time he had seen Gianera. Kathy Francis didn't know it, but after she had told him where to find Jim, had shut the door, and had gone back to bed, Herb had lingered on the porch and heard her voice, telepathically. "We are prepared to die," it said. "My children and I don't mind being killed to prevent an earthquake."

He determined then to return and murder them if he was successful in the search for his primary victim.

Five days after the Gianera-Francis slayings, Herb walked into the secretary's office at Saint Stephen's Lutheran Church in Santa Cruz and asked to talk with the pastor. He was clean-shaven, neatly dressed in a suit and tie, and carried his brown leather briefcase. A few minutes later he was ushered in to see the Reverend George Flora.

"What can I do for you?" the minister asked, after showing him to a chair opposite his desk.

"I'm interested in learning about the Lutheran faith," Herb answered.

"Are you a Christian?"

"I was born and raised in the Catholic church, but, you know, I don't think it's what I want anymore," Herb said. "I've read a lot about religion, and I was very impressed with Martin Luther. I was wondering if you had any books about him I could borrow."

"Of course. Is there anything about him that interests you in particular?"

"Well, I'd like to know more about why he left the Catholic church. I know he wrote pieces against the selling of indulgences and wanted the Bible translated for all people instead of just the priests, but what I guess I really want to know is if the Lutheran church still follows his teachings, you know, if you're still quite faithful to the things he felt so deeply about."

"I think we are," the minister said. "The library is downstairs in the secretary's office. Let's go down and see what books we can find that might answer your questions."

Herb looked at his watch and then glanced at a clock on the wall. It was noon. "I have an appointment," he said. "Maybe I could come back and pick them up some other time."

"Certainly. Why don't you come to one of the adult Bible classes on Sunday, and maybe attend the service afterward. I could give them to you then."

"What time?"

"The classes start at 9:00 A.M., and the service is at 11:00."

"OK, I will."

The minister was impressed by the young man's courtesy and sober interest, but he nevertheless had almost forgotten about him by Sunday, February 4, when Herb arrived again at his office door. The Reverend Mr. Flora was scheduled to teach another class, so he introduced him to the Reverend Timothy Hillerman, the associate pastor, who conducted a Bible study group made up primarily of older women.

The Reverend Mr. Hillerman found it unusual that a man Herb's age would arrive at church wearing a business suit and a heavy tweed overcoat and carrying a briefcase. Herb sat in the background and said nothing during the beginning of the discussion, which this day centered on the power of prayer over evil.

Two of the ladies in the class, Mrs. Minerva Christmas, a dressmaker, and Mrs. Betty Ray, who played the piano for Sunday School services and sang in the church choir, noticed that the newcomer neither smiled nor frowned, and that his eyes betrayed no expression. Everyone in the room was somewhat startled when Herb spoke up during a lull.

"The devil can get into people and cause them to do things they wouldn't do otherwise," he said. "I have the power to cast out demons."

The Reverend Mr. Hillerman, suddenly worried that Herb might be a missionary from another church carrying a briefcase full of tracts, quickly changed the subject.

Mrs. Christmas stared at him. That man is crazy, she thought.

By early February, Herb's briefcase was full of more than turned-down employment applications. He wrote to the army and requested information about regular enlistments and the ROTC program in California colleges. Convinced that his criminal record was responsible at least in part for his failures, he also corresponded with the legal aid society in Watsonville, asking if there were any way to have his records sealed. On February 6, a lawyer wrote back advising him there was not.

On February 7, Herb was gathering firewood for his parents along the north side of Felton-Empire Road a couple of miles west of Highway 9. He was unconcerned when a green car bearing a government license plate pulled into the turnout and stopped.

"Did you know this was state park property?" Ranger Wayne Dennis asked as he approached him.

"No," Herb said. "There's never been a park here."

"It's not developed yet, but it's Fall Creek State Park," Dennis responded. He looked into the back of the station wagon, which was almost full. "I'm afraid you'll have to put the wood back."

Herb stared at him silently for a long time. The ranger became uneasy. "Look, I'm sorry about this, . . ." he began apologetically.

"No," Herb barked, "you have to follow the rules." He began jerking the pieces of wood from the car and hurling them with all his strength down the bank. Dennis backed away and watched. When he had finished Herb, panting, got into his car and drove away.

Dennis, who had not asked his name, copied his license number in his notebook.

The next day Herb found the encampment of the four boys while he was wandering in Cowell State Park. The shelter was located almost exactly where he had been rousted by a ranger three and a half years earlier. His new experience with another forester brought it all back to him. If he had to obey the law, so would these interlopers.

When he returned the following day, Herb truly meant to evict the four young squatters. But after they argued with him and went back into the tent, he heard a telepathic voice. "It's all right," it said. "We know we have to die. We are prepared for the sacrifice."

Herb couldn't remember whether it was the voice or the damp chill that woke him early on the morning of Tuesday, February 13, 1973. A threatening gray overcast covered Santa Cruz, the dank air redolent of salt from the Pacific a couple of blocks from his apartment. Wisps of fog hung in the tops of the redwoods, creating a sort of artificial rain as the moisture condensed and fell in heavy drops on the steaming earth below.

He shivered as he adjusted the load of firewood in the back of his battered station wagon parked on the street. He had been gathering it near Smith and Empire grades the day before when he had seen the patrol car scream past him on its way to the spot where the teen-agers had found the skeleton of Mary Guilfoyle.

The words came again, annoying, persistent. It was the voice of his father. He sounded irritated.

"Before you deliver the wood, I want you to kill me somebody. Don't deliver a stick of it until you kill somebody."

Herb gazed sightlessly into the pearl-colored twilight of the morning. "Who do you want me to kill?" he asked, his lips not moving.

"I still want you to kill your Uncle Enos."

"I don't want to kill him. I told you that before."

"Well, kill somebody before you bring the wood."

I don't want to kill Enos, Herb repeated to himself silently. But he would have to murder someone, to satisfy the command, to prevent the earthquake. He needed a thirteenth victim. He decided it would be the first person he saw.

It was Fred Perez.

Not long after Herb's arrest, the police found a bizarre proclamation among his personal papers. At the time, none of us knew what to make of it. Now it made sense, in a twisted, horrible way.

Let it be known to the nations of earth and the people that inhabit it, this document carries more power than any other written before. Such a tragedy as what has happened should not have happened and because of this action which I take of my own free will I am making it impossible to occur again. For while I can be here I must guide and protect my dynasty.

34

The Panic Button

ON MAY 14, 1973, Judge Franich convened a hearing to consider the reports of the two psychiatrists—John B. Peschau of Agnews State Hospital and Charles I. Morris of Oakland—appointed to determine whether Herb was competent to stand trial. They both said he was, at least within the definition provided by state law.

Peschau tended to blame his conduct on LSD. "Without the drug there is only a vestige of [paranoia] in evidence," he wrote. "Certainly not enough to interfere with his ability to understand the nature and purpose of the action against him or to cooperate with his attorney in a proper defense, if he will do so. Therefore, in my opinion, the defendant is legally sane . . . and is competent to stand trial."

Dr. Morris disagreed, finding that Herb suffered from "schizophrenic reaction, paranoid type, in a partial remission." Nonetheless, he believed he was competent to stand trial: "This individual suffers and has suffered with a mental illness for an undetermined period of time and at present is still suffering with the effects of the illness. However, he does not suffer at the present time with a mental defect, state, or illness of such a severity or of such a nature that he would be unable to understand the nature of the charges brought against him. . . . It is not anticipated that his present mental state will change materially in the future."

Their opinions did not come as a surprise. Competency to stand trial is not necessarily the same as innocence by reason of insanity. Besides, it was in the nature of things that the two court-appointed psychiatrists had spent a total of fewer than four hours with Herb between them.

After accepting the two reports, Judge Franich set July 9 for the beginning of Herb's trial. On May 29, Jim Jackson filed a discovery motion asking for a list of prosecution witnesses and to review the evidence in the DA's possession. At the same time he told the court he saw no necessity for seeking to transfer the trial to another city, and the judge agreed to give him unlimited challenges of prospective jurors.

On July 13, Jackson formally changed Herb's plea to not guilty *and* not guilty by reason of insanity. In California defendants who enter insanity pleas must also maintain they are totally innocent. The result is usually two trials—the first to determine actual guilt and the second to decide whether a convicted criminal is legally insane. Because there was no question that Herb committed the murders, Jackson, the prosecution, and the court all agreed to combine both trials in a single proceeding.

I was particularly anxious that Herb have a single trial, since I had found that the standard method can backfire. Harold had talked with several of the jurors who had found Frazier legally sane. I had taken no part in his first trial, during which Peter Chang was required to try and prove he was guilty. When I took the witness stand during the sanity trial and testified that Frazier had confessed to me, some of the members of the jury felt that the defense had withheld evidence. It made no difference to them that it would have been unethical and improper for Jackson, in effect, to throw the first trial, and they paid little attention to the psychiatric testimony.

On June 15, as a result of the new plea, Judge Franich reappointed Peschau and Morris to reexamine Herb.

June 20, 1973, was an interesting day for me, to say the least. By then, I was not only interviewing Herb at the jail but also was seeing

Ed Kemper, who was being held at the same facility.

The two shared an abiding mutual hatred. For some whimsical reason, the jailers had for a time placed them in adjoining cells. The huge slayer of coeds tormented the slightly built Mullin and called him a "creep with no class." During one interrogation at the sheriff's office in Santa Cruz, Kemper even offered to inform on Herb, telling Sergeant Medina he would be happy to pass on anything he overheard him say in jail. Mullin in turn loathed Kemper as a brutal, immoral animal. His own murders had been for a purpose, not simply sexual gratification.

As Jackson had told me, Kemper was rational and straightforward and conversed in an easy, intelligent style. His answers to my questions were concise and reflected a sort of guardhouse lawyer's knowledge of psychiatry picked up during his years in the state hospital.

Since the two were at the same place, I tried to schedule my appointments with Herb on the same days I was having my initial sessions with Kemper.

Although all of his psychotic symptoms had been fully established before the murders began, Herb had not formalized and structured all of his theories until after he was arrested and had the time to think about them. By now he was convinced that his father telepathically had ordered Dean Richardson to commit suicide, and that somehow, through telekinesis, had caused the car to crash.

June 20 was a Wednesday, mild and sunny. It would be the last day I had to spend with either Mullin or Kemper before Herb's trial. Classes had ended at Stanford, and my five sons were out of school for the summer. For weeks Marilynn and I had been planning a trip with them to the mountains, and I was anticipating this vacation, frankly, with a sense of relief.

When Herb was brought into the interview room, he handed me a thick sheaf of neatly handwritten notes, which he said would explain all about his parents' evil influence over him, earthquakes, the Bible, and homosexuality. I cursed under my breath, but he didn't seem to notice. The last thing I wanted at that moment was a briefcase full of foolscap to take with me to Fallen Leaf Lake.

"You know my father is a mass murderer, don't you?" he asked unexpectedly.

"I don't think I was aware of that, Herb, no."

"I want his fingerprints to be taken and compared with all the murders which occurred in California and Oregon since 1925," he demanded.

"That might be a pretty tall order," I observed.

"I don't intend to testify at my trial until Martin William Mullin answers questions and is indicted for mass murder," he declared.

"I'll talk to Mr. Jackson about it," I assured him, anxious to keep him from becoming more agitated. "I'll see what we can do."

"My Aunt Bernice told my father in 1947, when I was born, that she would marry him in the next life if he would retard my socio-psychological-sexual development and maturation." He said it all without stumbling over the words once.

"Where would that leave your uncle?" I asked.

"Enos would marry my mother if she would help my father in this effort," he explained.

"I see." I wondered how often psychiatrists say that just to fill time.

"I've overheard their telepathic messages to each other," he went on. "They all had their first orgasms at the age of six or seven. The fact that I didn't have my first orgasm until I was fifteen proves how successful they were in retarding me and controlling all aspects of my life."

"I suppose this is all in the written material you gave me," I said. "Yes."

"OK, Herb, I'm going to be out of town for a while, and I probably won't see you again until the trial." He suddenly looked disturbed. "Don't worry," I added, "I'll go over all of what you've given me, and if I have any questions, I'll get in touch with you before then.

"I hope you'll cooperate with Mr. Jackson. It's important, and he really wants to help you. I think it's essential that you agree to testify. You can explain it all better than we can."

"Just make sure my father is indicted for murder," he said.

After Herb was led from the little room, I sat in a chair, eying the red button next to the heavy steel door. It was supposed to summon help if an attorney or psychiatrist or any other unfortunate soul suddenly found himself with a violent prisoner on his hands. I had mentioned it to Marilynn a couple of nights earlier. She had asked me, too casually I thought, what sort of protection I had if either of these two, especially Kemper, turned on me. I had laughed at the notion that they might attack me. They had no reason to do so, and besides, the panic button would bring a squad of deputies instantly.

It almost seemed as if Kemper had read my mind when he finally shambled into the room. "Has it ever dawned on you that I'm a foot taller and weigh damn near twice what you do?" he inquired, grinning.

I smiled back. "It never occurred to me that someone with your brains would be dumb enough to try anything in here," I said pleasantly. "Now then, where were we the last time?"

"I was telling you that I hope they execute me. I had better get the death penalty. If I don't, I'm gonna kill somebody in prison to make sure that I do."

"Don't you think that's a little extreme?" I asked quickly.

"I've fantasized about catching somebody off-guard. It would be easy."

"Have you been having a lot of fantasies lately?"

"Well, I've been having a little trouble sleeping. The stuff the county psychiatrist has been giving me doesn't seem to be strong enough. Maybe you could talk to him about it."

"Sure. What are you taking?"

"Two hundred milligrams of Thorazine three times a day, and then chloral hydrate at night." As I jotted down the prescriptions I happened to notice the doctor Kemper had referred to, Marc Abramson, passing in the hallway on the other side of the bulletproof window in the door.

"Hey, Marc!" I shouted. Naturally, he couldn't hear me outside the soundproof room. "Damn! Just a minute, Ed," I said, pushing the red button next to the locked door.

For the next seven minutes, Kemper and I stood facing each other silently. Traces of a smile played at the corners of his mouth. Finally I heard a key in the lock, and the massive door swung open. A small, unarmed man in a gray uniform stepped inside.

"You want something, Doc?" he asked.

"Yeah. I'll be right back, Ed."

When the door clanged shut, I let out a long sigh. I could feel sweat dripping down the inside of my shirt.

"Shit," I murmured.

"Something wrong?" the deputy asked.

"We'll talk about it later," I snapped. "Where the hell is Dr. Abramson?"

35

A Busy Writer

AS IT TURNED out I need not have taken Mullin's voluminous writings with me on our vacation because, for a number of reasons, it was early August before my testimony was required. The proceedings did begin as scheduled on July 9, but it took ten days to empanel a jury, and then the trial was delayed until July 30 after Peter Chang, the district attorney, had to undergo an emergency appendectomy. Even with the postponement, Chang didn't recuperate in time to take part in the prosecution, which eventually was handled by Art Danner and another assistant, Chris Cottle, who was brought into the case at the last minute. Thus, I had plenty of time to examine the material Herb had given me.

Almost from the time of his arrest Mullin had written constantly, sometimes thousands of words a day. He composed a detailed autobiography that revealed extreme paranoia. He framed questions that he demanded Jackson ask of different witnesses, including his relatives and friends, in which he projected the blame for his madness and the murders on everyone but himself.

Although the DA saw none of Herb's writings after he was in jail, he did send samples of what had been seized with search warrants, including his backward writing from San Francisco, to Robert H. Noce, a psychiatrist in Salinas.

"Most of his writings are dissociated in nature, some are copied," Dr. Noce reported. "Evidence of a thought disorder is observed. He has written about art, philosophy, engineering, mathematics, psychiatry, homosexuality, religion, and history. His writings are voluminous and in great detail. He has expressed delusions of persecution and 'kill or be killed.' "

Although he thought some of the material probably was written while Herb was taking drugs or experiencing LSD flashbacks, Dr. Noce's diagnostic impression was "schizophrenic reaction, paranoid type, with paranoid delusions."

I sharply disagreed with Dr. Noce's conclusion that Herb's writings, and the psychosis they symptomized, were the result of drugs or flashbacks. He obviously had taken no drugs after his arrest, yet he wrote about the same things. His maunderings repeatedly revealed acute paranoia. For instance, a couple of months after he was taken into custody he wrote:

> When I was five years old I feel intuitively that Bernice and Enos Fouratt talked my parents into ignoring me. My parents actually did not tell me the necessary facts of life, sex and death rate, social conversation techniques, etc. Bernice and Enos did not have any children.
>
> Why did Bernice and Enos convince my parents that I should be shunned? My guess is that my cousins and sister were having orgasms at age six. When I was five Bernice and Enos wanted to stop my mental and physical growth. They did not want me to mature.
>
> Why?
>
> . . . I think they were jealous and envious of the fun I and my parents were going to have when I started to grow up normal. I think they believe in reincarnation and that by confusing and retarding me they might improve themselves in their next life.

Other symptoms that revealed themselves in Herb's postarrest writings included grandiosity. He theorized that one of the reasons that his family "retarded" his awareness of sex and the social arts was jealousy because he was more "vivacious" and "smart" and "good-looking" than others.

He had decided that at least 95 percent of the population, including his parents, were bisexual, but that the information had been withheld from him maliciously. Describing his first homosexual encounter, he wrote:

> [He] chased me until we had an experience. It was my first. I was repulsed and scared. . . . [He] walked up to me and wanted to kiss me—I refused and he screamed in my face, "I'm a homosexual." [Later] I ask [another man] to make love with me—I feel maybe with him I could accept homosexuality. He refuses. I withdraw into myself and am confused. I've asked Loretta for a quiet wedding. She refuses . . .

He blamed the emotional pain of his first sexual intercourse with a man, which took place following an LSD trip, on his father:

> I believe my father has been unequally blamed for my failures. But surely, if he had given me the six-year-old homosexual "blow job" oral stimulation that I was entitled to, like most other people get, I would never had taken LSD without his permission.

He composed hundreds of questions (and answers) for his parents and other witnesses which he submitted to Jackson but which, for obvious reasons, were never asked in court. For example:

> Mr. Mullin, why did you threaten to kill anyone who helped Herbert mature correctly?
> Ans. I believe that Bill was afraid that Herbert would improve mentally, physically and spiritually if people helped him mature. Bill said—I will kill you on the next in-on-it [next life] if you help Herbert.

The trial was surrounded by controversy from the start. Because prospective jurors would be asked probing personal questions about their attitudes toward subjects such as homosexuality, mental illness, and psychiatry, the defense had requested that the *voir dire* examinations be conducted in chambers, away from the public and the press.

It was obvious to me that a venireman, with a reporter from the local paper sitting in the front row taking notes, might not respond candidly to such questions as, "Have you ever seen a psychiatrist?" or, "Has there ever been any mental illness in your family?" By the same token, at one of several late-evening strategy session, we had agreed among ourselves to hold nothing back, including the fact that

Herb had committed murders with which he was not charged. We needed to know whether prospective jurors were Catholics, and if they believed the killing of a priest was more evil than taking the life of a layman. When Judge Franich agreed to this admittedly unprecedented method, it caused an enormous uproar among some attorneys and the press.

"I may be wrong about this," the judge said, "but one has to take a few chances in life, and I am hopeful this procedure will eliminate the hesitation and evasiveness we see so often in courtrooms.

"We have too often worried about the comforts of the judge, defense, and prosecution, but seldom about the jurors. These people serve for five dollars a day plus travel expenses one way, and I think they deserve some consideration.

"With the sensational amount of publicity this case has received," he concluded, "I felt this was the best procedure."

Spokespeople for the American Civil Liberties Union and the California Newspaper Publishers Association didn't see it quite his way.

"It's unconstitutional," said Charles Marson, the San Francisco legal director of the ACLU. "If he doesn't back down, we're interested in going after him."

"It sounds like he's writing a new law in an area where we already have too many laws," added the publishers association general manager Ben Martin. "It's another erosion of press freedom and the public right to know."

I had a hard time myself trying to convince a number of my friends at the Stanford Law School that the idea was not to circumvent the Constitution but to assure the defendant of the most unbiased jury possible.

In the end, however, it was neither the media nor my colleagues who challenged Judge Franich's decision, but Evelle Younger, the Republican state attorney general, who, at the time, was entertaining much higher political aspirations.

"A trial is a public event which transpires in a courtroom and is public property," Younger intoned piously. "The people are as much entitled to a fair trial as the accused. Like the accused the people are entitled to have that right safeguarded by holding open the courtroom doors."

The state court of appeal quickly upheld Franich, pointing out that both sides "have agreed, and the trial court in its discretion has found that because of questions about the intimate personal lives of the jurors, the public be excluded. . . . This is the paramount duty of the court. . . ."

Although he didn't try to interrupt the jury selection, which already was under way, Younger took his objections to the state supreme court. His action perplexed Chang, who had wholeheartedly assented to the idea and who happened to be the elected representative of "the People" in Santa Cruz County at the time. He said he found the challenge by the attorney general "mysterious, without precedent, and without knowledge of the true situation."

Judge Franich was a little more blunt, calling Younger's position on the issue "hidebound." He said it was "possibly motivated by the fact that he needs a freedom of the press issue to help make him governor."

In a few days the Supreme Court upheld the closed questioning of potential jurors, which was just about over anyway, and the tempest quickly died down. We were all more concerned by that time with the health of Peter Chang, who was taken to the hospital early on the morning of July 16 complaining of severe abdominal pain. When it was learned he had appendicitis, the judge postponed the trial; but after Chang had to undergo a second operation because of an infection, Franich ruled that the trial would go ahead without him. That order ruined any plans Chris Cottle might have had for the summer. Although Danner had worked with the DA on the case from the beginning, Cottle, a tall, soft-spoken ex-football star from Stanford with a keen legal mind, was forced to cram twenty hours a day for the week preceding the trial.

Although I was worried about Peter's condition, I was forced to admit to myself that I also was disappointed. Analysing my feelings, I realized that, without really thinking about it, I had been looking forward to jousting with him again.

Finally, on July 30, 1973, the court and jury were ready to hear the opening arguments.

36
Reasonable Conversation of a Madman

THE FIRST DAY of testimony began with a little routine infighting in the judge's chambers between the lawyers over whether the prosecution should be allowed to introduce into evidence a particularly lurid photograph taken in the Gianeras' bathroom before their bodies were removed. Jackson argued it was inflammatory, since Herb had confessed. After a compromise was struck, the defendant, attorneys, judge, and stenographic reporter all trooped into the heavily guarded courtroom where the jury of six men and six women was waiting, along with a standing-room-only crowd of the curious.

Judge Franich began by explaining the first four of the five verdicts open to the jurors: first-degree murder ("willful, deliberate and premeditated killing with malice aforethought"); second-degree murder ("malice aforethought when there is . . . an intention to kill . . . but the evidence is insufficient to establish deliberation and premeditation"); voluntary manslaughter ("an intent to kill regardless of any thought beforehand"), and involuntary manslaughter ("which neither requires malice aforethought and intent, and doesn't require any of these mental states we are talking about"). He went on to explain that if the jury found that Herb had diminished mental capacity, it would have to take that into account to determine the degree of guilt.

Since he had already confessed, the only other option left for the jury was to find him innocent by reason of insanity.

"Legal insanity means a diseased or deranged condition of the mind which makes a person incapable of knowing or understanding the nature and quality of his act," the judge read, "or makes a person incapable of knowing or understanding that this act was wrong.

"So if either one of those two things is true," he added, "you'd have to find him insane."

Danner delivered the opening remarks for the people. His words were spare, restrained, and straightforward. With the luxury of overwhelming evidence, he could afford to be brief.

"We will prove to you that the defendant committed these crimes in a manner which shows in every instance that he knew and understood the nature and quality of his acts of murder, and that he knew and understood that each act of murder was wrong," he said.

"And we will further show you the way in which each one of these crimes was committed. We will show you that Herbert William Mullin, each time he killed, killed with deliberation and premeditation."

Using a map and photographs of the ten victims killed since January 25, Danner synopsized each murder. He concluded simply, "We will show you all of these things and more, and then we will ask you for a proper verdict. I thank you."

In contrast, Jackson's statement was long and far more colorful, reminiscent of some of the more dramatic courtroom scenes in motion pictures. He didn't pull any punches. The jurors listened attentively and appeared to be impressed.

"The evidence in this case will show that Herbert William Mullin wrote prolifically," he began. "On the 22nd of August 1972, he wrote the following message: 'Today at 12:15 P.M. I feel that my good friend Maurice Chevalier has been conceived to a very wealthy family in Boston, Massachusetts. He will be in the same grammar school as Albert Einstein. Because of different vibratory feelings, I feel fraternal experience has been achieved in maybe triplets.'"

Jackson put down the paper and leveled his eyes at the jury. "On

Friday the 13th, October 1972, Herbert William Mullin took a baseball bat and clubbed one Lawrence White to death." The jurors stirred. The name had not been on the list in the indictment. "On the 24th of October, 1972, he picked up one Mary Guilfoyle, stabbed her to death, took her to a remote area, opened her up, and looked at her internal organs." By now the jurors were murmuring to one another, electrified and confused by this new admission. Except for the mention of Father Tomei a few days after Herb's arrest, the newspapers had said nothing about his having killed anyone else. That was because the authorities didn't know that he had. Jackson's statement also took the prosecution by surprise.

Jim paused for effect while the judge restored silence with his gavel, and then he continued. "On All Souls Day, November 2, 1972, he went to a church in Los Gatos, entered a confessional, and stabbed to death Father Tomei. Thereafter, he killed Mr. and Mrs. Gianera, Mrs. Francis, and her two children. On the 9th of February in killed four people in Felton, and on the 13th of February he killed Mr. Perez.

"We do not, as you know, intend to argue the proposition that he did not commit these killings. You now know there are thirteen dead and not ten. You know that Mr. Mullin's defense is that he is neither sane nor capable of deliberation and premeditation. . . .

"You will see with your very eyes a videotape of approximately one hour in which Mr. Mullin details his beliefs." (Jackson was referring to the tape we made in May. Danner had already objected to its introduction into evidence, and the judge ultimately sustained him because the prosecution had not been on hand to cross-examine Herb. The jury would never see the tape.)

"Mr. Mullin believes, among other things, the following," Jackson said, pacing. "The State of California will fall into the ocean unless it is prevented from doing so by the intervention of a figure who will make a sacrifice in order to prevent earthquakes. . . .

"You have perhaps all heard of Jesus Christ, but you perhaps did not know why Jesus Christ died. He died to save the city of Jerusalem from an earthquake. You have heard perhaps of Albert Einstein. Albert Einstein died on the birthday of Mr. Mullin. And do you know what the significance of that is?" Jim's voice rose dramatically. "The significance is that Mr. Mullin could not thereafter be killed in Vietnam. And why would Mr. Mullin have been killed in Vietnam? He would be killed in Vietnam because his father would send him there to die because his father practices killjoy sadism . . . he learned that he possessed telepathic powers, that these powers had been taken from him as a child, were withheld from him because of his parents' practicing killjoy sadism."

Jackson took the jury through a list of Herb's symptoms and bizarre conduct and related them to the case of Daniel M'Naghten, whom he called "the most famous paranoid schizophrenic of all time."

"Dr. Lunde, a psychiatrist, and Dr. Marlowe, a psychologist, will assure you that Mr. Mullin is equally mad if not worse," he said.

"We will not at any time expect you to believe that when Mr. Mullin took a gun and pointed it at a fellow creature that he did not intend to kill him. Mr. Mullin intended to kill thirteen times, and he killed thirteen times with success. We will not contend that he did not know it was a gun, nor will we contend that he did not know the effects of a bullet.

"We will say he did not know and understand the nature and quality of his act or that it was wrong because these acts, for Mr. Mullin, were not acts of murder but acts of sacrifice agreed to by the victims for the most part, expected of him by society, and acknowledged by more than 90 percent of the people on the face of the earth."

Jackson picked up the photographs Danner had used in his opening argument. "Although it may appeal to the prosecutor to show you these pictures, they are as dead as they would be without them, and we will not contest it. They are horribly dead, and the evidence will show that Mr. Mullin at no time identified with his victims. He at no time looked at them as people, but rather as objects in his delusions. . . .

"The evidence will show that he is at certain times, or oftentimes, lucid and quite sane. You will be concerned when the psychiatrists tell you this, because they will be saying to you, much as Anatole France did, that it is the reasonable conversation of a madman that scares us most."

Jackson gestured toward Herb, who had his face averted. "He can act outside of his delusional area perfectly reasonably and rationally. He can drive a car, he can buy a gun, he can buy groceries, he can remember it is Valentine's Day, he can remember it is Christmas, he knows how old he is, he knows where he is, he knows all of these things that most people know, unless what he deals with falls within his delusional system.

"The premises he works from are real. His activities are crazy. . . .

"I say to you that the evidence shows, and the doctors will say, that he is mad," Jackson thundered, "stark, raving mad.

"He has no appreciation of right and wrong. . . . As he sees it, he is as right as Abraham was right in trying to sacrifice Isaac, as God the Father was right in sacrificing his Son, as Herbert Mullin is right in sacrificing human beings. That his how he sees himself. That is Herbert Mullin."

Jackson paused. "That is, ladies and gentleman, I suggest from the evidence, a person insane. That is a person who, in those funny words of the law, has diminished capacity.

"I suggest to you that the evidence will show that he is insane, and most certainly diminished."

Following the opening statements, the jurors were excused for lunch, and the attorneys and defendant stayed behind to allow opposing counsel to bicker over a few procedural points. When they were finished, Jackson turned to his client with a look of resignation.

"All right," he asked, "do you want me to ask the judge concerning the instructions?"

"Yes," Herb said, "I want the instructions in writing at this point."

Judge Franich, as he would be throughout the trial, was very patient with Herb. "Well, I can't give the jury instructions in writing at this point, Mr. Mullin, because I don't know what instructions they are going to need. I have to wait until the end and . . ."

"The thing I wanted to speak about," Herb interrupted, "was that I requested that my father's fingerprints be checked against the homicides in California since 1925. I wonder if that has been done yet."

Judge Franich glanced at Jackson, who was examining the shine on his shoes. "I haven't the slightest idea, Mr. Mullin," he said. "That was the first time I ever heard of it."

"That's the first time that we heard of it also, your honor," Danner said helpfully.

"I think you had better talk to Mr. Jackson," the judge told Herb, "because I can't help you on that score." With that he departed for lunch at the Elks Club.

The first witness the next morning was Bob Francis, who told a shortened version of the story he had told the detectives, including the fact that Herb had bought drugs from Gianera. Herb's reaction to his testimony was interesting. Instead of scowling as he had during Jackson's opening statement, he smiled and nodded occasionally as if to confirm details related by the witness.

Francis left the stand, glaring at Mullin with unconcealed loathing. Following his appearance, Danner and Cottle quickly worked their way through the parade of prosecution witnesses. Since the trial would turn on the psychiatric testimony during the defense and rebuttal phases, establishing the facts of the case was perfunctory. There were no surprises, and the state wound up its case in less than four days. The only hitch in the otherwise smooth presentation was provided by Mullin, who rose at one point, picked up a pathologist's diagram of Joan Gianera's wounds, and argued loudly with Jackson that they were improperly located on the chart. The lawyer assured him that it didn't make a hell of a lot of difference, and Herb sat quietly after that, smiling each time the pathologist said it was his opinion a victim had died quickly.

He wasn't doing himself a lot of good with the jury.

37
The Defense Begins

I WAS THE first witness called by the defense. I arrived at the courthouse early and then cooled my heels in the hallway for nearly an hour while the attorneys, judge, and clerk went through the complicated task of identifying and marking pieces of evidence. Although I was excluded from the courtroom because I was a witness, my oldest son, Monty, then thirteen, was inside occupying a front-row seat. A budding artist, he had come down to Santa Cruz with me to watch the proceedings and the work of those of his future colleagues who were sketching the trial for the media. He sat with Don Juhlin, a talented man who was making drawings for a television station in San Francisco. Monty was fascinated by their speed and accuracy, and the artists more or less adopted him as a mascot, letting him hang around with them during breaks and showing him how they worked.

When I finally took the stand, Jackson started the routine chore of qualifying me as an expert witness, asking me to list the dates I earned my bachelor's and master's degrees in psychology at Stanford, honors received, when I got my medical degree, and when and where I served my residency as a psychiatrist. As we were droning through an inventory of hospitals where I had worked and my history as a faculty member at the medical school, Judge Franich, who had heard my testimony in the Frazier trial, suddenly rapped politely on the bench with a pencil.

"May I just interrupt," he said. He turned to the prosecution table. "Mr. Danner, is there any question of Dr. Lunde's qualifications?" he asked.

"I would like the jury to hear what he has . . ." Jackson started to say.

It wasn't Danner but Cottle who answered the judge. His short statement put me on notice that I was in for some grueling cross-examination.

"The psychiatric testimony is going to conflict," Cottle said, "and I'll stipulate that Dr. Lunde is a licensed physician in the State of California but nothing more."

Thanks a lot, I thought. "Mr. Jackson apparently feels it is necessary to bring out his qualifications," the judge said.

"I think it is," Cottle agreed.

"Go ahead," the judge told Jackson.

When Jim had finished painting a glowing picture of my credentials, Cottle asked a number of questions obviously aimed at proving that most of my psychiatric experience had been academic rather than clinical, even though I had worked in half a dozen university, county, state, and federal hospitals. He stressed that all of my scholastic training had been at Stanford, which I thought a little ironic, since I knew he and I both belonged to the same alumni association. Then he inquired about a course I taught with Tony Amsterdam, a brilliant and nationally known law professor, called "Defense of the Mentally Disordered Criminal Defendant."

Tony had recently been in the headlines again, this time for arguing successfully before the Supreme Court that California's capital punishment law was unconstitutional. The decision had just come down.

"Mr. Amsterdam is sort of defense-oriented, wouldn't you say?" Cottle asked.

Jackson shot to his feet. "Objection!" he barked. "That calls for his opinion and conclusion. Mr. Amsterdam happens to be a lawyer who vigorously opposes the death penalty, among other things. Does that make one proprosecution or prodefense?" We all looked at the judge.

"Yes," Franich said slowly, "I think there is probably a technical problem here, Mr. Cottle. We ought not to get into this. I am concerned where all of this could lead, getting various opinions."

When Cottle reviewed my record as a forensic psychiatrist, he appeared to be disappointed when I told him that much of my work as an expert witness had been for prosecutors.

At the beginning of his direct examination, Jackson asked me to read the definition of paranoid schizophrenia contained in the *Diagnostic and Statistic Manual of Mental Disorders,* a book drawn up by the American Psychiatric Association to standardize the terms for different illnesses and symptoms:

> This type of schizophrenia is characterized primarily by the presence of persecutory or grandiose delusions often associated with hallucinations. Excessive religiosity is sometimes seen. The patient's attitude is frequently hostile and aggressive and his behavior tends to be consistent with his delusions.
>
> In general, the disorder does not manifest the gross personality disorganization of hebephrenic and catatonic types, perhaps because the patient uses the mechanism of projection which ascribes to others characteristics he cannot accept in himself.

Herbert Mullin had every symptom contained in the jargon of those two paragraphs.

As we went over a list of the materials I had reviewed in the case, I mentioned the videotape that Jackson had alluded to in his opening statement but that he had failed to get into evidence. This time it was Cottle who stood up quickly. "May I approach the bench?" he asked.

"All right," the judge said. The whispered discussion that followed provides an example of the intensity with which the opponents fought every point during the trial.

"I'm objecting to the mention of the videotape," Cottle told the judge. "You have excluded it, and if it is mentioned in the way Dr. Lunde is mentioning it here, it's going to be unfair to us because the jury is going to wonder what happened."

"I'm going to have to explain to the jury that it has been excluded," the judge said.

"Wait a minute," Jackson interjected, gesturing toward me. "He's entitled to review anything he wants. If he wants to sit down and listen to fairy tales, that's fine. If he's reviewed it, he's reviewed it. You can't start excluding things he's reviewed because it's unfair.

"This is not an ecclesiastical court," he added, his voice rising.

"Keep your voice down!" Cottle hissed.

"If he has a legal proposition, he should state it," Jackson said, jerking his head toward the prosecutor. "Otherwise, if he doesn't . . ."

"Would you instruct Mr. Jackson to keep his voice down," Cottle appealed.

Judge Franich sighed. "Keep your voice down," he said.

"Is there a fair decibel level you would like me to adhere to?" he asked. Franich ignored him.

"At this time I think I can only tell the jury that it has been excluded, and the fact that he has reviewed it," the judge said. "I don't think there's anything we can do about that."

"You can't tell them it's been excluded," Jackson insisted. "He's had conversations with me, and those have been excluded too, I suppose."

"I'm going to tell the jury it has been excluded," Franich told him. Cottle began walking back to his counsel table.

"The record should reflect the district attorney has left the side bar conversation," Jackson said to Cottle's retreating back.

"Isn't he supposed to have handed in a thesis of what was said in the videotape?" It was Herb, who had been standing next to Jackson during the argument.

"I don't know what you're referring to, Mr. Mullin," the judge said tiredly, "but he has offered the whole . . ."

"Do you remember the words on the videotape?" Mullin asked Jackson.

"He's offered the whole videotape," the judge explained.

"It's been excluded, but the words in the videotape can be put in writing and he can refer to that," Mullin said.

The judge made a gesture of dismissal. "Not under the circumstances," he said. After Franich told the jurors to forget about any videotape, Jackson resumed.

"Do you consider yourself sufficiently equipped in the field of psychiatry, or magic for that matter, to talk to a defendant for one or two hours and reach a psychiatric conclusion as a legal conclusion?"

"No," I answered. "There are certain instances when a brief interview would suffice to meet the requirements of a trial. For instance, in the situation where you simply are asked to give an opinion as to, say, whether somebody is a narcotic addict or not. In that case you can do it on the basis of a brief interview, but when you have a very complicated case such as this one, and a complicated defendant, I think it would be impossible for anybody to be very knowledgeable and to form any kind of accurate opinion on the basis of a one- or two-hour interview."

I looked at Danner and Cottle. "In that respect I'm wholeheartedly in the agreement with the comments that Mr. Chang has made," I said, invoking the name of their absent boss, "about psychiatrists who tend to spend only a very short period of time with someone and then get up and give very definitive statements. I don't think that's proper or possible in a complicated case such as this."

Jackson introduced into evidence the tape recording of my interview with Herb on April 10, the one in which he first explained his so-called Jonah Theory. Because of the low fidelity of the tape and the size of the courtroom, Jim and I did a sort of dramatic reading from a transcript, in which he played the role of the defendant, before the jury heard the actual recording. It was obvious from Herb's expression that he was disturbed by our performance.

When we went to lunch, I told Jackson that I had noticed another psychiatrist among the spectators. He was Dr. Joel Fort, founder of a controversial self-help organization in San Francisco called the National Center for Solving Special Sociology and Health Problems, more popularly known as Fort Help. Among attorneys and his fellow practitioners, Dr. Fort had a reputation as a proprosecution witness who believed in a very narrow interpretation of legal insanity. Before court reconvened for the afternoon, Jackson asked for a conference in chambers and objected to Fort's presence. Although he was not on the DA's list of potential witnesses, it was obvious he wasn't there as a casual observer. If the prosecution intended to call him, Jackson said, he should be excluded.

Cottle argued that since the prosecution had not yet had an opportunity to have a psychiatrist of its own examine Herb (Peschau and Morris were appointed by the court and would testify later; under the rules the defense did not have to make the defendant available to a prosecution psychiatrist until after I finished my testimony), Fort should be allowed to observe Mullin's conduct in court to help form an opinion about his sanity. I had already expressed my opinion of such methods.

Suddenly Herb, who also was in chambers, interrupted the debate. "If I may make a statement," he said, "I renew my objection to the use of my tapes in court and transcripts of my tapes, and also I will not talk to a court-appointed psychiatrist until such time as an investigation of Martin William Mullin's fingerprints and all the unsolved homicides in California since 1925 has been completed."

"Well, just for your information, Mr. Mullin," the judge said, "when the defense of insanity is interposed here and you are examined by a psychiatrist hired by your own counsel, the information that he uses must be made available for the trial, and that is why it was done this morning.

"I appreciate and understand your objection, but the tape is admissible."

"We are here in pursuit of the truth," Cottle began, "and obviously doctors can give more intelligent testimony having been in the courtroom and having seen . . ."

"One of the largest farces in the history of American jurisprudence was the case in which Alger Hiss was prosecuted for perjury," Jackson reminded him, "and the defense had a psychiatrist sitting in the courtroom who, at the conclusion of Whittaker Chambers's testimony, came to the stand and testified in his opinion, based on his observation in the courtroom, that Mr. Chambers was a pathological liar.

"If that assists the court in the search for the truth, I fail to see how."

"I tend to agree with you," Franich said. He turned to Cottle. "I think this way about it: that we can kid ourselves, but it does provide for an advantage that I think must be precluded."

When I finally resumed the witness stand, Jackson had me identify what amounted to a bushel of Herb's writings, including the letters he sent the previous fall to HEW and the U.N. to get demographic information to bolster his theories about death rates and natural disasters. The dates on the form-letter replies proved he had formed the delusion many months before his arrest. Then Jackson turned to another subject.

"Doctor, have you noticed the number 13 coming up in connection with your investigation of Mr. Mullin?"

"Yes," I answered, "it recurs in various contexts and in various documents I have reviewed, and I think it is consistent with Mr. Mullin's disorder that he gets involved with numerology and certain specific numbers.

"Now, the number 13 comes up, for instance, in connection with the fact that there were 13 victims in this episode of killings. The first victim was killed October 13 and the last victim was killed on the 13th of February.

"It comes up many other times," I continued. "For instance, the letter to the United Nations was written on a 13th. . . . In Mr. Mullin's writings there are lists of 13, for instance the twelve disciples plus Herbert or somebody else. . . ."

"Has he spoken to you in terms of twelve plus one?

"Yes, he has."

"Can you tell the ladies and gentlemen of the jury in what context that came up?"

"Well, various. It was referred to on the tape played this morning, that there were twelve men on the boat plus one, and he identifies himself with Jonah as the thirteenth person . . . and then in reference to the twelve disciples and Christ being the plus one. . . ."

"Is there a pattern as far as you can tell? Who was the plus one of the twelve plus one?"

"You mean in Mr. Mullin's thinking?"

"Yes."

"Well, I think it's himself in most cases."

"What other delusions are you aware of that haunt Mr. Mullin?" Jackson asked.

"Delusions regarding his sexual identity, and then the sexual identity of other people, particularly those closest to him." I glanced into the audience and saw Bill Mullin. He was watching me intently. I shifted my gaze back to Jackson as I completed the answer.

"There has been for some years a confusion in his own mind as to whether he was heterosexual, homosexual, or bisexual. There is evidence both in what he has told me and again in writings of his that he believed—this is what I referred to earlier as projection—that his father was homosexual and that his mother and sister were lesbians and that they had been so since a very early age, but that they kept this information from him as part of a conspiracy to keep him from maturing and discovering the secrets of his power. . . ."

"What things are there about Mr. Mullin specifically that he projects on to other people?" Jackson asked. "Is Mr. Mullin, for instance, a homosexual?"

"Mr. Mullin has had homosexual involvement," I said. "There is some reality as he applied it to himself, but as far as I know there is no reality when he projected it to other people. . . ."

At this point, Herb interrupted again. "I will stipulate that I am a bisexual," he said in a clear voice. Jackson looked at me. He decided to change the subject.

While I was answering a question about Herb's hallucinations, Judge Franich interjected a query of his own. "What you're saying is that he can't shut them off, but that he actually believes that there are voices speaking to him?"

"Yes." The judge motioned for Jackson to proceed.

"Can a person choose not to be a paranoid schizophrenic?" Jim asked.

"Not at all," I replied.

"Can a person who is a paranoid schizophrenic function in normal physical ways?"

"In many aspects of life, yes."

"Now, in your experience in mental hospitals and with mental patients, what have you noted that committed insane mental patients in hospitals are able to do?"

I waited a beat for the expected objection from the prosecution. The question was patently improper, since the jury was not supposed to consider what might happen to Herb if it found him innocent by reason of insanity. Strangely, neither Danner nor Cottle said anything.

"Well," I began, "at Atascadero, the state hospital where the criminally insane, that is, those who are found not guilty by reason of insanity, are committed, there are some extremely talented and productive people." I avoided Cottle's eyes. Still no objection. "I can recall individuals who can paint very well, who are talented artists and who not only painted but discussed art history at length and were quite knowledgeable about it.

"There are men who work in the machine shop and the wood shop down there," I continued, "and operate equipment that requires skill and complete dexterity."

"Are mental patients entitled to take courses from university extensions, for example?"

"Oh, yes, and some do . . . they can take courses at the college level and complete them successfully, and yet are insane both legally and mentally."

Jackson took me through Herb's history of hospitalizations, quoting from the opinions of other psychiatrists who had treated him over the years. He asked me about the drugs that had been prescribed for him.

"The specific ones that he received were Thorazine and Stelazine," I explained. "I should note that in other hospitalizations he was treated with the same medication, and when he was taking it he was much better.

"As I said, just as the diabetic would appear much better on insulin, the apparent schizophrenic does very well as long as he stays on the right medication, and on the right amounts.

"The problem here," I concluded, "was that when he left he stopped taking the medicine, nobody was supervising him or providing it, and so he would deteriorate after he left the hospital."

Jackson picked up the report from Mendocino. "I see the prognosis in this case is 'grave.' What does that mean?" he asked.

"It means 'serious.' "

"And what does that mean in terms of what Mr. Mullin or anybody so diagnosed is going to do in terms of improving?"

"It means he's not likely to improve, particularly without proper care, and that he was in need of rather extensive treatment and hospitalization at that very time."

Before Jackson could ask another question, the judge interrupted. "How do you account for the discharge, if I may ask the question? I think it's obvious to everybody."

Jackson was amazed. He looked at Franich as if he couldn't believe his ears. "I didn't hear you," he said, trying not to grin. I was equally delighted. One of the reasons I had taken the case in the first place was to draw public attention to the chaotic mental health system. I never expected to be given the opportunity by the judge.

"How do I account for the discharge?" I repeated.

"Yes," Franich said. Cottle frowned at the legal tablet on the counsel table in front of him, but said nothing.

"I'm glad you asked that, your honor," I said. "The reason for the discharge from these various hospitals during this period is twofold, and I think it's an extremely important issue that applies not only to Mr. Mullin but generally to psychiatric patients in the state of California.

"We have had two major developments in our state mental hospital system in recent years. One is a changing of the commitment law which makes it impossible now to keep anybody in a hospital who is dangerous to . . ."

"Was this true in 1969?" the judge interrupted again.

"Yes," I replied. "The law was written in 1967."

"This is the Lanterman-Petris-Short Act?"

"Yes, the LPS. It was in effect certainly at this time. It is now impossible to commit somebody for a prolonged period in the state of California, even though you know, as was mentioned repeatedly here, that the patient is dangerous to himself or to others.

"The law provides very limited, very specific numbers of days that your can keep somebody. Beyond that, even though a person may continue to be obviously dangerous, he must be released. The second reason . . ."

"You oversimplified a little," the judge chided gently, "because there is a procedure for conversatorship."

"That only applies to gravely disabled persons, your honor, which refers to people who are senile or, as defined in the Welfare and Institutions Code, unable to provide food, shelter, and clothing, and are totally mentally incompetent."

"They are determined mentally ill when they are mentally dangerous to others," the judge argued.

"But you can't appoint a conservator for persons who are dangerous to others," I said, "only those who are disabled, which refers to people who are senile or in a gravely disabled condition, such as after a terrible automobile accident. Does that explain?"

"No," the judge began, "but . . ."

"I'll be happy to furnish the proper sections from the . . ."

"I'm not going to quarrel with you," Franich said, "because the Lanterman-Petris-Short Act is something I've quarreled with for a long time myself."

"Let me go on and answer your question," I continued, "because the second part of my answer is really more important in that it makes the provisions of the LPS law pretty unimportant anyway, from a practical standpoint.

"About this time, namely 1969, I can recall very well, I was working on a part-time basis at Santa Clara County Hospital, and Santa Clara County didn't have any locked wards. Agnews was the state hospital for this geographical area.

"Well, the word came out at about that time that Agnews was going to be closed, that is, closed to psychiatric patients. It's still open for mentally retarded only, but not for psychiatric patients.

"The word was also put out that all the other state hospitals would be closed, and subsequently in Northern California, state hospitals have been closed. Mendocino, where Mullin was a patient, has been closed. DeWitt State Hospital has been closed. Stockton State Hospital is now closed. Napa State Hospital is the only one left in Northern California, and it is also scheduled to be closed.

"In other words," I went on, warming to the subject and wondering when somebody was going to cut me off, "we have a situation where all the state hospitals are simply being closed down. So, as a practical matter, whether somebody is dangerous or not, there is no place to put him. There's no place to send them unless people are extremely wealthy and can afford private mental sanitariums, and besides, most private sanitariums can't hold anybody legally against their will.

"There were reports recently of hearings in Sacramento relating to the effects of the closure of state hospitals. It had been brought out, for instance, that a number of people had been killed in California by patients who had been turned loose from mental hospitals. There are many, many more people who have been released and who are going to be released when Napa closes down, and there's no place for these people to go.

"They are living in ghetto areas of the large cities, such as San Jose and San Francisco, and some of them, as we are aware now, are living in Santa Cruz."

The court had finally had enough. "Doctor, I think that is a sufficient explanation," Judge Franich said. "I think we've gone along with that, and I won't quarrel with what you said." Cottle looked relieved.

"Could I ask a couple of questions so that the answer to the question the court asked is not totally misleading in terms of what goes on here?" Jackson requested.

"All right," the judge said. Jackson turned toward me. Cottle, alert now, was standing.

"Will that situation prevail," Jackson began, "should Mr. Mullin be . . ."

"Your honor, I object!" Cottle interrupted. "If we're going to get into what is going to happen to this man if the jury decides one way or the other, we are avoiding the issues."

"Mr. Jackson," Franich said, "we are going to have to stay away from this. We're going to have to trust the normal processes and hope that at least they do a better job in the future than they have in the past."

"No, no," Jackson complained, "that's exactly the impression I don't want the jury to have. It's not true. This man can't go into that kind of commitment."

Jackson did not want the jurors to believe, erroneously, that if they found Herb legally insane, he might be freed eventually because the state hospitals were closing. There was little doubt in my mind that if he were hospitalized, he would spend the rest of his life at Atascadero.

The prosecutors, for their part, did not want the jury to believe that a finding of insanity would have the same effect as a guilty verdict—that is, would safely remove Herb from society. They opposed the insanity verdict because they genuinely believed he didn't fit the legal definition. Moreover, an insanity verdict would amount to an acquittal, which district attorneys are in the business of trying to avoid.

"If he's allowed to do this," Cottle demanded, "I want to be able to go into what happens if this man goes into state prison, what the state prison has available for him."

"Gentlemen, we're getting off on a tangent," the judge said. "I'm not going to get into this further."

"I'll grant you, it is an interesting subject," Jackson insisted, "but it's irrelevant to what's going on here. At least grant that."

"Hey, let me ask you a question," a man called from the audience. Everyone, including Herb, was startled. "This guy sitting over there," the spectator continued, pointing toward me, "you, the doctor."

"No questions," Judge Franich roared, finally out of patience with all of us. "I'll have you removed from the courtroom if you insist, sir."

The man sat down, Cottle returned to his seat, and Jackson

resumed his questions about Herb's psychiatric diagnoses over the years. They day ended with no further outbursts or objections from either side.

Jim walked with Monty and me to my car after court adjourned for the weekend.

"How long do you think this will take?" I asked him.

"Bring your lunch," he said. "I'll be finished with you early on Monday, but Cottle's not going to take any of this lying down. He'll be all over you like the hives on cross examination."

My son grinned. "Can I come back with you Monday?" he asked. "I think I'd like to see that."

38
Cross Examination

OVER THE WEEKEND, Jackson reread the reports of the court-appointed psychiatrists and the doctor who had given the district attorney the report on Herb's writings. On Monday morning he started with a few questions that anticipated their testimony.

"Are you familiar with what an LSD flashback is?" he asked.

"Yes, I am."

"Have you any evidence that supports the idea that Mr. Mullin at any time was undergoing LSD flashbacks?"

"No, and the reason for that is that an LSD flashback is a reliving of a prior LSD trip, usually a bad trip. It's a specific, time-limited repetition of a previous experience that starts and stops and then the person is quite normal for most of the time. That's quite different from Mr. Mullin, who has been delusional, hallucinating, and so forth at virtually any time I've gone to see him.

"He has always shown the symptoms of paranoid schizophrenia, which is totally different from the limited flashback experience."

I believed it was critical for the jury to understand that Herb had not committed the murders because of drugs. He was a tragically ill man who had been denied treatment, not a crazed junkie.

Jackson had me explain how the brain processes information by taking it in through the senses, comparing it with what it has learned before, and finally ordering a response. I used the example of a person withdrawing his hand if he feels extreme heat, because experience has taught him that burns hurt.

"In Mr. Mullin's case, if you are dealing in an area of his delusions, what happens to his input?" Jackson asked.

"Well, the difficulty in someone like Mr. Mullin is that on the input side what he thinks is coming in, what he thinks he is hearing, is incorrect. It's a hallucination. It's a false sensory input."

"What happens to it once it gets in, or once it's there?"

"The next source of disorder is in the association areas, and here I'll use a simple example.

"If you take a telephone switchboard, with its incoming lines and its outgoing lines and an operator who is supposed to plug the caller into the right phone, what happens, in effect, is that the operator has gone berserk. The input has become too jumbled, and the lines are being connected to the wrong areas, and hence the wrong associations are being made.

"There are now more sophisticated analogies or models that are employed based on computer technology," I added, "but I think they are basically elaborations of this simpler model.

"It's as if the whole system had overheated and gone haywire, and therefore the output doesn't make any sense, at least to an outside observer. It can only be understood in terms of the internal mechanisms having gone berserk."

"In your opinion is that what happened with Mr. Mullin?" Jackson asked.

"Yes. I think that's what happens in chronic schizophrenia."

"Is Mr. Mullin, in the state you have described, capable of mature and meaningful reflection and deliberation?"

"Absolutely not."

"Do you have any doubt that he intended to kill the thirteen people that are dead now?"

"No."

Jackson had me relate Mullin's account to me of all the murders, including his telepathic commands. We had not gone very far when Herb grasped Jim's sleeve, and they held a long, whispered conversation. Jackson frowned and turned to the judge.

"May we approach the bench, your honor?"

"All right." I could hear the conversation from the witness stand.

"Mr. Mullin has requested that I terminate my examination of Dr. Lunde at this point," Jackson explained, "and I have told him that I'm not able to, due to the fact we have not as yet covered the insanity portion. Mr. Mullin has wished that an objection be lodged to that."

"Mr. Mullin, Mr. Jackson cannot terminate it at the present time, and I am saying this strictly on your behalf," the judge said.

"May I make a statement at the side bar conference?" Mullin asked.

"All right," the judge sighed. "Go ahead."

"The reasons behind my desire to terminate the examination between Dr. Lunde and Mr. Jackson is that so far they have only gone into the derangement aspect of my particular case, whereas in conference they explained that they would portray the reasons for my derangement.

"Also, I notice that different aspects and different facets of the story which I related are being portrayed completely false as to how I made them."

"That is an opinion you may undertake, but under the circumstances this is not a sufficient ground for stopping any interrogation," Franich told him.

"Now, Mr. Mullin, with the advice of your attorney, of course, you have the right to take the stand, make claim to anything you wish. But these witnesses also have the right to make the statements they are making based on their observations. That's it."

I was pleased. It looked as if Herb might agree to testify after all, even though his father had not been fingerprinted and interrogated about imaginary mass murders, as he had demanded.

Jackson's final questions dealt with the legal definition of insanity.

"Does Mr. Mullin, in your opinion, feel he is speaking the truth when he speaks?" he asked.

"Yes. He thinks it's the truth as he knows it."

"Now in terms of M'Naghten, is it your opinion that Mr. Mullin knew or understood the nature and consequence of his acts?"

"No."

"Does Mr. Mullin compare with your idea of what the word 'understand' means?"

"No, not at all."

"Do you have an opinion as to whether or not he knew and understood his acts to be wrong?"

"I have an opinion, yes," I said. "My opinion is that he did not understand that his acts were wrong. He felt that he was doing something not only right, but something very good, namely acts that would not only prevent things like earthquakes, but which also bring power to his family's dynasty."

"All right," Jackson said, "your witness, Mr. Cottle."

The prosecutor rose and put on his glasses. "Mr. Bailiff, do you mind putting a white sheet up on the board?" he asked. The deputy scurried to find a large piece of tablet paper.

On the board, Cottle listed the dates of my eight interviews with Herb and then went over what he had told me on each occasion. It soon became apparent that he was implying that the notes I brought to court, because they were typed and phrased in complete sentences, were incomplete, and that I might have left out incriminating material. I had learned years earlier that the best course after a psychiatric interview of a criminal defendant is for me to return to my office, immediately dictate a summary of my notes, and destroy the originals. I do this not to conceal anything germane to a case but to protect the defendant's, and my own, confidentiality in case of subpoena. On any given day my notebook might contain anything from unlisted telephone numbers, to false accusations by a defendant against innocent people, to a shopping list Marilynn gave me on the phone. Also, I am a doctor, after all, and very few people can decipher my home-grown shorthand.

Specifically, Cottle bore down on whether I had lied when I said Herb was not particularly close to Gianera. Jackson objected, but the judge overruled him.

"I'd be happy to answer that," I said when I finally got a chance, "because I think it's very clear from both the reports I have read and my interview with Mr. Francis that Mr. Gianera was well known as a drug dealer. Therefore, it doesn't surprise me that Mullin might have gone there, or might have said he went there to buy drugs.

"It's like saying, 'I went to Safeway to buy some groceries.' Everybody knows that Safeway sells groceries, but that does not imply that you are friends with the clerk at the checkout stand. Gianera was well known in Santa Cruz, and particularly at Cabrillo College in those earlier years, as the man you went to see if you wanted to buy drugs."

In was obvious from his next question that the prosecutor would contend Herb killed Gianera purely for revenge, which the jury might find a compelling motive. The problem was Herb had no rational reason for wanting retribution.

"Did you get the impression from the reports of Dr. Peschau and Dr. Morris, that is, the statements attributed to Mr. Mullin, that Mr. Mullin had some very vengeful feelings about Mr. Gianera?" Cottle asked.

"He had some vengeful, bitter feelings about Mr. Gianera," I agreed. "I think the important thing to distinguish, though, is whether or not they were based on reality. In my review of everything I can get a hold of relating to that relationship, it would appear to me that those vengeful thoughts were based on hallucinations.

"There is nothing I can find from anybody who knew the two of them that would relate them in an ongoing relationship, positive or negative, that could have accounted for such feelings."

"He never talked about hallucinations when you first talked to him about his feelings, did he?" Cottle asked.

"When we first talked he wouldn't discuss that with me at all. And," I added, "that's typical with a paranoid patient. By definition they are suspicious. They don't trust people, and they're not about to convey their hallucinations and delusions. You see that with paranoid patients in hospitals, too."

"Are most people charged with ten murders rather paranoid in your experience?" he asked acidly. "Or even one murder?"

"Not necessarily," I replied evenly. "Then, not too many people are charged with ten murders."

"Just to change the subject for a moment," Cottle said, picking up a copy of the trial transcript, "it reminds me of a question that was asked by Mr. Jackson of you Friday. The question was, 'Do you consider yourself sufficiently equipped in the field of psychiatry, or magic for that matter, to talk to a defendant for one or two hours and reach psychiatric legal conclusions?' And your answer to that was no, is that correct?"

"Mr. Cottle, I don't have the transcript, but I know that you know that my answer was explained not in terms of this case, and I went on to explain that in a complicated case, I think you would have to make a number of visits."

"Have you ever reached the conclusion that somebody was insane in a single interview?"

"Have I?"

"Yes."

"I can't recall a specific cause. It may be, because again there are some situations where you have documentary evidence available to you beforehand."

"Maybe I can refresh your memory as to one case, doctor, and then we'll talk about a couple more."

Cottle produced two court files from Alameda County. They were cases in which I had been appointed by a judge to determine whether two robbery defendants were competent to stand trial. I had written after single interviews that in my opinion they were not. Why, he wondered, was it necessary for me to spend 100 hours preparing for the Mullin trial?

"I think something should be made clear, here," I said. "I know that you don't want to leave an improper inference, Mr. Cottle." He smiled.

"As you know, there are probably some 75 to 100 reports of mine on file in Alameda County of this sort, and these two—selected, presumably, for certain purposes—were reports submitted to a judge to guide his thinking. They were not preparation for trial. Neither of these cases went to trial, and I did not do any preparation for going before a jury."

"Apparently most of the 100 hours that you have spent have been spent so you could convince this jury that your opinions are right, is that correct?"

"I will repeat what I said, that I spent a considerable amount of time in preparation so that I could answer any questions that would come up. I had no idea what line of questioning you would cover, what particular reports. As I said, it is quite different from just writing a report to a judge."

"Doctor," Cottle said, "if we can't get on a yes-and-no basis, we are going to be here for a long, long time. Would you try when you can?"

"I'll try, yes, but I think some questions require an explanation, and that was one of them." Jackson had been right, I thought. If this guy figures out a way to get his foot on my neck, he won't let me up. I had to admire his tenacity, however.

"All right," the prosecutor continued, "now the second part of what you said, you have 75 to 100 reports on file in Alameda County?"

"I would think so."

"Now, doctor, isn't it correct that the overwhelming majority of those—and I am talking about just on the insanity issue—were one-interview conclusions?"

"The answer is yes, if you're talking about those that involve simply a report to a judge in a nontrial case."

"Doctor, you testified in December, 1971, in the case of *People* v. *John Frazier,* did you not?"

"Yes."

"It was a rather complicated case, was it not?"

"It was more complicated than those robberies your have referred to. It was less complicated than this case. It would fall in between, yes."

"A less complicated case because there were only half a dozen victims?"

"There was only a single incident on one day as opposed to what we have here," I said. "With Frazier there was only one day involved. Here we have many."

"Nevertheless, John Frazier was also a person who claimed he heard voices and was acting with grandiose delusions and who did all of these things that you have mentioned that Mr. Mullin has done, is that not correct?"

"Objection!" Jackson strode toward the bench. "Complex and compound. If the question is was his diagnosis paranoid schizophrenia, the answer is yes, but . . ."

"All right," Judge Franich told Jackson, "You're not the witness here. But I think the question is complicated. Will you rephrase it, Mr. Cottle?"

"I mean, he was a complicated schizophrenic phenomenon, was he not?" he asked.

"I think I answered the question," I said. "He was more complicated than those two robbers, he was less complicated than Mr. Mullin. I would not begin to equate Mr. Frazier and Mr. Mullin in terms of psychology, or the comingling of the issues."

"Doctor, you concluded the same thing that you have concluded in this case, did you not?"

"No, and Mr. Cottle, I wish I had the transcript in front of me of that trial. I have read it recently, and I am familiar with it enough to say this: that the questioning there and the subject matter you are referring to was put differently, in the first place, by Mr. Chang, and my answers were different. In fact, if you will recall, he got very upset and moved that my whole testimony be stricken, which was then overruled." He looked as if he were framing another question, but I plunged ahead.

"The reason is that Mr. Chang asked the question, 'Did he understand in the context of right and wrong that laws are enacted to protect organized society?' Now, in regards to Mr. Frazier, the answer to that was yes. In regard to Mr. Mullin, of course, the answer is no.

"Mr. Mullin thinks that these laws have to do with increasing your power in the next life and preventing earthquakes and so forth . . . He thinks the law exists to keep people from getting too powerful in the next life and things like that, which is quite different."

"Did Mr. Mullin know it was unlawful to commit murder?" Cottle asked. "Did he know it was unlawful to kill somebody? Let's put it that way."

"He talks about his understanding of the laws, and he uses the word 'law' and the word 'murder,' but the context in which he uses them—namely that those laws are passed so people don't get too powerful in the next life, and a certain number of deaths have to occur, though, to prevent earthquakes—is a wholly different context, and does not constitute what I would consider a mature, meaningful understanding of the consequences of his actions, which is what the law requires in M'Naghten."

Cottle returned to the list of my interviews with Herb and to his accounts of the murders. Then he asked, "Doctor, you had warned Mr. Mullin that conversations with visitors might be bugged?"

"Yes," I replied. "He asked me the question, and I told him a truthful answer." Cottle smiled. Why, I thought, do I suddenly have the feeling I just led with my chin?

"Did you always give him truthful answers?" he asked.

"As far as I know, yes."

"Did you believe that the tape recording which you took from Mr. Mullin would not show up in the courtroom last Friday?"

I glanced at Herb. He was gazing at me unflinchingly. "The context of that was that I was not at that time court-appointed, and anything he told me at that time would not be turned over to the district attorney. Now, as you know, and as he has been told, and as Judge Franich explained on Friday, once the defendant puts his mental state into question, then the confidentiality is waived. But the question was in the context of that date, April 10."

Herb was on his feet. "Object," he cried. "That was not explained, not explained."

The judge, thinking Jim had made the protest, said, "I think, Mr. Jackson, the objection is understood."

"That should be explained," Mullin insisted.

The judge didn't look up. "I think the many phases on this type of question—this gets way off the track."

"You're hearing voices better than you're looking at people," Jackson told Franich, "because Mr. Jackson did not object."

The judge looked at Herb. "Well, anyway, I don't think there should be any connotation, Mr. Cottle, on that particular issue. I think this is nitpicking."

"Your honor, I'm sorry you're characterizing my cross-examination as nitpicking," Cottle began, "but . . ."

"I'm not characterizing it, but I think this particular representation that Dr. Lunde made, to classify it as being untruthful is carrying it away from what it really is. So that will end that. Let's go from there."

"Wouldn't a tape recording of a conversation between Mr. Mullin and somebody he trusted be one of the best kinds of evidence we could have in this case?" Cottle asked me.

"I'll object to that," Jackson said. "That's misleading. He trusts me. Why don't we bring the videotape in?"

"That's a different question completely," the judge said.

"He trusts Mr. Jackson?" Cottle asked incredulously.

"Do you want me to establish who I trust?" Herb snapped.

Judge Franich looked as if he might have a headache. "The objection is overruled," he said. "Let's not get into that now."

"Did Mr. Mullin early on and later on lie to you and withhold information from you?" Cottle asked me. "Let me ask that question, and why don't you think about it at noon, and when we come back we'll talk about that."

"Mr. Cottle has declared a recess," Jackson observed.

"He'd better," the judge said, looking at his watch, "because I wasn't aware of the time."

It was clear that the prosecution was going to attack every discrepancy in Herb's story as he related it to me, and to leave the impression with the jury, or at least hint, that his delusions and hallucinations might be as much a product of my imagination as his. This ignored the documentary proof from Mendocino State Hospital that he was hallucinating as early as 1969.

Cottle rephrased his question when we resumed after lunch. "Are you satisfied that when he told you that he heard voices that he actually heard them?"

"In his own mind, yes, and I think that part of the evidence of that is that he has acted on them, such as the incident where he shaved his head in response to the voices."

Cottle began to question me again about details of the murders, specifically the steps Herb took to conceal bodies or to keep from getting caught. I argued that his conduct did not show planning or careful premeditation.

"But would you go so far as to say that anything that a person does which might avoid detection with regard to the commission of crimes is *no* indication of their knowing or not knowing the difference between right and wrong?" Cottle inquired.

"Well, it might be," I said. "I perhaps can give you a single answer that will cover otherwise a series of questions about the specific acts.

"If you assume someone is rational, is normal, knows the law, knows and understands our system of justice and the rights of others, then it is fair to assume that if certain behavior takes place which indicates an effort to avoid detection, that is a reflection of a person who knows the consequences of his actions. This assumes he is a rational person.

"Another thing you would assume then is a rational person would be aware of the penalties for these acts, and of the fact he might be punished, and that such a person would be deterred."

I decided to try to use this line of questioning to get back up on my soapbox and wondered how long they would let me get away with it. "I think the reason we are seeing this sort of problem with Mr. Mullin and with other people in the community is that instead of providing treatment for the mentally ill which would prevent these kinds of things from taking place, we are closing down the mental hospitals, denying treatment to these people, deciding instead that we will offer punishment after the fact, after they've done something.

"Now the theory there, which I think is incorrect, is that a mentally ill person, like a normal person, would be deterred by the threat of punishment. I think it's very clear from this case that Mr. Mullin was not deterred by the threat of punishment, and that with mentally ill people that threat just simply does not influence their behavior.

"Now it is true that a normal person will either not do something because he doesn't want to get punished or will try to avoid detection, and would do it in a clever way.

"His conduct was hardly clever. As I pointed out this morning, Mullin could have left town, but he didn't do any such thing. In fact, he drove around here in broad daylight, in his own car with his own license plate, which made it very easy to trace him and to arrest him. He was simply not acting in accordance with the principles you are putting forth that a normal person would operate under if he were trying to avoid detection and to avoid punishment. Mentally ill people just aren't deterred by punishment," I repeated. "If we want to stop this sort of thing, we have to do it by treatment and not punishment."

"Do rational people always leave the area after they have committed a crime, Doctor?"

"A person who is a cold, calculating killer will have planned his escape in advance and certainly try to avoid arrest, yes."

"Wasn't Mr. Mullin avoiding arrest?"

"I think that's my whole point," I said, "but I've made it, and I think we just obviously disagree."

Cottle went on to Herb's statement not long after his arrest that he killed Mrs. Francis and her two children because they could identify him. It was later that he admitted having heard command hallucinations.

"So what you are saying is that he really didn't kill them because they were witnesses at all?" he asked.

"I don't think so. I don't think that was the reason, Mr. Cottle. I think the reasons are the ones I gave, and I really don't think you can make any sense out of all this whole series of events by assuming rational motives."

"Isn't it a very rational thing to kill people who may be witnesses to the fact that you killed somebody else?"

"Not if the initial killing is based on crazy reasons in the first place."

Cottle returned to the idea that Herb thought it was moral to commit murder. "Well, nobody really ever has the right to kill anybody, do they?" he asked.

"Nobody in their right mind, but . . ." I paused. I was beginning to get a little tired. "Well, I don't know," I said. "I think you would probably say yes, Mr. Cottle." He raised his eyebrows slightly.

"Obviously we consider the men in the military to have the right to kill," I continued, "and we draft people and train them to kill and send them to kill.

"Mr. Ehrlichman said over national television a week ago that he could conceive of a situation where the president could order someone to be killed in the interest of national security if that person had access to secret plans for the atomic bomb, so I don't think you could make a general statement about nobody hving the right to kill.

"I think that's one of the difficulties, that in our society we have emphasized that people do have a right to kill, and that we have glorified killing on television, and I don't think that has contributed to teaching our young children not to kill."

"Have you made a diagnosis of Mr. Ehrlichman yet?" Cottle asked dryly.

Judge Franich rolled his eyes. "Well, let's not get into that one," he said.

Cottle was leafing through the diagnostic manual that Jackson had me recite from when we began on Friday.

"There is one in here about antisocial personality," he said. "Would it be fair to say that some of the characteristics in that one apply to Mr. Mullin?"

"The answer is no, Mr. Cottle. I'm glad you brought it up because it is one of the points of distinction between Mr. Mullin and Mr. Frazier.

"For instance, the antisocial personality shows a lifelong pattern of criminality and antisocial behavior starting usually at an early age, often before age ten or twelve and continuing through the early teen years—juvenile delinquencies of various sorts, a record probably of having been in reform school, or in California the CYA—which as you know was the case with Mr. Frazier.

"In Mr. Mullin's case we have quite the contrary in his early history, which is totally incompatible with that of an antisocial personality. He was a first rate student. He was never in any difficulty with the law or authorities all through his school years, and did not run into trouble with the authorities, the mental hospitals, until late in life when the symptoms of mental illness came along."

"According to the manual," Cottle insisted, "one of the outstanding characteristics of antisocial personalities is that they tend to blame others for their behavior."

"Yes, but that's one of a whole long history of things, there is also a life history that has to go along with it, so you are taking one thing out of context."

"Well, I'm not trying to suggest to you that Mr. Mullin is an antisocial personality," Cottle said. "I accept your diagnosis that he is paranoid schizophrenic, but I am only trying to point out that the label paranoid schizophrenic contains certain aspects of personality and mental illness that are found elsewhere."

"I think you mean it the other way around," I said, "but I understand your question, yes."

Toward the end of the day, Cottle raised the specter of another of my earlier cases, this one from Contra Costa County, in which a mentally retarded defendant named Lopez mistakenly shot his crime partner during a robbery and was charged with murder. I had testified that tests showed he had an IQ of 54 when he was eight years old. Cottle made much of the fact that a later examination, administered when he was a teen-ager, attributed to him an IQ of 84. He wondered why I had used the earlier results in my testimony. I explained that I believed the first test was probably more valid, since Lopez had been tested several times after that, and his scores were bound to improve from simple practice.

"In the course of that trial wasn't it brought out that the IQ test was administered to Mr. Lopez when he was eight years old in an English-speaking school, in English, and that he was a Mexican-American?" Cottle asked. "Wasn't that brought out?"

"If you're implying that Mexican-Americans have a different IQ from Caucasians, Mr. Cottle, when they've been born and raised in Los Angeles, which is where Mr. Lopez came from . . ."

"I'm indicating Mexican-Americans have a little trouble with English, doctor."

"I don't agree with that, your honor, and . . ."

Cottle did not let up. "Why is it, then, we have recent legislation that . . ."

"I think we're arguing," the judge said coldly. "I'm going to sustain the doctor's objection because we're getting into argument."

Cottle walked back to the counsel table and sat down. "I have nothing further," he said.

"Are you through with Dr. Lunde?" the judge asked.

"Yes."

"Mr. Jackson? Anything further?"

"No."

"Dr. Lunde, you're through," Franich said, smiling. "Thank you very much."

"Thank you."

"It's a quarter to four, a little late to start another witness," the judge was saying. "We'll recess until tomorrow morning at 9:30."

"Hang around for a minute," Jackson mumbled through a pencil clenched in his teeth as he busily stuffed papers into his briefcase. "I'll buy you a drink."

"You're goddamn right you will," I said.

39

Conflicting Testimony

WE ALL THOUGHT the trial had gone fairly well so far. We had managed to make all the points we wanted to make, and we didn't think my cross-examination, though vigorous, had been damaging. On the other hand, mine was the only psychiatric testimony the jury had heard so far.

Patricia Bocca was the first defense witness the next day. Jackson took her over the same ground that Cartwright had covered in his interview. While she was describing Herb's weekend visits from Mendocino State Hospital, she made the tearful observation, "They handled him in such funny ways. Dealing with insane people, they seemed to just release them again and again."

She was followed to the stand by a succession of Herb's friends and relatives who recalled, in the words of Don West, a very capable reporter for the San Francisco *Examiner,* how Herb was "transformed from the nice kid next door everybody loved to someone who could admit to thirteen slayings." Enos Fouratt told of his nephew's disturbing and often frightening visits. Allan Hanson, who had spoken with Herb of reincarnation and telepathy when the two lived together in San Francisco in the late summer of 1971, remembered that Mullin stood in their kitchen one night for three or four hours, talking to God.

"I just don't understand what went wrong," he quoted Herb as saying. "Why, God? What did I do wrong?"

Dave Marlowe, the highly regarded clinical psychologist from UC Santa Cruz who had administered Herb's personality profile test and had interviewed him on several occasions, testified on August 8. His conclusions were basically the same as mine, and even though Cottle hammered at him on cross-examination, he told the jury repeatedly that in his opinion Mullin had been legally insane at the time of each crime. He conceded that Herb had first told him he was afraid Kathy Francis might be able to identify him as the man who asked for directions to the Gianera house, but insisted that his hallucination that she had agreed to be sacrificed probably was the main reason she was murdered.

Jackson wound up taking defense testimony on August 9. The first rebuttal witness called by the prosecution was John Peschau, the psychiatrist from Agnews State Hospital who had been appointed by the judge to advise him regarding Herb's mental state. His opinion had not deviated from the report he had submitted to Franich shortly before the trial. He had seen Herb three times, and by the third, he said, he was reasonably cooperative.

Dr. Peschau had told the judge that while he was recounting the murders of Mrs. Francis and the two boys, Mullin told him, "She was a witness, and I was afraid of prison." At the end of his story, Dr. Peschau said, Herb told him:

"Number 13 was Mr. Fred Perez. That one was unfortunate. I had the jitters. I was off welfare and had no job and had found out I didn't want the Gianeras dead. And my father was gigging me to kill someone. Mr. Perez was standing there and not saying anything. I killed him with the rifle I'd taken from the camp south of Felton. I was arrested ten minutes later. It was a foolish thing. He was well dressed with a haircut and looked the way I would like to look."

The psychiatrist concluded, "There is no doubt that the use of LSD had stimulated a mental illness of sorts, and that he was actively hallucinating. However, these hallucinations were incidental to his offenses and served as moral support for him. They were not hallucinations that he would be forced to follow such as those that are divine in origin. And in many of the killings he showed a frank awareness of the need to cover his tracks. . . ."

The other court-appointed expert was Charles I. Morris, M.D., of Oakland. His testimony filled most of the day on Friday, August 10. His diagnosis remained the same as it had been before, paranoid schizophrenia in partial remission.

Dr. Morris had told the judge, "At the time of the alleged offenses of January 1973, this individual did not suffer with a mental condition or state of such severity that he would not have known right from wrong or the consequences of his behavior. . . .

"As to October-November 1972," he added, "his mental state was such that he would have been unable to differentiate right from wrong, and would have been unable materially to reflect on his behavior.

"In February 1973, at the time of the alleged homicide of victim Perez, his mental state was such that he would have known right from wrong and that he was violating the rights of others. It is speculated that the homicides of the four in the cabin was directed by a feeling to rid the world of vermin, and in this period he was able to form intent. . . ."

All of which was no help at all, since Morris had concluded that Herb had been legally insane only during the first three murders, the ones with which he had not been charged.

After the jury was dismissed for the weekend, the attorneys stayed behind to debate whether the prosecution should be allowed to have Dr. Joel Fort examine Herb for possible rebuttal testimony. Jackson argued that since the two court-appointed psychiatrists had, in fact, testified for the state, it wouldn't be fair for the prosecution to have three expert witnesses compared with two for the defense.

The judge finally agreed to allow Fort to interview Herb Sunday night. He took the witness stand the following morning, after brief appearances by the Reverend George Flora, the Lutheran minister Herb had visited, and a Marine Corps recruiting officer and a physician who had examined Mullin at the induction center in Oakland.

Fort had spent two hours with the defendant the previous evening. He said he also had reviewed Herb's papers, the arrest reports, the California and Hawaii medical records, and all the previous psychiatric testimony contained in the daily transcripts of the trial. He related that Herb had cooperated with him, although there were a number of questions he refused to answer.

Basically, Fort testified that Mullin was legally sane at the time of the killings, legally sane now, and that most of his delusions were of recent origin, "an attempt to reconstruct . . . to explain it to himself, to try to understand just as we are trying to reconstruct, since none of us can enter his mind or were fully aware of what was going on there at the time of these thirteen killings. . . . And I realize that some have spoken about this concept of killjoy sadism as a delusion per se, but I saw it again as an example of a continuum . . . another way that he, in his attempted reconstruction of his own mental state and his background, talks about the conspiracy of his father and others."

Fort dismissed Herb's preoccupation with the date of April 18. He said his actual knowledge of seismology, Einstein, and especially astrology were superficial, "developed after the fact, and in his attempt to reconstruct what went on.

"And in part he attempts to do that and has attempted at least since March," Fort continued, "because it came across to me from our discussion that he, at times at least, feels horrified by this, that he one and the same time, for example, knows that he is supposed to love his father, that we are to do this, but hates his father and has tremendous hostility which he describes as strong resentment.

"He is unable to use the word 'hate.'

". . . the inability to express the hatred toward his father led to some of it being displaced on to other people that he saw as like his father, restricting his pleasure, keeping him from learning about a normal sex life."

Since Fort has a reputation as an expert on drug abuse, Cottle asked him what role he thought that played in the murders. The witness replied that Herb's answers to his questions on the subject had been guarded. "He did indicate, though, even though he didn't go into any detail, that they weren't involved in the killings," he added.

Throughout his testimony, Fort stressed what he repeatedly characterized as Herb's bitter enmity toward his father.

"It is possible," he told Cottle, "that his beliefs about his father are delusional. That would be particularly difficult to ascertain without having much more information about his family life.

"But at the very least it was my conclusion that there was a significant element of truth in that, of the authoritarian nature, the approval of at least certain forms of killing, the training in the use of weaponry and so forth. . . . Then, at some point in Mr. Mullin's mind, this moved into delusional thinking and may shift back and forth."

"And did you reach a conclusion with regard to whether he was mentally ill at the time of the offenses?" Cottle inquired.

"My opinion is that both now and at the time of the thirteen killings he has and had a combination of paranoid schizophrenia and what used to be called psychopathic personality, or in more modern terminology, antisocial reaction. . . ."

"All right. Are all paranoid schizophrenics, in your opinion, criminally insane?"

"Certainly not," Fort answered. "At the most a very small number of them would be. . . ."

"Have you formed an opinion on the question of whether he knew and understood the nature and quality of his acts when he killed, and on the question of whether he knew these acts were wrong?"

"I have formed such an opinion."

"And what is your opinion in that regard, doctor?" Cottle asked.

"That he knew the nature and quality of his actions and did specifically know that they were wrong . . . that he did and was capable of premeditating and deliberating."

Although Fort conceded that Herb probably had heard auditory hallucinations, he claimed "the voices at no time said kill this or that person. The telepathic communications were never that specific."

Under cross-examination by Jackson, Fort continued to fix on the father as the source of Herb's problems.

"The number-one factor that was involved in the killings was a long-standing, continuing, and growing aggressiveness, hostility, and hatred of his father," he said, "and this hostility and hatred, which I see as the prime force in his personality development, stem from the rejection, authoritarianism, the emphasis on violence and killing that came to him from his father. . . ."

"When Mr. Mullin killed Mr. White," Jackson asked, "did he think he was kiling his father?"

"I have no knowledge either from my interview or from the voluminous documents I reviewed that he did think he was killing his father," Fort said. "My own perspective on it is that at least in major part he was, as one of the factors involved, displacing the hostility, anger, and hatred that he feels and felt toward his father on to Mr. White and subsequent victims."

Jackson took Fort over the documents he had examined in preparation for interviewing Herb. When they got to a transcript of the conversation between Mullin and his father the night Herb was arrested, the psychiatrist made the comment:

"Well, of course, it is a limited sample of the human relationship, but I will say [it does] contribute, bear upon my statements.

"I find it strange," he said, "that a father of somebody just arrested as a multiple killer shows no love, compassion, or concern for him. I find the dialogue to be lacking in human feeling, and sort of rigid and controlled, and I find some expression in the transcript that I have read of his anger toward his father."

Bill Mullin, visibly shaken, rose to his feet and stepped into the aisle. He had been in court all day, sitting in quiet anguish as he heard himself described as the focus of his son's hatred and the possible cause of his mental illness. His face, livid with obvious rage, nonetheless betrayed the burden of years of trying of help his only boy, years of frustration. The courtroom was hushed; not even Judge Franich tried to speak. As every eye followed him, Bill Mullin started forward twice, as if he were going to say something. Finally, he turned, strode out into the hall, and slammed the big door behind him. A murmur followed a collective sigh of relief. Herb sat, motionless.

Jackson tried unsuccessfully to trap Fort on his definitions of premeditation and deliberation. Then, on redirect, Cottle asked, "What significance does the reloading of the gun have to do with deliberation, doctor, if any?"

"Well it has, I think, considerable significance," he said. "It is significant in terms of being able to see that more shooting is necessary in order to kill somebody. It shows an awareness of operating a complicated piece of machinery. In general, it indicates to me further confirmation that he was not insane."

"This young man hears voices," Jackson said during further cross-examination. "You will accept that?"

"Yes."

"And the voices he hears are generally the voices of his father or mother, is that correct?"

"Yes," Fort said.

"And I think you testified earlier that one of the conflicts in Mr. Mullin's life was that he wanted to obey the command, 'Honor thy father and thy mother,' isn't that correct?"

"That is right."

"No further questions," Jackson said.

Cottle rose again. "Doctor, Mr. Jackson mentioned one thing. Did you ever get the impression that at the time of the killings Mr. Mullin was hallucinating, at that time?"

"No, I had the impression that he was not hallucinating at that time, but the hallucinations had occurred in the recent to distant past, but were not immediately impendent on the killing."

"Which one was this?" Cottle asked.

"With any of them."

Jackson raised his palm before Fort could leave the stand. He had a few more questions. "And he does what the messages say, albeit not immediately?" he asked.

"No."

"He kills," Jackson insisted.

"No."

"The message says 'kill,' does it not?"

"The hallucination was at the most one component or one reason why he killed," Fort said.

"You're talking about a different subject," Jackson said. "The message was 'kill,' was it not?"

"No, the message was death by killing—by suicide, in a hospital, or on the highway—will replace or prevent an earthquake or flood." Jackson nodded, and was already returning to his chair as Fort completed his answer. "It did not just simply say kill out of context."

Court adjorned for the day. It was May 13, 1973. The only witness left would be Herb.

40
The Witness

ON TUESDAY AUGUST 14, the courtroom was jammed. Several times Judge Franich had to halt the proceedings and invoke the fire laws as the spectators tried to wedge into the already crowded benches. The hallway was strewn with cables and the other arcane paraphernalia of television news cameras. Though not yet fully recovered from his second operation, District Attorney Peter Chang sat at the prosecution table with Art Danner and Chris Cottle, compelled to watch the climax of a case he had built meticulously for more than six months but had been unable to try.

After refusing to be sworn but accepting an affirmation, Herb stood in front of the witness chair and waited patiently for Jackson to begin. He had said he would rather not sit.

When Jim asked Mullin to repeat his name for the record, he started instead a rambling recitation of the names of all his relatives, the members of his "dynasty." Jackson interrupted, gently.

"Maybe we could go about it in this way," he said. "Let me ask you why you killed thirteen people, Herb."

"All right. First of all you have heard me say before that I am a scapegoat, sort of an outcast who has been made to become a scape-goat."

"Are you answering Mr. Jackson's question?" the judge asked.

"Yes, sir," Herb said.

"All right."

"I don't know what a scapegoat is, Herb," Jackson said. "What is a scapegoat?"

"Well, a scapegoat is a person that is made to carry the guilt feelings of other people to an exaggerated extent," he explained.

"At the end of World War II my father was stationed in the South Pacific and he was—he turned himself in to a mental hospital feigning shellshock. Apparently the bombs were getting too close, and he did not want to give up his life for his country as he had stated when he went in. He said he was willing to organize and help in the organization of the war, but he did not want to die in it. And when the bombs started getting too close, he ran to the mental hospital and said, 'I can't hear anything,' or something. It was shellshock, you know.

"It bothered him when he got home. His wife and his daughter, they said there was nothing wrong with that. People are dying on the highways all the time. They're offering their lives so there won't be a cataclysmic earthquake and so that the earth will stay in orbit, don't worry about it. And it bothered him.

"So when he had a son—I am his son—he figured out the best way to eradicate this error of his, of being afraid in wartime in the military combat zone, was to put a yellow jacket on his son and let the pressure be so great by the different other boys in the communities . . ."

"What is a yellow jacket?" Jackson asked.

"A yellow jacket . . ."

"These people have never heard some of these terms," Jim explained, "so I will be interrupting you once in a while. What is a yellow jacket?"

"That is when one person is designated to experience the coward-ice of all," Herb went on. "In other words, it is forced out of him. Whereas the others don't feel the extreme pressure of bullying the one person does . . .

"Along with the yellow jacket there was a killjoy sort of philoso-phy that existed. Now this can be, as it was placed to me it can be, it is directly responsible for Mr. and Mrs. Enos Fouratt. Apparently they were extremely—how would you say—they were extremely disappointed at not having been able to have children in their life . . . so they said, 'Well, in the Bible it says that the suffering of Jesus, a person that dies, is offered up to God to accomplish our prayers, so we'd like a child.' And they asked my mother and father if they'd, you know, retard me, keep me unaware of the social and psychological and sexual functions of the normal Homo sapien.

"I don't know who, you know, whose fault it is as far as their not being able to have children. As far as I know, they could have just chose not to, you know.

"But like I say, nothing has been explained to me. I've been kept unaware. So what I'm trying to do is show you what, you know, what my mind was like when I received the command to kill. You know, what type of person does these things." The jury watched and listened to him intently.

"You saw the pictures, the people," he said. "They died quickly, but no one likes to die that way. So I'm trying to explain my mind, how my mind got to the position where I could commit such acts.

"I believe myself since Moses' time, six-eight thousand years ago, people on earth, we Homo sapiens, have been practicing bisexuals. In other words, we have experienced homosexual and heterosexual experiences, most of us since we were seven, eight, nine, ten years old.

"One of the first rules is that you're not supposed to talk about it. If you talk about it, then you're breaking a rule and you're committing a sin and you will incur the anger and the punishment of the other people in the community. . . ." He spoke earnestly, trying to make them all understand.

"Herb, when did you move from San Francisco?" Jackson asked.

"We moved to Felton in September of 1963, about nine years and eleven months ago."

"Why did you move?"

"I don't know . . ."

"You don't know why?" Jackson asked.

"No, I mean, as far as I am concerned, it was to uproot me, you know, take me away from the friendships that I was forming with different boys and girls in the city and to take me away from the city at a time when I was about to get my driver's license, so that I could not drive around the city and see what San Francisco is like at such a young age."

"Why didn't someone want you to drive around and see what San Francisco was like?" Jackson knew from experience that with Herb, he had to follow, not lead the questioning.

"Well," Herb answered, "I guess it is based on a concept of reincarnation, a belief that you have a soul that travels from body to body. In other words, the soul that is living in your body now lived in a body that had been buried, and will live in a body in the future, you know. The whole change of—it never started and will never stop, supposedly."

"I don't understand what that has got to do with moving out of San Francisco," Jackson prodded.

". . . Well, the person's enjoyment has been stolen away, even though he doesn't realize it . . ."

"And what has that got to do with moving out of San Francisco?"

"Well, a substantial amount of my enjoyment was spoiled."

"And as a result of that what happens?"

"Well, a person is caused to belong to a group of people that are suffering from *dementia praecox.*"

"What is *dementia praecox?*"

"It is a state where you are unaware of Jonah's philosophy. You are unaware of the healthiness of bisexuality."

Jackson asked Herb what method his father had used to spread the word among his youthful acquaintances that he should be shunned and belittled.

"Telepathy, I imagine," he answered. "On some occasions he even probably went door to door asking them, you know, to refrain from teaching me the facts of life."

"Why did that happen?"

"You know, the way normal children experience this learning of the facts."

"How do normal children do that?"

"I don't know. I am not a normal child."

"And what is it they have learned?"

"They have learned Jonah's philosophy that one person committing suicide or getting in an automobile accident or jumping off a bridge, or any of the other ways of being—of exterminating life from the body, that keeps the coastal areas from experiencing earthquakes, either small or large, to some extent."

"How many people you figure know about Jonah's philosophy?" Jackson asked.

"Every human that is out of *dementia praecox* . . ."

It was Herb who brought up the fact that "one of my favorite friends was killed in an automobile accident."

"Who was that?" Jim asked.

"Dean Richardson."

"So he died. How?"

"It was an automobile accident," Herb repeated. "It was called an accident."

"I would call it an automobile accident," Jackson said. "What would you call it?"

"I don't know. I have gone over and over and over and over this again in my mind. Sometimes it looks like as if he tried to commit suicide."

"What for?"

"Just Jonah's philosophy. He believed in Jonah's philosophy so much that he felt that he should give an example to the other people in the San Lorenzo Valley that were scheduled to die in the next ten years, you know."

"Why were they scheduled to die in the next ten years?"

"Well, if you believe in Jonah's philosophy . . ."

"All right," Jackson said. "I already told you that I don't."

"Well, OK," Herb replied argumentatively. "Whether you do or not, every second somebody dies on the planet earth, you know. Somebody is dying every second. There is 175,000 people born every-day, well, maybe 200,000. Maybe it is more than that, you know. So every second somebody dies. Every hour four people die by gunshots in the United States. Every hour four people die on the highways because of automobile accidents. Every hour four women die in hospitals because of breast cancer. Every hour five or six people die in the hospital because of cancer. Heart attacks, four or five an hour.

"So there is a steady flow of death to keep, you know, the coastline from cataclysmizing and keeping the earth in orbit."

Jackson had Herb explain that when the death rate was not high enough, natural disasters were a threat. He had him describe each murder and, as the jury sat enthralled, tell of the voices he heard, either from his father commanding him to kill, or his victims acquiescing.

On cross-examination, Cottle bore in on the voices, trying to get Herb to admit he had made them up after he was arrested, since it was only then that he hit upon the Book of Jonah as the Rosetta Stone for his philosophy of death.

"Had you ever received messages from your father before the killing?"

"Yes," Herb said.

"And when were those?" Cottle asked.

"In October," Herb insisted, "first part of October, seventh, eighth, ninth, tenth. . . ." Herb said that after White, Miss Guilfoyle, and Father Tomei had been murdered, he received a message from his father to kill again in December, but he was able to resist it.

"Can you tell me why?" Cottle asked.

"I felt," Herb began, "I felt as if I just didn't want to kill anymore. You know, I was—I didn't think it was right."

"You probably thought back about those people," Cottle suggested, "that you had killed those people, those three people, didn't you?"

"I thought . . ." Herb sounded uncertain. "I thought that I had killed three people, yes."

"Did you ever think back and remember how Mr. White looked after you batted him to death with that bat?"

"No, sir, I didn't. I remembered his picture in the paper when he was buried."

"And how about Mary Guilfoyle?" Cottle asked. "Did you ever think about her and how she looked when you left her body?"

"No, sir, I didn't."

"You never thought about it?"

"No, sir."

"What did you think about when you thought about the people that you killed, when you were thinking about it in December?"

"Like I said, I didn't think about it," Herb said. "I just thought I didn't want to kill anymore."

"Do you remember why you didn't want to kill anymore?"

"I didn't think it was right."

"Did you know it was a violation of the law?" Cottle was stalking him now.

"I didn't think about that," Herb said.

"Did you know?"

"Well, if I did know, I didn't think about knowing."

After getting Herb to admit that he was aware that murder was against the law, Cottle turned to questions about premeditation, and Herb's efforts to conceal his guilt. He asked him why he took the empty shells with him when he left the Gianera house.

"Were you aware when you left the residence that you had left one casing there?" he asked.

"No, sir."

"What had you done with the other casings?"

"When I reloaded I put them in my pocket, I thought."

"And why did you put them in your picket?"

"Just to keep them, I guess."

"You knew at that time enough about guns to know that the casing of a bullet that is fired from a gun can be traced to that particular gun, did you not?"

"No." Herb was positive. "I did not know that."

"Do you remember what you thought about when you put those casings in your pocket?"

"No, sir."

"Had you known one of them had fallen to the floor, would you have picked it up?"

"Probably."

"Why?"

"It belonged to me."

"Why?" the judge asked him, somewhat taken aback.

"Because it belonged to me," Herb said. "I brought it with me."

Returning to premeditation, Cottle asked, "When did you decide to kill Mr. Perez?"

"Well, if I decided, it was probably thirty or forty seconds before I did."

"Well, did you have some question in your mind as to whether you decided to kill on that particular day?"

"Well, let's say there is a glass picture window, and there is a five-year-old child, or a six-year-old child, and a twenty-year-old male, and . . ."

"Mr. Mullin," Cottle interrupted, "I would rather that . . ."

"I wonder if Mr. Mullin could finish his answer," Jackson said, rising.

"It's not responsive," Cottle said.

"Well, Mr. Mullin thinks it is."

"Let him finish, Mr. Cottle," the judge ordered, "and we will see what comes out." He turned to Herb. "Make it brief, Mr. Mullin," he added.

"The twenty-year-old tells the five-year-old to throw a rock at the window, and that it is all right, that he should throw the rock at the window and break it. And the child thinks about it and then breaks the window. Now, did the child decide to break the window or did the twenty-year-old decide to break the window?"

"Well, who decided to kill Mr. Perez, Mr. Mullin?" Cottle asked.

"Martin W. Mullin . . .

"You mean that you were instructed as to how to go about this killing, then, by the voice?"

"The thought I heard that morning was, 'Don't deliver a stick of it until you kill something.' So does that . . . ?"

Cottle interrupted him again. "Would it be fair to say that every decision made thereafter was yours?"

"I don't believe decisions were made," Herb said. "I think it was . . ." He stopped for a few seconds and looked around the courtroom.

"A rock doesn't make a decision while it's falling," he said. "It just falls."

41
Alone with His Madness

JUDGE FRANICH GAVE the jurors a day off before hearing final arguments, which were impassioned, eloquent, and thorough.

Cottle, as expected, based his summation on the distinction between medical and legal insanity, describing Herb as a "sick, sick guy" who nonetheless "knew that what he was doing was wrong." He derided my spending 100 hours examining Herb, reconstructing his background, and interviewing other witnesses, implying that the effort was aimed at adding unnecessary weight to my testimony. He insisted that two hours was long enough for any psychiatrist to determine that Mullin knew right from wrong.

For his part, Jackson urged the jurors to resolve the conflicts between the experts by trusting their own observations. "You listened to the defendant for longer than any of the prosecution psychiatrists," he reminded them.

The only melodrama, predictably, was provided by Jackson. It came during his rebuttal of the state's claim that Mullin not only planned each murder but also tried to avoid detection and arrest. Recalling that Mrs. Stagnaro said Mullin had stared at Perez for as long as forty-five seconds after shooting him, Jackson picked up the rifle from among the prosecution exhibits and asked, "Do you know how long forty-five seconds is?"

Several of the jurors flinched at the sharp, metallic click as he pulled the trigger of the unloaded weapon. "Mr. Perez has just been shot," Jim said, and sat down. People in the courtroom fidgeted and looked at their watches as the seconds ticked by slowly. After what seemed three-quarters of an hour rather than three-quarters of a minute, Jackson stood and addressed them again: "There is your sane man, who is supposed to know exactly what he was doing. There is your sane man who planned every detail."

In the end, it was probably not the final arguments that swayed the jury, nor even the psychiatric evidence. I believe the most compelling element leading to the verdict was the arrest of Edmund Kemper.

The public mistakenly believed that this brutal giant had been committed to Atascadero for murdering his grandparents, and that the hospital had released him to take the lives of eight more people. In fact, he had only been sent there for safekeeping. He had been released by the parole board, not a panel of psychiatrists. Nonetheless, in the summer of 1973, I don't think any jury in California, much less Santa Cruz County, would have turned Herb over the the state mental health system.

On August 19, 1973, the third day of deliberation, the jury found Herb guilty of two counts of first-degree murder for the slayings of Jim Gianera and Kathy Francis, guilty of eight counts of second-degree murder in the other killings, and sane throughout his crime spree. I never was able to divine how the panel resolved that he was suffering from diminished capacity when he shot and stabbed Mrs. Gianera and Kathy's two boys at the same time he was murdering her husband and their mother respectively, but, then, I wasn't on the jury.

Judge Franich set September 18 to receive the recommendation of the county probation officer and to pass judgment. He thanked the jury and admonished its members to go home and expunge the trial from their memories. "Don't even think about it," he urged.

One juror would find himself unable to follow that advice.

Alex H. Quartly, a Santa Cruz County deputy probation officer, spent the next month conscientiously compiling his presentencing report for the judge. The day after Labor Day he drove to the

California Medical Facility, the euphemistically named state prison at Vacaville where inmates are held temporarily for evaluation before they are assigned to a permanent facility. Herb was polite but firm in his refusal to talk with Quartly. "I have already made my statement," he said.

After an exhaustive study of the facts, the probation officer concluded:

> There can be no doubt the defendant is mentally ill, and that he was deeply involved with drugs. Whether the drugs caused the illness, or precipitated a dormant illness, or whether the illness would have occurred and progressed to the state it did without drugs, are questions which could be debated but never answered.
>
> After the onset of his illness, the defendant was hospitalized four times, yet the illness progressed to the point that the defendant took the lives of thirteen humans. It could be argued, then, that the illness is either untreatable or that the defendant must be constantly medicated and treated to prevent him from killing again.
>
> In either case, the defendant presents such a threat that he should never be permitted to join the community.
>
> Accordingly . . . it is respectfully recommended that Herbert William Mullin . . . be committed to the Department of Corrections for the terms prescribed by law."

Judge Franich sentenced Herb to life terms for the deaths of Gianera and Kathy Francis, to be served concurrently, and imposed consecutive sentences of five years to life for the eight second-degree murder convictions. Assuming a minimum of seven years for first-degree murder, Herb would be eligible for parole in the year 2020.

During the weeks between the verdict and the sentencing, Herb was indicted for murder in Santa Clara County for killing Father Tomei. It was a patent waste of the taxpayers' money, since the case was solved and he already had been found guilty of ten other murders. Peter Chang had no intention of piddling away his office's time prosecuting the White and Guilfoyle murders; he was just grateful the two cases were closed. But the DA in San Jose persisted, and eventually Herb was allowed to plead guilty to another count of second-degree murder. That boosted the date of his potential parole to fifty-two years into the future, sometime after his seventy-third birthday.

The juror who could not keep himself from being tortured by the Mullin case was Kenneth Springer, the foreman, who lived in the San Lorenzo Valley. The conservative owner of two television stores, he went home after the trial and tried to sort out what he had seen and heard. Then he sat down and wrote an open letter to Ronald Reagan:

> I hold the state executive and state legislative offices as responsible for these ten lives as I do the defendant himself—none of this need ever have happened.
>
> We had the awesome task of convicting one of our young valley residents of a crime that only an individual with a mental discrepancy could have committed. Five times prior to Mr. Mullin's arrest he was entered into mental facilities. At least twice it was determined that his illness could cause danger to lives of human beings. Yet in February and January of this year he was free to take the lives of Santa Cruz County residents.
>
> According to testimony at his trial, Herb Mullin could and did respond favorably to treatment of his mental illness. Yet, the laws of this state certainly prohibit officials from forcing continued treatment of his illness, and I have the impression that they, as a matter of fact, discourage continued treatment by state and county institutions.
>
> In recent years, mental hospitals all over this state have been closed down in an economy move by the Reagan administration. Where do you think these mental institution patients who were in these hospitals went after their release? Do you suppose they went to private, costly mental hospitals? Or do you suppose they went to the ghettos of our large cities and to the remote hills of Santa Cruz County? We know where Edmund Kemper went when he was relased from a state mental institution!
>
> I freely admit that I write this at a time when my emotions are not as clearly controlled as perhaps I would like them to be, but I cannot wait longer to impart to anyone who may read this my convictions that the laws surrounding mental illness in the State of California are wrong, wrong, wrong.

Springer concluded by pleading with his fellow Californians to write to Reagan. "Don't let another person in our country lose his life because our governor needs a balanced budget," he implored. "Please, please write."

The trial of Herbert Mullin helped galvanize the California legislature, which passed a bill several months later blocking the governor from closing any more mental hospitals. Reagan tried to veto the measure, but in an unprecedented show of cooperation between the members of his own party and the Democratic opposition, both houses voted to override him, and the savaging of the state department of mental health was halted. It was the only veto override during his eight controversial years in office, and only the second in California since World War II.

But, to mutilate a cliché, not only had the horse already been stolen, most of the barn had been torn down. The hospitals that had been closed were not reopened, the remaining facilities became hopelessly overcrowded, and the subsequent administration of Jerry Brown has, if anything, exacerbated the problem.

Since Brown took office, all of California's state psychiatric hospitals have been decertified because they cannot meet minimum federal standards. Thus the state has lost millions of dollars in federal aid that would have been used for treatment. California has dropped from among the top to twenty-ninth out of the fifty states and last among the eight largest states in per capita expenditure for mental health. Meanwhile, patients who are turned away from hospitals are often being held in jails.

Brown's excuse for failing to keep a 1978 promise to seek new funds for psychiatric care has been the passage of Proposition 13, California's property-tax-cutting initiative. He has ignored the results of a statewide poll taken the same day as the election that showed the people ranked mental care, along with police and fire protection, among those services they do not want reduced.

But it is easy not to think about mental illness. It is politically convenient to ignore it.

Today, Herb sits in a cell at San Quentin prison, alone with his madness and helpless against the delusions that have tortured him since he was in his early twenties. Because he was found to be legally sane, he can receive no meaningful treatment or therapy. At times, when his condition deteriorates and his conduct becomes bizarre, he is shipped to the prison system's medical facility at Vacaville to be sedated until his symptoms subside and it is determined he can be returned to the penitentiary without being a threat to himself, his guards, or the other inmates.

He is in his thirties now, a piece of human wreckage who already has cost the taxpayers more money than they would have had to pay to make him, if not useful, at least not dangerous. The price in terms of human suffering is incalculable.

He is one of society's failures, swept under society's rug. The question remains: How many other, potentially deadly, similar mistakes are we making every day?

There is no simple answer to the conundrum posed by the Herbert Mullins of the world. If long-term treatment had been available for him, he probably never would have killed. On the other hand, mental patients have civil rights too, and to consider laws that would allow people to be locked up indefinitely for something they *might* do suggests an almost medieval abuse of power.

As always in a free society, the question comes down to the fragile equation that has never been and perhaps never can be adequately solved: how do we protect both the liberties of the individual and the safety of the majority?

But there is an obvious place to start: we must understand that without adequate, competently staffed mental hospitals, none of us will ever be safe.